# Creating Capitalism

# Explorations in Social Structures

General Editors: Patricia Crone and John A. Hall

State and Society in Soviet Thought
*Ernest Gellner*

Creating Capitalism: the State and Small Business since 1945
*Linda Weiss*

# Creating Capitalism

*The State and Small Business since 1945*

Linda Weiss

Basil Blackwell

First published 1988

Basil Blackwell Ltd
108 Cowley Road, Oxford, OX4 1JF, UK

Basil Blackwell Inc.
432 Park Avenue South, Suite 1503
New York, NY 10016, USA

*British Library Cataloguing in Publication Data*
Weiss, Linda
  Creating capitalism : the state and small
  business since 1945 — (Explorations in
  social structures).
  1. Small business — History — 20th
  century  2. Capitalism — History
  — 20th century
  I. Title  II. Series
  338.6'42      HD2340.8

  ISBN 0–631–15733–6

*Library of Congress Cataloging in Publication Data*
Weiss, Linda, 1952–
  Creating capitalism : the state and small business since 1945/
  Linda Weiss.
    p.  cm. — (Explorations in social structures)
  Bibliography: p.
  ISBN 0–631–15733–6
  1. Capitalism.  2. Industry and state.  3. Small business.
  4. Capitalism — Italy.  5. Industry and state — Italy.  6. Small
  business — Italy.  I. Title.  II. Series.
HB501.W4728  1988
338.6'42 — dc19
                                                            87–35517
                                                                 CIP

Typeset in 11 on 12 pt Bembo
by Columns of Reading
Printed in Great Britain by TJ Press, Padstow

# Contents

*To my mother*

# Preface

This book is intended as a contribution to the larger debate on the state's relation to capitalist development. Its aim is to show how national configurations of contemporary capitalism – from the spread of micro capitalism in Italy to the consolidation of big business economies more generally – are linked to the domestic and geopolitical activities of states. My initial interest in this area began with the small-firm economy of Italy and the attempt to explain why industry in that country was peculiarly blessed with small enterprise. But the more I pursued that task, the less 'exceptional' Italy appeared to be. Indeed, the more relevant question seemed to be why small capital was not more prominent in western capitalism generally. The result is an attempt to establish the pre-eminence of states in the making of twentieth-century capitalism.

I wish to thank first of all those who supervised the doctoral thesis out of which this project grew. I am profoundly grateful to Michael Mann whose supervision, teaching and research opened up a new world to me, convincing by example that sociology need never be dull, trivial or abstruse, that it does indeed have something important to say and that it can be said with clarity and vision. I also count myself fortunate that Colin Crouch shared the burden of supervision. His comparative knowledge, advice and encouragement I value very highly. Along with other like-minded researchers, both he and Michael Mann made the LSE Sociology Department an especially stimulating environment for postgraduate study. My warm thanks too to all my fellow postgraduates who formed the core of the informal seminar group, in particular, Kim Lewis, Nancy Nason-Clarke, Dave Docherty and Di Parkin.

Along the way, my research was facilitated by many people: fellow researchers, archivists, administrators and various 'gatekeepers' of Italian institutions. I wish in particular to acknowledge the seminal articles of Suzanne Berger, which guided my initial forays into the Italian context. Among those who responded so generously to my requests, I would like to mention Carlo Dané of SPES-EUR, Marcello D'Alberti of Mediocredito Centrale, Sga. Hovaghimian of Artigiancassa, Giuseppina Alfieri of Istituto Sturzo, Piero Fazio of CENSIS and Giovanna Guidi of Confindustria. Special thanks are also due to Andrew Gamble, Marco Maraffi and Marino Regini who lent assistance in the early days of the project. And for much practical and moral support, not to mention their splendid hospitality in Italy, my deep appreciation to Fiorella Carra, David Moss and Lorenzo Speranza.

For helpful comments on various parts of the manuscript, I would like to thank Salvador Giner and Gianfranco Poggi. My greatest debt is to John Hutchinson who, in spite of similar commitments, always found time to lend a critical ear (even when his eyes glazed over) when it was needed most.

Still others have contributed in various ways to the publication of this book. My sincere thanks to Patrick Davis, Publications Officer of the LSE, for his helpful mediations on my behalf, and to the Publications Committee for its sponsorship. I am also grateful to the Overseas Commonwealth Scholarship Commission for financing the initial research in London and Italy, and to Griffith University for assisting in the preparation of the typescript. Lynne Ferguson's remarkable editing skills and precision were a great bonus in that process.

I am also indebted to Il Mulino for permission to quote material from G. Poggi (1968) and P. Sylos Labini (1878), and to Franco Angeli for permission to reproduce material from C. Barberis (1980).

Finally, I wish to record my appreciation of the advice and forbearance of my editor at Blackwell, Sean Magee. My deepest gratitude, however, is to Patricia Crone and John Hall. They gave the book their full support, spotted larger possibilities that I had missed, and encouraged me to extend and rewrite the manuscript in its present form. For whatever shortcomings that remain, I am, of course, entirely responsible.

# Abbreviations

| | |
|---|---|
| CDU | Christlich-Demokratische Union/Christian Democratic Union |
| CENSIS | Centro Studi Investimenti Sociali/Centre for the Study of Social Policy |
| CGII | Confederazione Generale dell'Industria Italiana/General Confederation of Italian Industry |
| CGIL | Confederazione Generale Italiana del Lavoro/Italian General Confederation of Labour |
| CICR | Comitato Interministeriale per il Credito e Risparmio/Interministerial Committee for Credit and Savings |
| CIPE | Comitato Interministeriale per la Programmazione Economica/Interministerial Committee for Economic Planning |
| CISL | Confederazione Italiana Sindacati Lavoratori/Italian Confederation of Workers' Unions |
| CNEL | Consiglio Nazionale dell'Economia e del Lavoro/National Council for Economics and Work |
| CSU | Christlich-Soziale Union/Christian Social Union |
| DC | Democrazia Cristiana/Christian Democrat Party |
| EEC | European Economic Community |
| ENI | Ente Nazionale Idrocarburi/National Energy Board |
| FLM | Federazione Lavoratori Metalmeccanici/Federation of Metal Workers |
| IASM | Istituto per l'Assistenza e Sviluppo del Mezzogiorno/Institute for Southern Aid and Development |
| ICAS | Istituto Cattolico di Attività Sociale/Catholic Institute for Social Activities |

| | |
|---|---|
| IRC | Industrial Reconstruction Corporation |
| IRI | Istituto per la Ricostruzione Industriale/Industrial Reconstruction Board |
| ISTAT | Istituto Centrale di Statistica/Central Statistical Institute |
| JETRO | Japan External Trade Organization |
| MEC | Mercato Europeo Comune/European Common Market |
| MITI | Ministry for Industry and Trade |
| MSI | Movimento Sociale Italiano/Italian Social Movement |
| NSDAP | National-Sozialistische Deutsche Arbeiter Partei/National Socialist German Workers' Party |
| OECD | Organization for Economic Cooperation and Development |
| PCI | Partito Comunista Italiano/Italian Communist Party |
| PDIUM | Partito Democratico Italiano di Unità Monarchica/Italian Democratic Party of Monarchist Unity |
| PLI | Partito Liberale Italiano/Italian Liberal Party |
| PNF | Partito Nazionale Fascista/National Fascist Party |
| PPI | Partito Popolare Italiano/Italian Popular Party |
| SBA | Small Business Administration |
| SVIMEZ | Associazione per lo Sviluppo dell'Industria nel Mezzogiorno/Association for the Development of Industry in the South |

# 1

# Forms of capitalism and the state

This book is about the political creation of forms of capitalism. It tackles a number of substantive issues in order to extract theoretical and practical lessons: why does the extent and importance of small capital vary so remarkably within mature capitalism? Do all societies have similar potential for the development of a small firm economy; or are some more likely than others to witness its rise and expansion? Why, in particular – and in contrast to the prevailing pattern of development – has micro capitalism become such a weighty force in some advanced industrial settings, such as Italy? And why, more generally, has the ascendance of big business and the demise of petite industry become the dominant trend of twentieth-century industrial capitalism? In addressing these questions, the book develops a state-centred argument about the national configurations of contemporary capitalism.

Its central claim is that capitalist development is inherently neutral. The development of capitalism does not necessarily favour any one particular economic outcome. More than one form of capitalism is (and has been) possible. What matters is the way in which states, in pursuit of their own objectives, have inserted themselves in the economic process. The study therefore explores the conditions under which national political agencies have regulated the market to favour concentrated or dispersed forms of production.

This argument has implications for two areas of sociology, theories of capitalism and theories of the state. Nowadays there is no need to labour the point that our theories of industrialism and capitalism have overstated the degree of homogeneity within and between societies. This applies equally to Marxist and liberal-Functionalist traditions, each of which has posited some law-like tendency to produce similar economic and social structures.

Though such theories disagree about the political outcome of such tendencies they are united in denying significant space to small producers. In these theories of demise, big business capitalism – symbolized in mass production, the large factory and the giant corporation – is the superior economic form destined to dominate, if not exhaust, economic space. By contrast, small capital – with its cottage industries and craft workshops, its mini factories and micro plants – is at best an anachronism destined for the dustbin of economic inefficiency. Along with other institutions and practices considered 'traditional', it is assigned a transitory role in the move towards a fully mature economy, the assumption being that as the exigencies of production become paramount, homogeneity within and between national economies increases, and the demise of the 'traditional' paves the way for the 'new' middle class.

Although these determinist and essentialist notions still linger in the literature with surprising tenacity, there is now less need to do critical battle with a set of theories whose defects have been so lucidly exposed elsewhere (see Berger and Piore 1980, especially chapter 5; Abrams 1982, chapter 1; Goldthorpe 1984). What does need stressing, however, is that while powerfully aware of the inadequacies of the conventional models, even the most theoretically explicit critiques succumb to the classical habit of invoking a logic of capitalism. It is not that social scientists today ignore the existence of small capital. On the contrary, they worry over the conditions of its survival – *given* the preponderance of big business capitalism. And therein lies the nub. For rather than rejecting wholesale the classical rule, they have (unwittingly it would seem) reinstated it with a theory of dualism. Small independent production is possible because it is functional, even necessary, for capitalism proper (Berger and Piore 1980; Goldthorpe 1984). I shall return to this point later. But the thrust of all the literature, including critiques of convergence, should be clear: the classical position misled because it underestimated the functional value of the small firm sector, its economic and political uses for 'modern' capitalism.

This study takes a different approach. It suggests that if our theories of capitalism are wrong, this is not because they overplayed the dominance of big business or the decline of the workshop economy. It is because they underestimated the role of the state in that process. One implication of this position is that the survival of small producers is not especially problematic. If anything, what is really puzzling is not that they persist, but that they have declined so greatly in most – *but not all* – industrial settings of western capitalism. This suggests that the pre-eminence of big business capitalism is no more theoretically or historically inevitable than is the general retreat of its petite counterpart. Thus, if we take seriously the proposition that capitalist development is inherently neutral, then we need to consider the various ways in which states as historical actors have shaped national configurations of contemporary capitalism.

The argument thus has considerable implications also for theories of the state's relation to capitalism. As Mann (1984) and Skocpol (1985) have noted, most such discussions have been highly abstract. They have argued over the state's capacity to act autonomously, over the nature of the functions it performs and over whether it is bound to support capital accumulation. But whatever the nature of the disputes and distinctions, all such general theories share a common point of departure. They all tend to take as given the structure of the economic setting in which states carry out their activities. States may be more or less autonomous, but the consequences of that autonomy are rarely seen as transformative. Since the economy appears to have a direction of its own, the state's role is merely to help it along the way: clearing the path of obstacles, managing crises and contradictions. States may distort or stimulate, retard or accelerate the accumulation process, but on the forms that process takes, they appear to have no decisive influence.

One central implication of this study, however, is that states do not simply support accumulation in an undifferentiated way. They actively channel and mould economic activity into particular forms. Moreover, whether states typically sponsor concentration or foster dispersion, 'what gets done' in the policy arena is not readily explained in terms of society-centred demands, needs or interests. As much recent research emphasizes, states – as organizations controlling socio-spatial units which exist within a multi-state system – are potentially independent sites of policy-making activities. Whether to maintain domestic order, to establish international position or to defend national sovereignty, states attempt to meet such challenges in ways that highlight their powers as society-shaping forces (see Skocpol 1985 for a review). In adopting a similar perspective from which to analyse the state's relation to capitalist development, this study therefore lends support to a growing body of research that depicts states, past and present, as weighty actors in economic and social development (for example, Mann 1980, 1984, 1986; Hall 1985, 1986; Giddens 1985; Evans et al. 1985).

To develop the argument I have outlined, my discussion focuses on one national case which departs significantly from the big business norm. Italy is the centre of a vast and vigorous small firm economy. In that setting (as in Japan), small capital does not simply 'survive', it contributes massively to economic development and employment. It is well to admit, however, that social scientists have been impressed far more by cross-national similarities than by variations in industrial structure, for these appear to vindicate the classical vision of a relentless drive towards concentration and the mass-collective worker. On the whole, they have been far less excited by differences, for these appear to be the product of 'historically specific' circumstances, at best illustrating the tenacity of tradition or the power of politics to divert the 'natural' course of development, but otherwise offering little in the way of general practical or theoretical lessons.

In this study, it is the departures from the prevailing pattern that are of especial significance. At the very least, the ability of some nations to combine vast small business sectors with highly successful capitalism clearly testifies to the fact that more than one form of capitalism is possible. Such cases may therefore illustrate aspects of capitalist development that, when examined in comparative perspective, can be grasped in more general terms. In keeping with the wider aims of the study, the Italian case will therefore figure not as a manifestation of the particular, but as a particular manifestation of a more general phenomenon: the role of the state in generalizing and consolidating specific forms of capitalist activity.

To pave the way for that analysis we need first to break with the 'revisionist' response to theories of demise. I therefore set out and criticize the dualist argument for small firm survival, drawing finally on the research of Charles Sabel to historicize the rise of Fordism.[1]

## The revisionist critique: from demise to dualism

Rather than chorusing the demise of petite capital, social scientists nowadays are more inclined to probe the reasons for its survival. Indeed, among the most influential and sustained attacks against unitary conceptions of industrial capitalism, we find precisely those which invoke the persistence of petite production (Berger and Piore 1980; Goldthorpe 1984). Why does it continue to occupy a place in the modern economy? In tackling that question, these analysts take on board two assumptions of the conventional models they seek to demolish: first, that the preponderance of big business is necessary to (and synonymous with) capitalism; second, that small enterprise is a backward, inferior form of economic life. The problem then is how to reconcile their coexistence. The result is a theory of industrial dualism.

The thrust of the dualist argument is that small business, however weak and deficient, survives because it performs a variety of functions essential to the political economy of capitalism. The latter's requirements, it seems, are far messier than the unitary conceptions allowed. For the logic of capitalism does not eliminate the inferior, 'traditional' segments. It exploits and reproduces them. Capitalism does not create a uniform world; on the contrary, it recreates forms of dualism.

This promiscuity stems from the very nature of modern (mass production) technology (Piore and Berger 1980: chapter 2). For one thing, the specialized equipment that mass producers require to turn out their standardized goods cannot itself be mass produced. For another, a mass production economy generates an organized labour force that cannot be readily dismissed in times of slack demand. Above all, Fordism must avoid markets for whose products demand is fluctuating and uncertain. The subsequent displacement of risk thus produces a segmentation of the market: on one hand, a core of large and powerful firms with well-protected workers; on the other, a periphery of small subordinate units whose labour force is highly *disponible*. As Goldthorpe puts it, 'the logic of capitalism has required, as the counterpart to the evolving mainstream or primary labour force, the creation of a further body of labour that is still capable of being treated essentially as a commodity' (1984: 335).

Capitalism, then, requires forms of dualism and these can be supplied by race, ethnicity or small firms. Which form prevails in a particular setting will depend on the resources that nationally specific histories have bequeathed. Thus the structures that distribute risk in one context may rely primarily on a distinction between firms, large and small; in another, on divisions between workers, native and foreign, black and white. In all cases, the result will be to render permanent the 'traditional' cleavages, institutions and practices that in conventional models were supposed to disappear.

To summarize, the main point of the dualist argument is that there is a logic to the development of capitalism, but it is one which sets limits to Fordism's capacity to fill economic space. In so far as small firms meet that problem by populating the periphery of economic uncertainty, their survival is therefore crucial to modern capitalism.

Some of this reasoning is perfectly sensible. No doubt some small firms can be subsumed under the residual risk-shifting category. But to consign the small economy *tout court* to the traditional sector, and to conceptualize it as a form of dualism, is to disregard a great deal of evidence to the contrary (see Sabel 1982: 194–227; Curran and Burrows 1986: 271, 273). Moreover, it is extremely doubtful that capitalism has any such requirements. Viewed historically, the long-run tendencies of capitalist development suggest quite the reverse. Indeed, the only solid evidence for 'dualism' in the labour market is that structured by gender, and this is traditional (Blackburn and Mann 1979: 301).

One final criticism is worth stressing. By construing the small firm sector as the subordinate periphery necessary to the mass production core, the dualist theory merely saves the classical rule of concentration by providing it with a 'functionalist' exception (Sabel and Zeitlin 1985: 138). Perhaps the rescue operation is unintended. Yet the nature of the question posed makes it unavoidable. To ask why small capital survives is tantamount to inquiring why big capital has not completely captured economic space. There are, however, sound historical and contemporary grounds for problematizing its supremacy. This is precisely the point at which Sabel (1982) and his co-author (Sabel and Zeitlin 1985) have arrived.


## A radical view: from survival to subordination

Whereas most writers have pondered over the small firm's survival, the investigations of Sabel and Zeitlin are driven by a radically different kind of question. Arguing for the independent vitality of small, craft-based production – both today and in the past – they probe the reasons why it lost out to an alternative paradigm.

In a highly suggestive set of analyses these writers provide simultaneously an account of the rise of Fordism – a system of mass production matching single-purpose machines with unskilled workers to meet standardized demand, and the eclipse of the workshop economy – a system combining flexible technologies with skilled workers to meet differentiated demand.

Drawing on numerous historical examples from the famous industrial districts of Europe and America, they show that the nineteenth-century mechanized forms of craft production were technologically vital and capable of significant increases in productivity (1985: 142). In principle, it seems they could easily have figured as the core of an alternative economy. Thus, Fordism was not foreordained by the nature of technology.

So why was the workshop economy submerged? Sabel and Zeitlin argue that it was not the inherent superiority of one form over another which overshadowed the system of flexible specialization, but an historically contingent set of conditions. For this system had no time to prove itself before the emergence of Fordist techniques blinded manufacturers to alternative possibilities. Once Fordism was installed, belief in its superior efficiency and in a 'rough-and-ready technological determinism' held sway. Thus, instead of being championed for the flexibility it provided, the workshop economy became almost universally regarded as a 'vestige of an inefficient age, fated at best to play a secondary part in a superior order of production' (Sabel 1982: 434). If one single factor can be isolated, it seems then that small capital lost out to a 'vision'. Belief in the brilliance of Fordism acquired the force of an irresistible paradigm and 'this vision helped change the course of events precisely by declaring one future inevitable' (Sabel and Zeitlin 1985: 172).

What makes Sabel and Zeitlin's approach superior to existing accounts is its ability to cut through the conventional wisdom surrounding the small firm and to demonstrate that craft production has all along been a viable alternative. This is a finding of exceptional importance, not least because, in historicizing the rise of big business, it clears space for a completely different set of questions.

What seems less convincing is the explanation they advance for the decline of the workshop economy. One of the main difficulties stems from the force it attributes to visionary ideas. Indeed, if craft principles were equally viable, then the existence of an alternative 'paradigm' would be unlikely to convince numerous producers to abandon their time-tested practices. As Poggi (1983) reminds us in his reading of Weber, visions, like ideologies, however enthusiastically propounded by their exponents, rarely gain momentum unless embodied in some powerful collective force to carry them forward in practice. To do that, seemingly utopian visions (however mundane) usually have to meet some widely felt need, and thereby offer solutions to real problems which are collectively experienced.

## Bringing in the state

That theoretical point suggests that alternative principles of organization are most likely to gain force in periods of great crisis. For the important issue, as Sabel and Zeitlin make clear, is not just the *existence* of mass production, large factories and giant corporations, but the way they become *generalized* throughout society as a pre-eminent feature of economic life.

It is well to admit, however, that certainty on this issue is probably unattainable. Nevertheless, historical analysis can add weight to the theoretical point. For the European trends indicate a very considerable economic space for small capital right up to the First World War (and, for some countries, well beyond). Thus, if we are looking for a prime mover under the 'crisis' category, then we would do well to start with war. And war is *par excellence* the business of states. More specifically, with the advent of total war this century, each time states have engaged in international struggles to strengthen or defend national sovereignty, they have pushed economic co-operation and concentration to new heights: institutionalizing mass production techniques, combing out small producers, standardizing production processes, initiating centralized economic management – the whole gamut of features familiar to contemporary economies, but initiated in near-panic circumstances of mass mobilization warfare, and carried through in peacetime to meet new international rivalries in the economic arena.

This suggests that it is international relations, relations between states, rather than within markets, that have provided a decisive impulse to scale and concentration. As I shall attempt to indicate in chapter 8, power relations between states have typically led governments to sponsor the creation and consolidation of large-scale undertakings. At certain moments, however, international pressures may be offset by challenges internal to nation-states and by the powers and projects of their political managers. Thus, chapter 7 shows that where issues of domestic political integrity took precedence over international considerations, as in post-war Italy, governments endorsed a small-scale strategy of industrial order.

The point of that contrast is not to insist that a particular source of threat (domestic or geopolitical) requires or calls forth a particular type of industrial strategy. That would be a perverse requirement indeed given the current industrial decline of Britain. As the widening crisis of Fordism indicates (Piore and Sabel 1984), the economic structures that may help win the war in the trenches do not necessarily clinch the battle in the market-place.

Rather, that contrast serves to emphasize the two general points developed in this book. First, that the dynamics of capitalist development are not independent of national politics, nor indeed of the role of nation-states. Whether in pushing concentration generally or promoting dispersion in particular, states have helped to generalize distinctive patterns of industrial ownership and organization that society-centred forces alone would very likely not have produced. The second point bears on the notion of autonomous state action. While we should not be dogmatic about something as historically contingent as state 'autonomy' (see Mann 1984), at the same time we cannot intelligibly read off distinctive strategies for industrial order from the 'needs of capitalism' or the 'interests of class'. The policies states have fashioned to favour particular economic forms necessarily create power groupings and destroy others in ways that subsequently circumscribe state autonomy. But to explain the general bias towards bigness or the particular predisposition towards petite property, we will need to bring in to our account the international and domestic objectives of states (and their managers) themselves.

I develop these points in two parts. Part I focuses on one national case which did not travel far down the big business track and where the submergence of small-scale production did not take place. What accounts for the difference? These chapters first survey and reject society-centred interpretations via an analysis of the distinctive features of state support. The main argument of this section (fully developed in chapters 6 and 7) is that Italy's small business economy expanded and prospered because it had something its European counterparts lacked: a highly sympathetic state. While governments elsewhere celebrated its contraction or encouraged its elimination, the Italians created a distinctive category of small capital and set about populating and replenishing it. Chapter 6 examines the ideological resources which fashioned Christian Democracy's project for a property-owning democracy. Chapter 7 explores the political struggles which helped carry it forward.

Part II rounds off the discussion by developing the implications of the case study in two directions. First, in chapter 8, it attempts to generalize to other nation-states – Germany, France and Britain

(America appearing as the exceptional case here) – the argument about the state's relation to forms of capitalism. It concludes that if there is a 'logic' to the concentration process, its central locus has not been economic, but military and geopolitical.

Beyond these theoretical concerns, the book also has a practical thrust. It does not seek to add to the corpus of diagnoses and cures for the ills of western economies. Nor does it adopt the extremist position of ascribing the affliction of modern societies to big business 'rigidities'. On this issue the most that can be said is that the relation between industrial concentration and economic success is ambiguous. What we do know is that under modern conditions of international competition, what really matters is the ability of states rapidly to reorganize their national economies. It is called flexibility and its precondition is some form of social cohesion (Hall 1985: 178–9). The combination is an elusive one. The clever and efficient states like Sweden have achieved it with a good deal of political effort from above and much history on their side (Crouch 1986). This is known as corporatism. Its core is extensive collaboration between trade unions, employers and the state at national level. It is perhaps no coincidence that one of the least clever and efficient states stumbled on to a very different solution, micro-capitalist, sometimes misleadingly called 'dualism'. Its core is intensive collaboration between workers, employers and neighbouring firms at local level. Corporatism and 'dualism' are usually conceptualized as extremes, two alternative paths to economic and social flexibility, each embodying radically divergent ideological choices. Thus, whereas corporatism represents a political and collectivist solution, 'dualism' entails a retreat to individualism and market discipline (see Goldthorpe 1984).

Chapter 9 suggests that this rigid distinction – which also informs much of the current vogue for small business, especially in Britain – is misleading. It therefore concludes the study with a discussion of the practical lessons of the Italian experience for the so-called 'small' firm strategies currently being pursued elsewhere, notably in the United States and Britain. With some reservations, it argues the case for the exportability of the Italian recipe. To a large extent, the ability to re-create micro capitalism will depend less on special preconditions of social structure than on what these states do with what is already there. But if both big business corporatism and micro capitalist 'dualism' are predicated on social co-operation, and if the success of each is bound up with more, not less, intervention from above, what chance has the political economy of *laissez-faire*?

# PART I

# The Italian Case, 1945–1975

# 2

# The problem: its contours
# and Explanations

In 1945 Italy was a nation of smallholders and artisans. Despite the
industrial giants of Olivetti, Fiat and Pirelli, it remained one of the
few European countries in which agriculture provided the chief
source of employment. In 1975 Italy had become the west's sixth
industrial power. 'Despite' the proliferation and predominance of
micro enterprise it remained one of the few major OECD nations
in which manufacturing employment was expanding rather than
contracting. Since the fifties, it has more than doubled its share of
world manufacturing exports,[1] maintained one of the fastest
growth rates in the EEC and increased industrial productivity at an
annual rate (4.3 per cent) only slightly below that of France (5 per
cent) and Germany (5.4 per cent). Moreover, the growth of
industrial employment has been conspicuously higher in Italy than
among any of her European rivals.[2] That this performance has been
sustained on the basis of a vigorous and burgeoning regime of mini
manufacturers must surely challenge our received notions about the
nature, dynamics and direction of capitalist development.

The task of this chapter is twofold. Beginning with a brief survey
of international data on trends in industrial structure, it foregrounds
the distinguishing differences that set Italy apart from most other
countries. It then outlines the three main approaches to the national
differences in question, which have emerged from the Italian
debate. The issues these raise for further analysis and how they
relate to the development of my own argument will be considered
in the final section.

Table 2.1　Trends in small enterprise sector, 1951–1971 (industry)

| Census | No. of firms (1–100) | Share of total (%) | Employed (no.) | Share of total (%) |
|---|---|---|---|---|
| 1951 | 636,500 | 99.4 | 2,088,000 | 51.6 |
| 1971 | 737,700 | 99.5 | 3,515,000 | 53.3 |
| Increase (%) | (+16) | | (+68) | |

Sources: 1951 data from ISTAT (cited in CNEL 1961: 7); 1971 data from ISTAT (1978: pt 7).

## Small enterprise: definitions, importance and trends

Information on the size-distribution of enterprises and establishments affords a glimpse into the social stratification of an economy. In particular, it can tell us whether small independents are a significant or marginal element of a nation's class structure; and it can be used for evaluating the degree to which labour is concentrated in industry, thus enabling greater or lesser levels of organization and protection.

Consider first the definition of small enterprise. In Italy there are two such categories. The artisan firm is a legal classification, applied generally to plants with a maximum of ten to twenty personnel (depending on the number of apprentices engaged).[3] Forming the vast majority of Italian enterprise, the artisan sector in 1976 embraced some 1.5 million concerns, employing in excess of 3 million people in industry and services – that is, roughly 15 per cent of the entire working population (Germozzi 1978: 204). Small industry, comprising over 95,000 firms in 1971, is conventionally defined – for the purposes of government assistance – as those concerns employing fewer than 100 workers.

The trends in firm and employment growth in industry are represented in table 2.1. Most notable is the fact that whilst the number of small firms increased by 16 per cent over the twenty year period from 1951 to 1971, the population employed in them rose over 68 per cent.

Even a glance at the table reveals the increasing weight of small firms in Italian industry. Of the 744,725 industrial enterprises censused in 1971, 99.5 per cent have fewer than 100 employees; and these firms account for over 53 per cent of the entire industrial workforce. In manufacturing industry, by far the most important branch, with over 80 per cent of the industrial workforce, the pattern for 1971, as shown in table 2.2, is essentially the same. More than 54 per cent of employment is concentrated in small firms, 23 per cent of which is contributed by the tiniest concerns with fewer than ten persons employed. Despite the clear importance of small business to the Italian economy, even this data, however, tends to grossly underestimate the reality. It has been estimated, for example, that if cottage industries could be included in the official tabulation, the number of artisan concerns would be some 30 per cent higher. Since many artisans live and labour under the same roof, a vast proportion of the artisan economy thereby escapes the census taker (Barberis 1980: 19).

To round off these observations on Italy, we might note that between 1971 and 1981 the trend to smallness increased. By the mid-seventies the number of craft concerns had risen by 11.4 per cent (Germozzi 1978: 204), while the number employed in micro units (with fewer than twenty persons per plant) was estimated to be in excess of 4 million, just under 50 per cent of the total industrial workforce (Barberis 1980: 53). According to the census of industry in 1981, the number of industrial firms appears to have risen by 21 per cent during the preceding decade. In addition the size of firms was markedly reduced as the average number of employees per firm fell from 77 in the early 1970s to 57 in the early 1980s (OECD 1984).

## Italy in international perspective

The significance of the Italian phenomenon can be readily appreciated when comparatively viewed. Table 2.2 shows that in the 1970s, the share of manufacturing employment in small Italian firms was at least two to three times greater than in any other major industrial power. The one noteworthy exception is Japan, strikingly similar to Italy, with over half of its employment concentrated in small units. Since there are striking parallels between the two countries, particularly with regard to the state's treatment of small manufacturing capital, the significance of the Japanese case for the argument of this book will be taken up in the final chapter.

With the exception of Japan and Italy, the figures reflect a general

*Table 2.2  Contribution of small firms to employment in manufacturing, in six countries*

| Country | Year of data | Manufacturing employment in small firms (1–99) |
|---|---|---|
| Italy | 1971 | 54.4 |
| Japan | 1970 | 51.6 |
| West Germany | 1970 | 28.8[a] |
| France | 1976 | 25.2 |
| UK | 1976 | 17.1 |
| USA | 1977 | 16.2 |

[a]German statistical data in this and the following table refer to establishments (sites) rather than to enterprises.
*Sources*: Commission of the European Communities; Dept. of Industry (cited in Storey 1982: 8); the Italian and US data are from Bamford (1984: 98) and Granovetter (1984: 328) respectively.

decline in the relative importance of small firms since the end of the war. More precisely, small business in most countries has been 'pushed' into non-manufacturing areas (Bruchey 1981). The picture is however a mixed one, which tends to defy the implications associated with 'early' and 'late' industrializing countries. Thus, whilst in Britain at least this trend has recently been arrested and reversed (Storey 1982: 8–10), in France, Germany and the United States the shrinkage of the small sector has continued, accelerating since the 1960s.[4]

Whilst comparable data for the various countries are not available, table 2.3 gives a snapshot view of the different trends – in four countries – in the small firm's share of manufacturing employment since the early sixties. Most notable is the fact that over a ten-year period, Italy's dispersed manufacturing sector not merely continued to provide the bulk of manufacturing employment, but actually widened its share to just under 55 per cent of the workforce.

Whilst France and Germany at the beginning of the 1960s still employed a significant share of the workforce in small plants (46 per cent and 36 per cent respectively), by the 1970s the push towards concentration – boosted by public policies – had induced notable shifts in the proportional distribution of jobs. Employment

Table 2.3   *International shifts in manufacturing employment in small firms, 1961–1971*

| Country | Year of data | Manufacturing employment in small firms (1–99) |
|---|---|---|
| Italy | 1961 | 53.0[a] |
| | 1971 | 54.4 |
| Japan | 1961 | n.a. |
| | 1971 | 51.6 |
| West Germany | 1961 | 35.8 |
| | 1970 | 28.8 |
| France | 1962 | 46.2 |
| | 1976 | 25.2 |
| UK | 1963 | 13.6 |
| | 1976 | 17.1 |
| USA | 1963 | 22.1 |
| | 1977 | 16.2 |

[a]The 1961 figure refers to establishments, not enterprises (Fuà 1976: 52). For Italian firms the difference would be at most three percentage points lower.
*Sources*: Adapted from Storey (1982: 8); Bamford (1984: 98); and Florence (1972: 41).

in Germany's small firm sector had shrunk by 7 per cent, working to the advantage of the largest category of enterprise; whilst France witnessed an even more spectacular decline as the share of employment in small enterprise contracted by 21 per cent. Firms with more than 1,000 workers increased their share correspondingly (Zysman 1977: 207).

The comparative resilience of Italy's small-scale economy seems all the more remarkable in relation to a country like France whose industrial and employment structure, until quite recently, closely resembled that of Italy. In 1951, for example, the non-agricultural independent workforce, including unpaid family helpers, was just under 2.5 million for both countries; and in proportional terms their weight was similarly distributed, accounting for 19 per cent and 21 per cent respectively of the active non-agricultural population (Hildebrand 1965: table 65). By 1978, however, the differences were truly dramatic. Whereas Italy's share had risen slightly to almost 23 per cent, the French figure had plunged sharply to just under 6 per cent (Boissevain 1984: 22).

We see then that in defiance of all conventional expectations about the marginalization of micro capitalism, Italy's petite producers have carved out an ever-widening space in the post-war economy. Elsewhere (excepting Japan), the landscape is much less crowded, but by no means so sparsely populated as the 'theorists of decline' were wont to predict. Indeed what this rapid comparison suggests is that Italy is by no means an 'anomalous' case. In the early post-war years at least small capital still colonized a significant space in the European economy. Since then the major Italy–Europe differences have become *more*, rather than less, pronounced. So that today Italy is the most outstanding example of an industrial economy organized predominantly around small-scale production.

What accounts for this distinctive departure from the general post-war pattern? Why did Italy move further down the small business track while most other national economies were pushing in the opposite direction? A purely economic analysis would be of little use here. Since small firms find economic conditions of existence everywhere, their differential weight and importance across nations cannot be adequately explained by economic factors. Economic analysis can identify a whole range of circumstances which work to the advantage of micro units. But, on the question of why the importance of small, family-linked capital varies so considerably from society to society, it has little to say. For what such analyses do not consider are the varying opportunities and constraints present in different national settings.

Clearly any adequate explanation requires some historical sweep. It would not do to focus, for example, on the political and economic events of the last decade or so. The wave of worker militancy, world-wide recession, the disintegration of mass-product markets and industrial restructuring – these processes have embraced most of the advanced capitalist countries. But the responses they have called forth have varied considerably depending on the resources available in a given national setting. Thus, for instance, when exposed to severe foreign competition, the textile industry in Italy and in Germany reacted in entirely different ways: whilst German firms went bankrupt or transferred to low-wage countries, Italian companies were able to transfer industrial production to the existing myriad of micro workshops. One may well argue that small capital was thereby mobilized and 'invigorated' by the political and economic events of the 1970s, but the crucial point is that the small sector already had plenty of life in it *before* these developments were under way. That is the crux of the issue.

As indicated in the previous chapter, my argument centres on what the Italian state has done for small capital and why. It tackles the 'small business miracle' from an historical perspective, examining the state's role since 1945 in forging a supportive structure to foster and diffuse small-scale production. On the basis of primary research it establishes a relationship between the activities of the state and the reinforcement of micro capitalism and explains that relationship in terms that emphasize the independent powers and purposes of state elites: on one hand the ruling party's project of small ownership; on the other hand, the internal challenges posed by organized labour.

To see how this argument differs from and builds upon existing approaches, we must turn to the Italian debate.

## The rediscovery of small business

In Italy the academic rediscovery of the small enterprise sector and its independent occupants received stimulus in two important ways. Following the release of the 1971 industrial and commercial census data, a noted Italian economist, Sylos Labini (1975), produced a major statistical and interpretative work on the Italian class structure, underlining what he referred to as the 'hypertrophy' of the independent classes.

At the same time, another important development had taken place: big business was in crisis. The Hot Autumn struggles of 1969 had culminated in a legal statute which enforced the rights of labour in industry; and workers in the corporate sector had begun to turn their militancy and newly won status to secure job protection and greater economic advantage. With higher labour costs, chronic absenteeism and the constraints on dismissals, employers felt they were losing control; and large industry began in some areas to transfer work out of the factory to the small firm sector where wages, benefits and job security were generally outside the control of trade unions.

These events, in combination with official inquiries, brought into prominence the importance of the small firm and gave rise to a lively debate in which both political and academic issues were raised. The political debate turned around the question of alliances. The Communist Party (PCI), which for over a decade had been seeking to cement an alliance between workers and the productive middle strata in the name of an anti-monopoly strategy, redoubled its efforts both in the public arena and at local government level to be seen as the spokesman for small business.[5] On the other hand, trade unionists within the Marxist left began to oppose the party's across-the-board coalition policy. Like their colleagues of different partisan persuasions, the PCl-affiliated trade unionists had long adopted a 'flexible' strategy in negotiating with small employers. But to continue to do so under the new regime of 'decentralization' would amount to giving big business a 'discount' (Federlombarda 1977: 64–81). In other words, it was now necessary for the trade union movement to differentiate the good from the bad, the genuine from the 'satellite' small industry which only existed for the convenience of the large.[6]

In response to these political concerns and to the alleged strategies of big business, one area of research accordingly turned its attention to the characteristics of small enterprise itself: for instance, its degree of autonomy, technological sophistication and contractual observance. These early initiatives have spawned a literature of vast proportions and we will draw on some of its findings at a later stage as they become relevant to the discussion.

By contrast, the academic debate turned on the question of survival and proliferation: why, despite several decades of intense economic development, Italy's small independent producers were still so numerous. From this literature, one can identify two types of explanation. Beginning first with a summary of the major positions, and where applicable their weaknesses, I shall then go on to outline the questions they raise for further analysis.

## Existing approaches

### The 'Three Italies' model

The first hypothesis (Bagnasco 1977) arises out of the discovery of a 'third Italy', as opposed to the traditional dichotomy of an advanced north and a backward south. The third Italy – the striped area in figure 2.1 – occupies the middle ground of the central-north-eastern regions and is noted for its booming economy of specialist workshops and mini factories, most of which has mushroomed since the end of the war. Here, traditionally rural regions – typically, the Veneto, Emilia Romagna, Tuscany and the Marche – have been transformed into centres of sophisticated cottage industry whose job creation, industrial exports, income and value added have increased at a rate well above the national

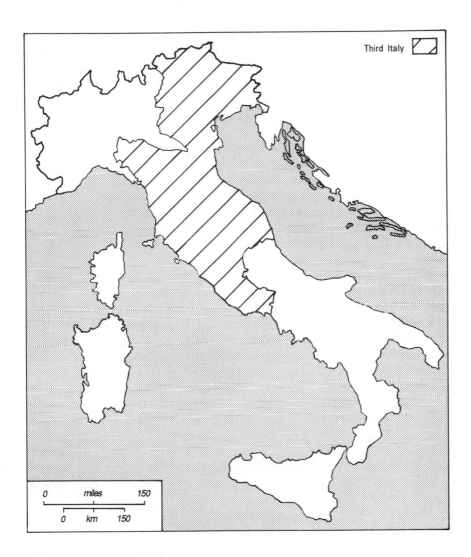

**Figure 2.1**   The third Italy

average.[7] Since small enterprise was conventionally regarded as the traditional, inefficient residue of an incomplete development, it was therefore something of a shock to find that it had declined only in the least developed region, but had multiplied everywhere else, especially so in the third Italy.[8]

Although small enterprise is widely diffused throughout the peninsula, its importance in this area of the country is particularly striking. For example, the percentage of the manufacturing workforce employed in plants with fewer than 100 workers is consistently higher than the 1971 national average of 54 per cent, ranging from 60 to 75 per cent (see Appendix I, table E). The relatively greater vitality of micro entrepreneurship in the third Italy is also graphically portrayed from a different angle in figure 2.2.

To return to Bagnasco's model, the persistence and renewal of the small firm is explained in terms of its relationship to the market, or source of accumulation; and from this it deduces three correspondingly different patterns of state–economy relations in Italy.

First, in the advanced north-west, it survives because of its subcontracting links with big industry, ties which supposedly have been reinforced and broadened since the resurgence of trade union militancy. In the mature industrialized triangle of the 'first' Italy, the state intervenes in support of monopoly capital. Hence the importance of small industry in this setting is due to 'other' factors, namely, class struggle and the consequent decentralization strategies of big business.

Second, in the central-north-eastern regions of the third Italy, it persists because it has conquered an independent space in the world market, specializing in those traditional goods which are the province of industrial 'latecomers' occupying a peripheral position in the international division of labour. Thus, in this recently industrialized area where large complexes are few, the state adopts a *laissez-faire* posture. Hence the flourishing of small-scale enterprise in this context exemplifies the logic of the invisible hand of the competitive (international) market.

Third, in the underdeveloped south – where neither of these market outlets are available – the small firm sector only manages to survive because it is propped up by state assistance. Thus, in the inhospitable environment of the Mezzogiorno, whose industrial structure is chiefly composed of small, local concerns and the giant complexes installed by public corporations, economic activities

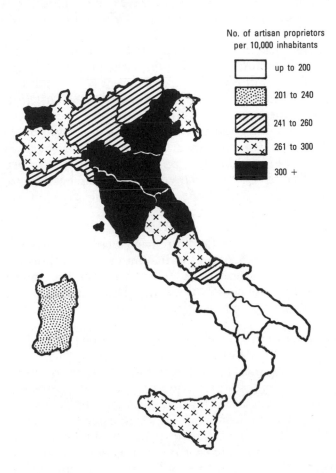

No. of artisan proprietors
per 10,000 inhabitants

| | |
|---|---|
| ☐ | up to 200 |
| ▦ | 201 to 240 |
| ▨ | 241 to 260 |
| ⊠ | 261 to 300 |
| ■ | 300 + |

**Figure 2.2** Regional density of artisan proprietors per 10,000 inhabitants, 1978 (from Barberis 1980)

largely depend on political power. Here, alone, the state intervenes with financial assistance to secure the 'survival' of a fragile small business sector.

In effect, with this tripartite scheme Bagnasco neatly systematizes on a territorial basis the main themes raised in the Italian debate. In order to extract from this model the hypotheses most useful for investigation, we need first to dispense with some of its assumptions.

Note first of all how the economic orthodoxy of economies of scale which predicts the decline of small enterprise reappears in this model in the guise of explaining persistence. Thus, it is claimed that small firms can only occupy the 'niches' left vacant by the large, or which the latter find it uneconomic to fill (for example, working on small commissions from big industry; specializing in 'traditional' goods subject to the changing dictates of fashion).

Now the main reasoning behind this position as argued by Paci (1979) and others is that as an industrial latecomer Italy has had to occupy a particular space within the international division of labour, which other countries have since vacated. Since that space is for products with a 'mature' technological content, and since such products 'are those for which small firms are particularly functional', it must follow that the size-structure of Italian industry and thus the preponderance of small producers are determined by the international division of labour.[9] The assumption, in short, is that small firms can succeed only in the spaces where economies of scale are inoperative.

Against such received notions, two points need to be made. The most general point is that whilst the economic and sociological literature is pervaded by the notion that big business is more efficient, this orthodoxy is increasingly questioned. If one reads for example Prais (1976: chapters 2 and 3), it is clear that the economic case for economies of scale is not at all established.[10] Second, research has revealed that small Italian firms proliferate in all branches of industry and operate with equal ease in both the consumer and investment goods sectors. Whether producing shoes, textiles and domestic appliances or automatic machines, machine tools and agricultural equipment, small manufacturers offer an extraordinary variety of items and specialize in virtually every phase of the production process (Brusco 1982). Indeed, at least since the 1970s, there has existed an extensive network of high-technology cottage industries. As Charles Sabel (1982: 226)[11] observes in this context, 'For most aspects of production, the small firms are not at a disadvantage because of their size; they have found that economies of scale exist at the level of one or a very few machines, not whole factories.' Overall, then, the dispersed economy encompasses an extraordinary variety of technical capacities and productive arrangements. In some areas, like Modena and Reggio Emilia, it involves dense conglomerations of high-technology engineering firms specializing in the design and manufacture of prototypes. In other parts, like Prato, Florence and Macerata, it centres on the craft-based, multi billion dollar export industries of footwear and textiles.[12]

This is not to suggest that dynamism and sophistication infuse every corner of the small firm sector. In some parts, like the vast back-street clothing industry of Naples, it centres on the figure of the middleman and the putting-out system. As the mayor of that city once boasted, 'Naples exports five million pairs of gloves a year, yet we do not have a single factory.'[13] But the sweatshop image that the Neapolitan system evokes is a far cry from the modern micro-capitalist regime. In this regime, flexibility is achieved not via 'sweating', which is 'the generic response of embattled firms – whether mass or small producers'; but through a fluid division of labour and a highly skilled workforce able to switch rapidly to new products and processes (Piore and Sabel 1984: 265, 269).

What needs to be stressed then is that the classic secondary labour market characteristics of low pay, poor conditions and primitive technology apply only to certain corners of the dispersed economy. For the core of this domain, notably the 'flexible specialists' of the third Italy, shares with the 'primary' sector not only its competitiveness on the world market, but also its advanced technology, its innovative capacity and, increasingly, its ability to pay high wages (Brusco 1982: 183; Solinas 1982).[14]

That conclusion can be reinforced by considering another crucial feature of the small firm economy: its largely independent market position *vis-à-vis* the corporate sector. This brings us to the final criticism of Bagnasco's model. Despite a widespread tendency to link the importance of small firms to the decentralizing strategies of big business via the process of subcontracting, there are at least two reasons why the extent of that practice should not be overplayed. First, even in Italy's most mature industrial regions of the north-west, the bulk of small firms produce directly for the market.[15] Second, the small firm's role in subcontracting is not generally that of recipient of orders from the large. More frequently, it is the initiator of such commissions. Indeed, all the research shows that it is the artisan or mini enterprise, not the large industrial firm, that typically acts as the major independent source of subcontracting.[16] For this is one of the time-honoured practices among small businesses, almost a structural characteristic of the Italian economy, by which dependent labour is kept to a minimum, the scale of operations contained and family control assured.

We can now leave aside these criticisms of the three Italies model and foreground instead its assumptions about the state's relation to micro capitalism. For as we have seen, it is more than a statement about the territorial distribution of three types of small enterprise, conceptualized in terms of their conditions of existence. It is also a statement about the role of the state in this process. For our purposes, the central point to be derived from this economy-centred explanation is that the small sector has expanded and prospered most where it has been left to its own devices. According to this view, state support has been negligible and irrelevant to small enterprise outside the south. Protection has been forthcoming for the most backward and inefficient small business strata of the country; yet, where the diffusion and vitality of small firms have been most pronounced, the hand of the state has been least visible.

### The danger thesis: state protection of the 'uneasy stratum'

The second type of interpretation which dominates the literature gives much more space to political factors. In particular, it assumes state 'protection' and invokes the supposedly belligerent tendencies of the independent stratum to explain the state's interest. Although no full-blown studies of this relationship exist,[17] what I have called the 'danger thesis' is so pervasive in the literature that it can be considered as part of the conventional wisdom. Its core theme and underlying assumptions are summarized as follows.

The small or 'traditional' economy is backward, inefficient and precarious. And the small business stratum which populates it is historically reactionary, unstable in its alliances and always ready for a Fascist adventure. Therefore, these two characteristics – economic backwardness and political danger – require the state to respond with political protection.

Adherents to this thesis typically invoke historic Fascism and its post-war variants as a key to understanding the petite bourgeoisie today and its relation to the state. Thus, for example, one of the leading students of the Italian and French traditional middle classes writes:

[Their] hostility to democracy and, even more, to socialism makes them willing allies of reactionary political forces. . . . In both France and Italy then, the mobilization of discontent in the traditional sector remains a major preoccupation of government. (Berger 1980: 111–12)

Viewed as a pivotal force in movements of the extreme right, it is believed to exercise a constant 'threat' potential, guaranteeing its protection throughout the post-war period. Thus, fearing the mobilization of discontent among the 'traditional electorate', governments of the post-war period so it is claimed have periodically responded with a flow of provisions that keep it from slipping to the right (Berger 1974: 306; 1980: 111–15; Sylos Labini 1975; Provasi 1976: 24, 91; Di Palma 1977: 258–60; Pizzorno 1980: 76–7, 83). Thus for those writers who have done most to advance 'political' explanations for petit bourgeois survival, both the reality and the ideology of danger combine inextricably as potent forces shaping political decisions.

This argument is applied at times to the petite bourgeoisie as a whole (Berger 1974: 1980), and most often, with special emphasis, to southern Italy. Since it is in the less developed south that small firms and employment are most precarious, that political alliances are so unstable and that neo-Fascism survives, it is here – so the argument goes – that the state has had to intervene on a massive scale to divert petit bourgeois unrest. Post-war governments, in particular the Christian Democrats (DC), have therefore doled out benefits to small businessmen on an individual, clientelistic basis, transacting resources for votes (Pizzorno 1980).

Common to all these political arguments, however different in detail, is the idea of a potentially belligerent class – frustrated and anxious, volatile and reactionary – which somehow has to be appeased. Most of these diagnoses flow from a widely held conviction that small business is, or at least has been for most of the post-war years, uniformly and ineluctably backward, inefficient and fragile; and its occupants thus precariously poised for flight into unpleasant politics. So rooted are these notions that even the few noteworthy efforts to explain the Italian small business phenomenon, as we have seen, tend to do so in terms that reinstate those very assumptions.

Consequently, although the danger thesis posits a role for the state in its approach to the small business phenomenon, it is not one which would lead us to expect the results in question. If little more than an exercise in pacification, prevention and protection, then we may well wonder at the extraordinary profusion of micro initiatives that so distinguishes the Italian economy today!

## The politics of unemployment

The third influential argument links the abundance of small firms to their strategic political functions in the labour market. According to this approach, politicians step in as necessary to cushion the small business sector for reasons of social order. Above all it is the fear of unemployment and its socially explosive effects resulting from a weakening of the 'secondary' sector which has called forth protective responses from the DC and its governing allies. This variation on the danger theme has two components, each of which may be found in combination, but with different emphases in the interpretative schemes of various writers.

In the first version, it is the small sector's function as a 'shock absorber' for the modern economy – absorbing or releasing labour as the economic cycle demands – which makes it crucial for resolving potentially explosive social problems (Castronovo 1976: 18–19; Berger 1980: 107–8). According to the most authoritative exponent of this thesis, the use of the small sector is strictly tied to the crises or limited absorbing capacities of large-scale industry. Protective measures are thereby 'conjuncturally conditioned and elicited' (Berger 1980: 124). In other words, their primary aim is not to promote, but rather to prevent the decline of small-scale initiatives. Political elites 'revert to protection of the traditional forms . . . when the road ahead looks bumpy' (1980: 108). What makes their use 'political', however, is the government's recognition that unemployment is 'the most serious problem susceptible to radicalism' and that this sector protects society from unrest and explosions that are 'feared to result from high levels of unemployment' (1974: 307; 1980: 109). For this reason, political elites and modern economic groups are 'willing to pay high costs for protecting the traditional remnants' (1974: 307; 1980: 110).

A slightly different version of the employment hypothesis is provided in Pizzorno's seminal article (1980) on 'I ceti medi nei meccanismi del consenso' ('The *ceti medi* in the mechanisms of consensus').[18] Like Berger, Pizzorno links the profusion of small business to a series of provisions in support of sectors capable of absorbing labour: 'agricultural policy, construction and public works policy, commercial licensing and credit for artisans and small industrialists . . . all have in view the danger which the insecurity of marginal workers represents for political stability' (1980: 83). In Pizzorno's version, however, post-war governments were not interested simply in managing unemployment, but in manipulating 'consensus'. The central presumption in this account is that the small firm is peculiarly susceptible to clientelistic interventions and this has made it especially functional for the DC's mechanism of vote-getting (Pizzorno 1980). Hence, if the state's political managers took an interest in the fate of small capital, this was not merely to avoid punishment, but also to curry favour with small employers and the workers they hired.

Putting these complementary positions together, it appears that the state protects the secondary sector not only to propitiate its dangerous owner-inhabitants, but also because of the functions it performs in the electoral and labour markets. Conversely, it is assumed that in the absence of these fears and pressures, the Italian state, and the ruling political party which has come to occupy it, would have shown precious little interest in these otherwise 'marginal' economic groups and structures.

Despite their differences, then, all three approaches share common features. They are all relentlessly society- and economy-centred. Even those accounts most sensitive to the 'state' factor – the 'danger' and 'fear of unemployment' theses – are fraught with reductionist difficulties. This is partly because of a deeply rooted tendency to take big business capitalism as a given and to see micro capitalism as an inferior form of economic life whose chief asset is the ability to generate constant political anxiety. From this perspective, the state is not a society-shaping force, but one that 'interrupts' the normal course of development. The more direct source of these difficulties, however, is that to date no systematic analysis of the state's involvement has been attempted.

This study fills that gap. My investigations into the nature, extent and effects of small business schemes revealed that after the reconstruction years the Italian state had put into effect a set of measures which not only actively promoted small undertakings, but positively discriminated in their favour. These, in turn, have had a substantial impact on the fate of micro capitalism in that country. The central empirical question, then, is: why was emphasis placed on increasing the chances for small capital, especially when governments of other major European countries moved decisively in the opposite direction?

Was the state's relation to small capital, as the literature argues, conditioned by problems springing from that sector itself: problems that threatened to explode should the small sector be left to its own devices? In other words, to what extent were governments of the post-war period pressed into action by fear of petit bourgeois discontent? Was there any objective basis for this fear? Did politicians perceive such a threat? Has the behaviour of the state been consistent with the fear of unemployment?

These then are the central hypotheses that will be put to the test in the course of the next three chapters. Each one is decisively rejected. The petite bourgeoisie has not been pathological but a pillar of society. The state has supported the most dynamic areas of the micro economy and with barely a concern for the employment factor. These chapters pave the way for the analysis in chapters 6 and 7 where I argue that the decisions which favoured a small-scale productive structure were shaped ideologically and reinforced politically by the internal challenge posed by organized labour.

Thus, to understand why, for example, the French petite bourgeoisie have found it necessary intermittently to mobilize against the state in order to exact concessions; whilst in Italy they have been almost invisible as a political force; or why European governments of the 1950s and 1960s launched modernizing programmes that sought to reduce and eliminate the small firm sector, whilst at the same time the Italian government sought to control the size of enterprises and to encourage their proliferation; or even why the United States, one of the few countries to champion the cause of small business, ended up encouraging giantism – from such contrasts as these, it would seem important to consider the differences in government stances towards small capital and also the quite different challenges to state power which have historically given it a more or less central place in the post-war state and economy. These brief comparative points will be pursued more rigorously in chapters 8 and 9.

# 3

# The petite bourgeoisie on trial

The petite bourgeoisie has had a bad press.[1] More than any other class or stratum, this particular social category has inspired a rhetoric of danger. Almost invariably, the representatives of small capital active in industry, crafts and commerce are presented as politically volatile and socially frustrated, economically uneasy and fearful of proletarianization, and by nature available to right-wing adventurism. As a corollary, the existing orthodoxy portrays the economic landscape inhabited by small property owners as pervasively insecure and threatening as its politics. What is thus referred to in this analysis as the 'danger thesis' is best summarized by the following statement:

Today, handicapped by technical progress and the development of large-scale industry and commerce, producing at non-competitive prices, or for a reduced clientele, a good part of this self-employed lower-middle class is economically and socially 'reactionary' and, consequently, politically discontented. Hostile to the 'financial feudality', fearful of falling into a proletarian condition, they feel that neither liberalism nor socialism defends their interests. Incapable of understanding their own political Malthusianism, they find a scapegoat in the political system, the 'impotent parties and Parliamentary system'. (Dogan 1967: 155)

More recently, this conception has been mobilized to make sense of a battery of government initiatives that, since the end of the war, have supported a growing multitude of small firms in Italy's advanced industrial economy. Such measures are typically viewed as an exercise in pacification, protection and prevention, a means of quelling unrest among a volatile stratum that might otherwise slip to the extreme right.

This chapter tackles the danger thesis from two different angles.

From the first, it analyses existing sources to determine in what measure the independent *ceti medi* actually supported Fascism and its post-war variants. From the second, it takes a more positive tack. Using a variety of evidence, including electoral and survey materials, the analysis counter-poses to the 'pathological' interpretation of the petite bourgeoisie an alternative profile. This stresses its confidence, its stability of allegiance and its commitment to centrism. The main argument is that, contrary to the claims of the threat hypothesis, small capital can in no meaningful empirical sense be portrayed as reactionary, exhibiting anti-regime positions. The basic premise of this claim – that the independent strata, either before or after 1945, were the willing allies of right-wing extremism – is rejected, and with it its explanatory value.

## Who were the Fascists?

Any serious attempt to demythologize the petite bourgeoisie must come to terms with historical and sociological interpretations of Fascism as a 'quintessentially petit bourgeois phenomenon', for these have deeply coloured accounts of its contemporary nature. Much of this literature views Fascism as a petit bourgeois response to economic decline and claims as confirmation the over-representation of the traditional middle class (also referred to as 'lower' middle class) amongst its supporters.

To what extent then were the independent *ceti medi* – particularly in crafts and industry – prominent or decisive constituents of Fascism? To tackle this issue I propose to examine the social composition of Fascism before it came to power. This requires looking at the occupational census of those who enlisted in the Fascist Party (PNF) at the height of its popularity as a mass movement (1921).[2] Such a strategy is dictated by two considerations. First, other kinds of material for constructing a convincing case about social composition are simply not available. On the question of 'who were the Fascists?' even the more recent Italian scholarship is inconclusive, owing in large part to serious deficiencies in the existing data base (see Larsen et al.: 1980). As several writers have pointed out, Italy remains 'the one huge gap' in the research on social composition. Consequently, most arguments about Italian Fascism tend to be inferential, drawn from what is known about the more solidly documented German movement (Lyttleton 1976: 134–5; Payne 1976: 385; Milward 1976).

The second reason for using membership data can be justified on

Table 3.1   Occupations of PNF members before take-over

| Occupation | Members % | Members no. | Population[a] (%) |
|---|---|---|---|
| Agricultural workers | 24.3 | 36,847 | 22.1 |
| Industrial workers | 15.4 | 23,418 | 25.5 |
| Seamen | 1.0 | 1,507 | — |
| White collar employees | 9.8 | 14,988 | 0.9 |
| Public employees | 4.8 | 7,209 ⎱ | 2.0 |
| Teachers | 1.1 | 1,680 ⎰ | |
| Professions | 6.6 | 9,981 | 0.8 |
| Students | 13.0 | 19,783 | 1.4[b] |
| Artisans and small traders | 9.2 | 13,878 | 11.9 |
| Industrialists and businessmen | 2.8 | 4,269 | 1.1[c] |
| Landowners and farmers (large, small, and tenants) | 12.0 | 18,084 | 31.0[d] |

[a] The column does not tally because some 'special categories' (e.g. religious and military) are excluded.
[b] Merkl's estimate (1980a: 260).
[c] Includes high-level managers and large landowners as calculated by Sylkos Labini.
[d] Population figure does not include large landowners, who have been incorporated in (c) as part of the 'big bourgeoisie'.
*Sources: Il Popolo d'Italia*, 8 November 1921 (cited in De Felice 1966: 6–7). Population figures from Sylos Labini (1978: 61).

methodological grounds. As Merkl points out, the founders or leadership of a political movement are not the best guide to understanding its social base, since in most cases, these tend to be drawn from the upper-middle strata. Whereas, 'If the membership at large could be shown to belong overwhelmingly to a certain class . . . the link-up would undoubtedly be much more significant' (1980a: 765).

Most important of all, however, the 1921 membership list shortly to be examined is the source most widely used to document the petit bourgeois interpretation (see, for example, De Felice 1966: 6–7; Tasca 1966; Togliatti 1970: 44–5; Linz 1976: 61–2). On that basis alone, the data provide a valid tool of analysis, permitting us to evaluate the danger thesis in its own terms, by challenging the way the material has been used and interpreted.

The occupational composition of PNF membership for 1921 is set out in table 3.1. Altogether, 151,644 people took part in the survey, representing roughly 70 per cent of the total membership at that time (De Felice 1966: 7). Now the case for interpreting Fascism as a petit bourgeois movement has been based on the claim that the traditional middle class was clearly over-represented among the PNF membership (Roberts 1980: 337). If we use this yardstick, that is, the percentage by which each occupational group exceeds or falls below the population average, then even a casual glance at the occupational figures ought to ring a few alarm bells.

Consider, first, the major groups which are *under*-represented in the membership. These fall into three main categories. Apart from the slightly excessive weight of agricultural workers which, combined with other rural elements, underlines the importance of agrarian Fascism (totalling 36.3 per cent of the membership), we find the expected under-representation of urban workers. More significant for our purposes, however, are the two remaining groups, for these have their basis in small independent ownership. Thus, farm owners, who make up 31 per cent of the population, provide less than 12 per cent of the membership; whilst small businessmen in trade and craft industry, which constitute almost 12 per cent of the population, comprise little more than 9 per cent of the total membership. Using the same criteria as other students, we see then that the independent middle class is clearly under-represented in the movement.

Most strikingly, however, the membership figures do confirm the disproportionate prominence of professionals, teachers and other white collar careerists. Considering that these groups comprise only 3.7 per cent of the population, their share of the total membership (22.3 per cent) leaves no doubt as to which social strata were the most predisposed towards Fascism. In comparison with other groups in the PNF, like tradesmen and independent artisans, and 'particularly considering the occupational structure of Italy' as Linz (1976: 63) observes, 'the number of white-collar employees, state and municipal civil servants, professionals and those engaged in teaching . . . is striking.' If we add students, then the membership of this 'learned' and salaried component contributed 3.5 out of every 10 members of the *Fasci* and exceeded its population weight sevenfold.

The weight of these groups, .Linz suggests, lends support to one of the earliest interpretations of Fascism. In *Nazionalfascismo* (1923), Luigi Salvatorelli argued that Fascism was largely a movement of the 'humanistic' petite bourgeoisie, identifying with this term those dependent strata of officials, clerks, teachers and other professionals whose function is, broadly speaking, more 'intellectual' than

*Table 3.2   Members' occupations in the German and Italian Fascist movements*

| Occupation | NSDAP[a] members (%) | 1933 pop. (%) | PNF members (%) | 1921 pop. (%) |
|---|---|---|---|---|
| Industrial workers | 25.0 | 54.6 | 16.0 | 25.5 |
| Agricultural workers | | | 24.0 | 22.1 |
| White collar workers | 10.0 | 12.4 | 10.0 | 0.9 |
| *Public employees* | | | | |
|   Civil Service | 11.0 | 5.7 | 5.0 ⎱ | 2.0 |
|   Teachers | | | 1.0 ⎰ | |
| Professions | 5.0 | 2.7 | 7.0 | 0.8 |
| Students | 1.0 | 0.5 | 13.0 | 1.4 |
| Independent traders and craftsmen | 26.0 | 15.5 | 9.0 | 11.9 |
| Big industrialists and businessmen | 12.0 | 0.9 | 3.0 | 1.1 |
| Farmers | 8.0 | 7.7 | 12.0 | 31.0 |

[a] 849,000 NSDAP members in 1933.

*Sources*: Merkl (1980a: 774). Population census data from Kater (1983: 241). The Italian data have been added.

'economic'. More to the point, perhaps, these groups are in the main dependent on the state. Since their interests and identities are more directly affected by its changing fortunes, they have a stake in preserving or enhancing its prestige. Hence one possible reason why the salariat is so prominent in a nationalist movement like Fascism. Whatever the explanation, the distinction between 'intellectual' and 'economic', or 'dependent' and 'independent', is a useful one for cutting through some of the conceptual confusion surrounding Italian Fascism.

Its importance becomes particularly clear at a comparative level. A comparison of the Italian (PNF) and German (NSDAP) movements at roughly comparable moments in their respective development (that is, prior to taking power) illustrates some very clear and crucial differences. As table 3.2 shows, the NSDAP, like its Italian equivalent, has a strong following among the salariat in both public and private sectors. Relative to the population at large, however, the level of support from this quarter reaches less remarkable proportions than that shown for the PNF. The most dramatic difference that leaps to our eyes is the prominence of small business in the German movement, accounting for 26 per cent of the membership yet only 15.5 per cent in the overall population. In sum, whereas German Fascism tends to draw considerable support from the independent middle class, the social base of Italian Fascism is much more clearly dominated by the dependent middle class.

For this striking difference historians and political analysts have offered little explanatory illumination other than to suggest that Fascism in the less developed countries like Italy was probably less a reaction to economic decline than it was in the more advanced Germany (Linz 1976: 678; Merkl 1980a: 259; Roberts 1980: 339ff). The minor presence of the independent middle class in the PNF compared with its disproportionate weight in the NSDAP certainly lends this view some plausibility. On the other hand, it may well be that 'economic crisis' played little part in either country.

Michael Mann (forthcoming: vol. 2, chapter 4) finds at least two clear-cut international trends to suggest that 'the narrowly economic fortunes of the non-agricultural petite bourgeoisie were probably not a major determinant of those turbulent politics.' First, there has been no *absolute* numerical decline of the petite bourgeoisie this century. Second, the greatest *relative* decline in most countries occurred around the *middle* of this century – that is, '*after* the politics of the *Mittelstand* and of Fascism had largely subsided'. Mann's detailed analysis suggests in fact a more plausible explanation of Fascism: not a reaction to economic decline, but a nationalistic response by the middle class, especially the holders of 'cultural capital', dependent on the state and interested in its glorification.

This argument, however, does not entirely solve the puzzle of German–Italian differences *vis-à-vis* small business support. But an explanation which resonates with Mann's interpretation can be ventured. It is possible that the 1933 NSDAP members categorized as small business operators were in reality closer to the lumpenproletariat – hurled into independence by the Depression as blue and white collar workers were being retrenched by large industry. As we will see shortly for Italy, it is precisely the urban poor eking out a subsistence on the far edges of the small business stratum that has provided a constituency for post-war neo-Fascism. The sources obviously blur this distinction, but it was precisely between 1929 and 1933 that self-employment underwent tremendous expansion in Germany. These points anticipate material presented in chapter 8 in the context of a quite different argument. The main point to emphasize here is that the puzzle of national differences in the extent of small business support for Fascism may well hinge upon little more than spurious classification.

My immediate purpose is not to settle this issue, but rather to expose serious flaws in the conventional accounts which, by lumping together dependent and independent strata, have made the petite bourgeoisie 'the keynote of the reigning interpretation'. In order to reinforce the validity of that distinction, it is worth very briefly considering material of a different nature, namely, the writings of respected contemporary observers.

According to Angelo Tasca, historian and prominent figure in the Communist Party, writing in 1938, Fascism found its chief support not among members of 'the middle class of the classical period of capitalism' but among those who have no direct share in production and who eventually form part of the immense Fascist bureaucracy which is now the country's ruling class' (1966: 342, 351). Tasca (1966: 342) went so far as to argue that those of independent economic standing, small property owners, 'remain antifascist'. In a somewhat similar vein, Luigi Sturzo (1926: 200), Catholic leader of the outlawed Popular Party (PPI), set down his observations regarding the sectors of society which, at the beginning of 1925, supported a dictatorship and the suppression of civil and political liberties. Apart from the big landowners and industrialists who feared a renewal of rural agitation and labour militancy, those singled out by Sturzo were the petty officials 'whose little hour of success was and is firmly bound up with the fortunes of Fascism'.

Prominent Marxists like Gramsci and Togliatti drew similar distinctions in their assessment of the sources of Fascist support. For Gramsci, the 'intellectual petite bourgeoisie' were the decisive components of Fascism, particularly in the south which, only in the last stages, rallied behind the Fascist coalition. In his 'Alcuni temi della questione meridionale', written in 1926, Gramsci argued that such support came from the southern petite bourgeoisie, by which he meant an 'intellectual stratum of rural small and medium landowners who do not work the land, but who draw income from land given in rent or share tenancy, and who seek to put their children through university, or the seminary in order to enter the professions or civil service' (cited in Catalano 1981: 165; see also Gramsci 1964: 797-819). Writing in 1923, Togliatti similarly described the main component of the Fascist movement as a 'small and medium bourgeoisie of professional people' (cited in Catalano 1981: 191).

However impressionistic, such observations add strength to the more objective data examined. Our analysis does not, of course, disprove that the independent *ceti medi* supported Fascism. It simply refutes the grounds for this assertion, namely, their supposed prominence in the movement. A valid criticism might be that such groups figured less prominently in the membership, not because they did not support the PNF, but because they were (and are) simply less disposed to join organizations of any kind. Yet, if one reads Sarti's (1971) account of the struggles for and against unification of business interests under one industrial leadership, it seems clear that most small business groups were organized if not always on a national, then almost certainly on a local or provincial basis.

Moreover, if such support was forthcoming, one wonders why the Fascists never drew more than 15 per cent of the popular vote, especially in the last fair election of 1921 when the movement had achieved a mass base. And this 15 per cent is a maximal estimate, owing to the united list system of that election (Payne 1980: 48).

It may be of course that once installed, the regime drew on passive support from small capital, but that is a much weaker argument than the one typically put forward. The case for petit bourgeois centrality it seems has been rested on little more than the lumping together of a motley of 'middling groups' – some employed in corporate and bureaucratic career hierarchies, others engaged in the professions, still others running small businesses.[3] Yet it is only the latter which properly constitutes the petite bourgeoisie or 'traditional' middle class. And this as we have seen is the crucial distinction.

## Right-wing extremism after 1945

Similar criticisms can be extended to attempts to link the independent middle class with neo-Fascist politics in the post-war period. Efforts in this direction have so far failed to do more than provide a list of right-wing political phenomena. Thus, the short-lived *Uomo Qualunque* movement of the mid-forties and the subsequent emergence of the neo-Fascists (MSI) are cited as examples of the 'political stirrings' of a discontented, easily mobilized small business stratum to which governments have rapidly responded with a flow of protective measures. Yet, as we will see in the following chapter, neither in the timing nor in the content of public policies is there anything to suggest such a relationship between 'reaction' and 'response'. Nor, as this argument implies, is there anything in the character of these move-ments evocative of a Poujadist-style protest movement. The *Uomo Qualunque* (literally, the 'ordinary man') emitted no protectionist outcry for small business interests. It adopted none of the protectionist demands usually associated with such protest move-ments. In short, the conventional association of *Qualunquismo* with small business discontent tells us more about the strength of a particular paradigm than it does about reality. To support this point, I shall very briefly discuss the three main features of *Qualunquismo*, which research has brought to light. These include the context of its emergence and decline; the interests to which it appealed; and the geographical distribution of its support.

In the most extensive treatment of the subject, Setta (1975) charts the rise and decline of *Uomo Qualunque* from 1944 to 1947. Its expansion and dissolution run parallel to the changing fortunes of the Communist–Socialist left whose initial dominance in the political arena gave way to increasing isolation following its eviction from government in 1947. Much more than a simple anti-communism, however, the movement was symptomatic of a widespread reaction to the growing disorder of public life and of a mounting aversion to the government – an 'anti-Fascist' alliance of Communists, Socialists and Christian Democrats – for its apparent incapacity or unwillingness to put an end to it. Numerous episodes of civil and partisan violence, land occupations in the south and agitations by the southern unemployed, the militancy of northern industrial workers – all worked to create a climate of increasing fear and uncertainty. What added to the general anxiety were the specific fears of the economic oligarchy, threatened by the proposals of the new Parri government which promised tough anti-monopolistic measures, as well as a more vigorous purgative action extending to private industry. In combination with the revolutionary rhetoric of the left and the discovery of unconsigned arms, such actions were seen by many Italians as dramatic proof of insurrec-tional plans being prepared for a dictatorship of the proletariat (Setta 1975: 54ff).

Against this background of internal tension and increasing political polarization, the *Uomo Qualunque* movement expanded, attracting the sympathies of the 'moderate' citizen disaffected with the parties in power. Disaffection notwithstanding, it polled only 5.2 per cent of the vote in the 1946 elections and quickly dissolved in the wake of the left's expulsion from power. As the leader of the Christian Democrats saw it, the major threat to the new democracy stemmed from the Communists' presence in the government. For De Gasperi, the Communist Party's (PCI) shaky democratic credentials and its apparent complicity in subversive activity undermined the legitimacy of parliamentary democracy and exposed it to 'a repetition of the phenomenon of 1922'.[4] In view of the actions taken by Christian Democracy to deal with the right-wing resurgence, namely, an intensification of anti-communism and repressive measures towards the labour movement, it would appear that small business disaffection played little part in shaping the political leadership's perception of danger.

To whom did *Uomo Qualunque* appeal? Beginning as a simple polemical journal (of a playwright and cartoonist) lampooning all the political parties, it moved ever more explicitly in 'defence of the bourgeoisie'. In particular, it appealed to the 'great leaders of Italian industry' and attacked the political leadership for the anti-Fascist purges taking place in the large industries of the north. In its propaganda *Qualunquismo* exalted the big bourgeoisie as the true agent of progress (Setta 1975: 130ff).

In short, *Uomo Qualunque* was no spokesman for the 'little man', for the small-scale entrepreneur. Even more to the point, it did not *need* to be: the government of the day was already sympathetically disposed towards small capital (see chapter 6). Suffice to note that one of the provisions that provoked hostility from big business towards the new government was an economic plan which, anti-monopolistic in spirit, envisaged the distribution of scarce primary materials in favour of the small and medium-sized firms (Setta 1975: 56; Abrate 1981).

The third important feature of the *Uomo Qualunque* and of its neo-Fascist successor, the MSI, is the localized nature of its following. As Linz (1976: 60) and others have pointed out, the far right-wing formations of the post-war era, in contrast with the 1920s movement, have found the bulk of their constituency in the undeveloped south and in the islands. Its southern resonance is most clearly reflected in the regional concentration of the vote. Of its 5.2 per cent share of the total vote in 1946, the *Uomo Qualunque* gained barely 2.3 per cent and 5.3 per cent in the north and centre respectively. But it polled 9.7 per cent in the south and Sicily, and 12.4 per cent in Sardinia (Setta 1975: 161).

Support for the MSI reveals a similar pattern. Averaging around 4.5 per cent of the vote in post-war elections,[5] it has consistently drawn the bulk of its support from the Mezzogiorno, most notably among the civil service personnel in the larger cities. Thus, in Rome, the seat of government administration, the MSI in 1958 polled 12.6 per cent of the vote, compared with 4.7 per cent in Italy as a whole. Informed trade union leaders have estimated that MSI supporters 'have been disproportionately four or five times more numerous among civil servants than among other voters in the capital'. Similar patterns were reported for other southern cities (Palermo and Bari), as well as in Trieste in the north (Dogan 1967: 153–4; Galli 1968: 341).

Reviewing similar evidence, Christopher Husbands' survey of right-wing extremist movements makes two important points for Italy that resonate with the preceding analysis. First, most analyses of the MSI tend to reason on an intuitive basis rather than resorting systematically to empirical data. Second, no consistent social base can be identified for the period as a whole. The only hard evidence of support that Husbands uncovers is that of poorer, rural strata in the 1950s, and of urban, upper and upper-middle class groups (contractors, free professionals and managers) in the 1970s (1981: 85–9).

One important conclusion, however, can be drawn: the essentially southern character of neo-Fascism is indisputable. As we have seen, it has consistently found its largest constituency in the metropolitan centres of the Mezzogiorno, especially among civil servants. Other students have suggested that an important reservoir of MSI votes is provided by the urban lumpenproletariat: the groups hurled into existence by poverty and under-employment. Made up of 'all those who survive by making ends meet on a day-to-day basis' – the mass of street vendors, marginal wage earners, small wheelers and dealers trading in the slum economy of southern cities – this is a world of 'penny capitalism' (Chubb 1982: 49; Allum 1973). Some of these groups are indeed situated at the far edges of the small business stratum, but they can hardly be considered as typical components of small capital.

With regard to the political perceptions of neo-Fascism, the writings of Christian Democrats, once again, identify the salariat and 'learned' component of the middle class. Writing in 1951 on the *ceti medi* – defined in this context as free professionals and public employees – Sturzo (1968: 66) argued that

The disorientation of the *ceti medi* in Italy (in alternate phases) is due above all to the heaviness of our post-war economy which has not yet shown signs of a promising overall recovery; and to the tendency (a terrible malady) of all wanting to become employees of the state and of public bodies.

Sturzo here alludes to the problem of the southern, unemployed intelligentsia and its connection with right-wing radicalism. In a similar vein, Baget-Bozzo (1976: 119–123), a leading spokesman for the left wing of the Christian Democrats, identified the 'Fascist danger' in 1949 with that part of the southern *ceti medi* who 'have a role in ruling and in social organization, especially with regard to the peasant mass'. According to this observer, the real menace stemmed not from any particular political movement. Organized neo-Fascism he referred to as a 'phenomenon of little significance . . . well confined to a nostalgic few'. Rather, the problem consisted in 'the unchanging political structure of the *ceti medi*', in their continuing clientelistic dependence on the large landowning class. This could be effectively dealt with only by eliminating the mono-polistic power base of the southern notables and incorporating those groups with 'a role in ruling and social organization' as agents of control for the state. By way of confirming the representative-ness of this view, it is worth pointing out that it perfectly describes the way the DC proceeded to gain control of the south during the 1950s.

To conclude these observations, let me summarize two principal weaknesses of the 'danger' argument. First, it alleges the complicity of the traditional middle class in Fascism (and its post-war variants). This is not established. Implicit in this claim is the assumption that the economically independent parts of the middle class were favourably treated under the Fascist regime. If it could be shown that small industry and crafts were among its principal beneficiaries, that substantial advantages accrued to these groups, then there would at least be a stronger case for this interpretation. For it might then be argued that in order not to alienate this class and to purchase its compliance, the DC had likewise to favour it.

On this point, however, the research is quite clearly in agreement. Fascism, whether Italian or German, pursued policies from which the petite bourgeoisie gained relatively little, if anything (Sarti 1971; Winkler 1976: 16; De Felice 1977: 180; Hagtvet 1980: 31; Milward 1980).[6] Indeed, the whole point of the new credit system introduced in the 1950s was to cater for smaller concerns whose needs under the existing banking structure had not been accommodated.

Finally, the danger argument presupposes economic precarious-ness which, presumably, ought to be evident in declining numbers of small independents. But the trend is that of *rising* numbers. Since the date of the last prewar census (1936) through to 1971, the non-agricultural petite bourgeoisie (small employers plus 'own account' workers) expanded by at least 1.1 million units (Sylos Labini 1978: 78).

A great deal of this post-war expansion, as the following chapters make clear, has been deliberately sought by government policies favouring an extension of small ownership. And it is precisely this aspect of state support which has been obscured by a discourse cast in the idiom of protection. The only clear example of protectionist legislation in post-war Italy is that applying to the retail trades, which restricts the number of department stores and supermarkets. Towards the small retailers themselves, however – as we shall see in chapter 6 – licensing policy has been altogether liberal, with the result that there are now more tiny outlets per head of population than in any other European country. Yet in vain might we look for something similar to the 'social protectionism' of the *Mittelstand* in Imperial Germany, with its guild-like regulations for the handicrafts (Winkler 1976); or indeed to the cartel principle introduced under Fascism, which effectively excluded newcomers from the market and left numerous small concerns struggling to survive on the margins of legality (Sarti 1971: 110–11).

Indeed, as I try to show in chapter 6, one of the reasons why small business has mushroomed in recent years, almost to the point of saturation in some sectors, is that the DC rejected protectionist legislation of the kind which, in Germany, continues to make entry into independent trade so difficult. As we shall see, some of the most important small business legislation in the post-war period, rather than protecting acquired positions, was more likely to challenge them.

### An alternative profile of the small business stratum

To draw an analogy from the court room, I have sought to undermine the danger hypothesis by putting the independent *ceti medi* on trial to prove its guilt. The evidence for the prosecution – the historical examples conventionally cited – has failed to establish its complicity in Fascism and its post-war variants. At this point, an appropriate verdict might read: 'a case of mistaken identity'.

To round out this judgement, we move now from the defensive

*Table 3.3  Comparison of four main electoral subdivisions, 1946, 1963, 1979*

|  |  | 1946 | 1963 | 1979 |
|---|---|---|---|---|
| DC |  | 35.2 | 38.3 | 38.3 |
| Right | (Liberals and Monarchists) | 9.6 | 8.7 | 8.2 |
| Left | (Republicans, Social Democrats, Socialists, Communists, Radicals,[a] Proletarian Unity[a]) | 46.6 | 46.7 | 45.0 |
| Fascists | (*Umo Qualunque* and neo-Fascists) | 5.3 | 5.1 | 5.3 |

[a] 1979 elections only.
Source: Galli (1966: 119). The 1979 figures have been added.

position to confront the danger thesis from a more positive angle. To restate its central premise: the petite bourgeoisie is strongly hostile to the left, inimical to organizational loyalties and, consequently, unstable in its alliances and easy prey to right-wing radicalism. By way of contesting these assumptions a variety of political data will be presented from which an alternative profile may be drawn.

### The pattern of electoral support: stability or instability?

If small property owners, who constitute a substantial part of the Italian electorate,[7] were the politically unstable creatures invariably portrayed in the literature, then one would expect to find significant oscillations between elections, especially to and from the far right. Yet one of the outstanding and undisputed features of the Italian electorate – at least until the early seventies – has been its overall stability (Galli 1966: 119; Martinotti 1978: 37ff). According to one study, the 'constant' electorate ranges between 70 per cent and 80 per cent, a proportion higher than in the United States, Great Britain, Canada and Japan (Barbagli et al. 1979: 118)![8]

As an example of electoral stability consider Galli's comparison of the 1946 and 1963 positions of the four main electoral subdivisions in Table 3.3. Although Galli's analysis covers only the period up to 1963, the 1979 figures show also the relevance of his observations for the later period. Thus he calculates that over a period of roughly twenty years during which numerous political, administrative and regional elections took place, redistributions of the vote involved displacements of only 5 to 6 per cent of the electorate. In this light, the contest between the Christian Democrats and the Communists, who have consistently drawn around two-thirds of the total vote, appears to be little more than 'a frontier battle on the confines of their solid electoral empire' for the acquisition of 'a marginal electorate'. Thus, the PCI wages an offensive battle on its right to snatch away fringes of the 'socialist' electorate; whilst the DC conducts a defensive campaign on its right to retain the most conservative fringe of its 'moderate' domain. *In each case no more than 3 per cent of the electorate is involved* (Galli 1966: 127–8).

From these brief observations, it can be tentatively concluded that the putatively 'unstable stratum' has repeatedly failed to live up to its collective reputation. Instead of significant *national* fluctuations, we find only marginal displacements. Even at a regional level, where such shifts have at times been considerable, it has been the moderate rather than the extreme right which has gained most from rightward displacements.[9]

That the small business sector is less volatile than conventionally portrayed gains further plausibility if we consider the absence of protest in a situation most likely to induce it. Between 1963 and 1966, southern firms were severely affected by the adverse business cycle, forcing numerous small operators in crafts and industry out of the market. In manufacturing alone, the south lost some 10,000 establishments between 1961 and 1971. Yet, in the 1968 elections, the DC did not suffer any mass defection of *ceti medi* supporters. It actually increased its strength in the south, whilst that of the MSI declined.

*Political preferences: the sociological composition of the vote*

For present purposes, it is more important to know *how* a particular class or category votes than to know *what* factors influence electoral preferences. Of the sources covering earlier years, the most useful is Poggi's (1968) study of various occupational groups, based on national survey material of 1963. As a good part of this data is of an inferential nature – owing to the traditional reticence of the Italian electorate in disclosing party preferences – its strength lies more in boldness of outline than in accuracy of detail. Yet, as we will see, its plausibility seems considerably enhanced when set alongside other findings.

Table 3.4 highlights two important patterns. First, the DC gains by far the greatest share of small business votes – around 40 per

Table 3.4  *Political preferences by occupation, 1963*

| Occupation | PCI (25.3)[a] | PSI (13.8) | PSDI (6.1) | PRI (1.4) | DC (38.3) | PLI (7.0) | PDIUM (1.7) | MSI (5.1) | Don't know | Total no. |
|---|---|---|---|---|---|---|---|---|---|---|
| Artisans | 17 | 19 | 8 | 0.5 | 40 | 7 | 2 | 6 | 0.5 | 187 |
| Shopkeepers | 15 | 15 | 7 | 2 | 40 | 11 | 1. | 7 | 3 | 177 |
| *Employees* | | | | | | | | | | |
| Clerical | 14 | 13 | 12 | 1 | 43 | 8 | 1 | 5 | 3 | 127 |
| Executive | 11 | 11 | 11 | 1 | 42 | 12 | 2 | 7 | 3 | 272 |

[a] Bracketed figures represent party's share of 1963 vote.
*Source:* Adapted from Poggi (1968: 47, table IV.4).

cent for both artisans and shopkeepers. Second, the large majority of these preferences are clustered around the centre and left of centre. Thus, rather than being oriented to the right of the political spectrum, a significant proportion of small independents tends to favour left-wing parties, particularly those *within* the governing coalition. Even allowing for the tendency of interviewers to attribute right-wing preferences to these groups when such information is withheld, there is little evidence to suggest pro-Fascist sympathies from this quarter. From other information supplied (Poggi 1968: 19), it would appear that the most likely sympathizers are the male professional, managerial and executive strata.

The same broad patterns can be traced in Sylos Labini's estimates relating to the 1968 elections, which are set out in table 3.5. From this, we see that almost 50 per cent of the independent stratum (including farmers) support the Christian Democrats. Compared with the Communists' share of the working class vote (40 per cent), it would appear that the support of the independent petite bourgeoisie for the DC is at least as, if not more, compact than that of the working class for the PCI. In addition to the pro-government stance of small business, the 1968 estimates reaffirm two other patterns which were identified in Poggi's data: the centre-left orientation of small business and its modest support for neo-Fascism. Thus, almost 80 per cent of its preferences go to the three major parties, but less than 5 per cent to the MSI. By contrast, the latter attracts in proportional terms more than three times as many voters from the salaried, executive and professional strata.

Having established the overall pattern, the regional distribution of support should be examined. This varies significantly not only for the petite bourgeoisie but for all social classes, highlighting one of the peculiarities of the Italian context. In other words, the 'class' variable is less important in influencing the vote than other factors like party organization and religious affiliation. The literature draws particularly on these variables to explain why, for example, the DC can count on a significant share of the industrial workers' suffrage; why the Communists are stronger in the more rural regions of the centre than in the industrialized north-west; and, more generally, why electoral outcomes can differ considerably between adjoining regions or towns with similar economic and social features.[10]

The implications of the 'organizational' factor will become clear as we examine the PCI's success among the small business electorate in Emilia Romagna, and if we recall one central

Table 3.5 Distribution of votes among Italian parties, subdivided by social class, 1968

| Percentage of total vote | Party | Petite bourgeoisie | | | | |
| | | (a) Bourgeoisie | (b) Employees | (c) Independents | (d) Special categories | (e) Working class |
|---|---|---|---|---|---|---|
| (31.4) | PCI–PSIUP | — | 23.5 | 23.7 | 20.0 | 40.2 |
| (11.5) | PSI | — | 13.7 | 6.5 | — | 12.1 |
| | PSDI | 14.3 | 3.9 | 4.3 | — | 4.4 |
| (2.0) | PRI | 14.3 | 2.0 | 3.2 | — | 1.3 |
| (39.1) | DC | 28.5 | 35.3 | 48.4 | 40.0 | 35.6 |
| (5.8) | PLI | 28.5 | 5.9 | 8.6 | 20.0 | 2.6 |
| (5.8) | MSI–Mon | 14.4 | 13.7 | 4.3 | 20.0 | 2.6 |
| (1.4) | Others | — | 2.0 | 1.0 | — | 1.2 |
| | Total | 100.0 | 100.0 | 100.0 | 100.0 | 100.0 |
| % of electorate | | 2.2 | 16.0 | 29.3 | 3.1 | 49.4 |

(a) big entrepreneurs, managers, professionals
(b) private and public
(c) artisans, shopkeepers, farmers, others
(d) religious and military personnel
(e) all sectors
Source: Sylos Labini (1978: 75, table 14).

assumption of the danger thesis: namely, that the independent middle class, being implacably opposed to the left and lacking firm organizational ties, are susceptible to the blandishments of the extreme right. The following material evinces a very different view.

It has increasingly become clear that, in the Red Belt where the Communists have established deep historical ties with the region, an extensive organizational network and considerable command over local resources, the party is able to attract wide consensus from the small business community. One measure of this ability is the proportion of *ceti medi* voters within the Communist electorate. Estimates vary quite dramatically, depending on the classifications used, but all suggest that the PCI both nationally and regionally has

Table 3.6 *Geographical distribution of political preferences of artisans and shopkeepers (aggregates only; percentage horizontally)*

| Area (% of 1963 vote) | PCI (25.3) | PSI (13.8) | PSDI (6.1) | PRI (1.4) | DC (38.3) | PLI (7.0) | PDIUM (1.7) | MSI (5.1) |
|---|---|---|---|---|---|---|---|---|
| North | 14 | 15 | 13 | 1 | 38 | 13 | 0 | 4 |
| Centre | 30 | 20 | 4 | 1 | 27 | 7 | 3 | 5 |
| South and islands | 11 | 18 | 2 | 1 | 48 | 6 | 1 | 10 |

*Source*: Poggi (1968: 52, table IV.12).

increasingly become an 'interclass' party like the DC.[11] According to the 1963 survey used by Poggi, the PCl received more preferences from this quarter than any other party in central Italy (see table 3.6).

More recent studies suggest that the *ceti medi* have become gradually more disposed towards the Communists since the early sixties. In Emilia Romagna, for example, this growing consensus is reflected in the PCI's steady electoral advance despite structural changes in the economy resulting in fewer wage earners and increasing numbers of independent workers and salaried personnel (Donati 1976: 66).

It is no coincidence that the expansion of this support has paralleled the PCI's increasing efforts on behalf of the small business community. As we shall see, its ability to penetrate that electorate is less a reflection of petit bourgeois 'instability' than of the skill and peculiarly adaptable nature of the Italian Communist Party. Forced to reckon with small capital as a permanent and expanding part of the Italian economy, the PCI began at this time to advance its anti-monopoly alliance strategy, championing small business interests nationally and assisting the self-employed in areas where it controlled local government resources. In parliamenrary debates, the Communists' solicitude for small industry has at times seemed almost a parody of the Christian Democrat position. In the same context, discussions of the results of financial incentives for small enterprise have frequently been used as occasions to 'expose' the DC as a pro-monopoly party and to hasten a split within the ranks of industrial employers.[12] That such charges have been largely unfounded is beside the point. What they demonstrate is the PCI's efforts to substitute the DC as the 'true' spokesman for this section of the population. This endeavour probably goes beyond what several commentators have considered as an anti-Fascist or 'neutralizing' strategy (for example, Hellman 1975: 382ff). As I shall presently suggest, so far from being based on the notion of an insecure, protectionist-minded petite bourgeoisie, the Communists' policy highlights the confidence and reality of *social mobility* that has characterized this stratum in Italian society over the post-war period.[13]

The power to capture and allocate resources at local level is no doubt one important element in the party's ability to attract small business consensus. Organizational loyalties and group identification add another crucial component, especially among the artisans of the region. In 1980, for example, 55 per cent of the 145,725 registered artisan enterprises in Emilia Romagna were members of the Communist- and Socialist-affiliated Confederazione Nazionale dell'Artigianato. Confirming earlier inquiries, Sabel's (1982: 229) research in the Red Belt also revealed that many of the small, innovative metal-working firms are run by their Communist and Socialist founders, formerly expelled from the large factories during the political purges of the 1950s.

This finding touches on one very important aspect of the small business world in Italy, namely, that a high proportion of independent craftsmen and small entrepreneurs generally have risen from a wage-earning position – a theme that chapters 6 and 9 will return to. The PCI's early appreciation of the 'mobility' factor has probably done more to influence its attitude towards the small sector than any 'pathological' theory of petite capital. Already in their analyses of the *Tendencies of Italian Capitalism* (Istituto Gramsci-CESPE 1962), a group of Communist deputies had begun to anticipate the discovery of a 'third' Italy, noting the crucial role of small enterprise in the economic expansion of Italy's central regions. What is of major interest here – both for its implications for Communist policy and for its remarkable parallels with the demochristian view – is their attempt to account for the growth of independent initiatives. According to these analysts, the fundamental factor was the presence of a highly skilled and politically progressive labour force whose 'spirit of initiative' had led to thousands of workers setting up independently. Their inquiries revealed that many of these new entrepreneurs in industry and artisan trades were none other than former factory workers who had resigned or been dismissed from their jobs in the preceding period. In sum, they concluded, these new entrepreneurial formations were the result of 'politically and socially advanced forces who have ruptured the old relations of exploitation, who no longer want to depend on a master, who want to acquire greater freedom, independence and prosperity and who demonstrate a capacity for initiative and adaptation hitherto unsuspected' (1972: vol. 2, 313). But for the term 'exploitation' and the admission of the unexpected nature of the phenomenon, one might be forgiven for attributing this statement to the PCI's arch rival which, for the past two decades, had been making almost identical diagnoses. In chapter 6 we shall see just how remarkably this understanding echoes the demochristian ideology of 'deproletarianization' and social mobility. The general implications of the Communist analysis seem clear. For if, as suggested, the small entrepreneurial class was recruiting significant numbers of workers to its ranks – including Communist and Socialist sympathizers – then all the more reason for a benevolent stance towards this sector.[14]

What conclusions about petit bourgeois politics can we draw from this material? First, the regional evidence leaves no doubt that the owners of small craft concerns are one of the *least* likely candidates of right-wing radicalism. Second, instead of a politically anchorless small business stratum, steadfast only in its aversion to the left, the Emilia Romagna experience suggests that even in the most Communist of regions, its constituent groups – including small industrialists and shopkeepers – have become increasingly integrated within the organizational net of a dominant party. This does not of course imply that the Communists enjoy overwhelming support from this quarter. What it reveals is that the independent stratum is far more stably inserted within the political system than the theorists of danger ever suspected.

One of the best examples of the *pro-regime* sentiments of small entrepreneurs is the extent to which they support the dominant party, not for its record on industrial policy, but as a means of ensuring the stability of the political system. A nationwide survey carried out in 1976 by the General Confederation of Italian Industry (CGII) – otherwise known as Confindustria – involving some 4,000 entrepreneurs, revealed that whilst only 18 per cent of the respondents considered the DC had been the party most sensitive to the problems of industry, nevertheless, 41 per cent said that they would vote for the DC above all others in order *to guarantee political stability*. These findings are set out in table 3.7 overleaf.

The different patterns of response solicited for each issue indicate that small industrialists draw a clear distinction between matters economic and political. Rather than seeking to penalize the major

*Table 3.7 Parties considered in order of reputed sensitivity to problems of industry, compared with those who should receive greater electoral support to ensure political stability*

|  | Party most sensitive to problems of industry | Party supported for greater political stability |
|---|---|---|
| Republicans | 31.4 | 18.7 |
| Liberals | 26.0 | 21.1 |
| Christian Democrats | 18.3 | 40.9 |
| Social Democrats | 8.6 | 4.1 |
| Neo-Fascists | 6.5 | 6.8 |
| Communists | 5.3 | 2.7 |
| Socialists | 3.8 | 4.0 |
| Others | 0.1 | 1.7 |

*Source*: CGII (1976: 33, 43).

party and reward others in accordance with perceived economic performance, they favour an enhancement of the DC's electoral weight – at both national (41 per cent) and local (48 per cent) levels. Consistent with their loyalty to the centre and desire for political stability is the constancy with which these entrepreneurs maintain their electoral preferences. Of the 2,100 respondents on this issue, 77 per cent confirmed they had elected in the 1975 administrative elections the same party as nominated on previous occasions. As the Confindustria inquiry concluded, even if they disagree or are dissatisfied with government policy, small industrialists still support the governing parties, above all, the Christian Democrats for their pivotal role in regime stability (CGII 1974: 41).

To what extent are such attitudes representative of small industry over the period as a whole? Despite the lack of comparable survey material for earlier years, it is worth noting that the 1976 findings are consistent with those reported in a smaller, regional survey conducted ten years earlier (Farneti 1970: 188–90). But one of the earliest, and perhaps strongest illustrations of the democratic, pro-government orientations of small industry is provided at an organizational level, in a context fraught with business antagonism towards the interventionist policies of the DC.

The setting is the first National Conference of Small Industry, held in 1956 by the small employers' representative body within Confindustria, the National Committee of Small Industry. Note the date: the same year in which Poujadism made its explosive debut in French politics. Yet what seems instructive here is the absence of parallels with the French case. Attended by 3,000 entrepreneurs and a heavy contingent of DC ministers, Members of Parliament and junior ministers, the conference had a purely symbolic purpose. Touching only briefly on specific economic problems of small industry, its chief aim was to demonstrate the unity of the industrial class in defence of private initiative.

To set this event within its wider context, as part of the DC's strategy to gain greater economic and political independence from big business and other interest groups, the party had begun to extend its hold over the state apparatuses and to expand the public sector. At the time of the conference, measures were before Parliament which would create a separate ministry for the State Holding Corporations; detach the latter from Confindustria and set up a separate employers' organization; and, finally, separate the artisanat from the rest of industry on the basis of firm size. At the same time, Confindustria, which lacked a specific political base either inside or outside Parliament, saw itself acting, according to the President, Micheli, 'in a permanent state of inferiority' (CGII 1956: 25). Thus, alarmed by what they saw as the state's encroachment into the domain of private initiative and attempts to divide the industrial world, the representatives of industry sought to show the government that the entrepreneurial class was a united bloc 'not to be fragmented by the interventions of the governing class'. As the spokesman for small industry complained: 'We are against political attempts to create a situation of privilege for the small-size firm since this divides the industrial category and would lead to an economic inversion, to a fatal contraction of productive activities' (CGII 1956: 30).

Yet despite this 'gathering of strength' and the strong opposition expressed towards certain government measures, the overall tenor of the conference as described in the press was one of 'moderate protest'. Instead of using the solidarity of the occasion to threaten a withdrawal of consensus, the organization assured government that the small industrialists were 'the natural and most staunch defenders of the State and of order . . . an irreplaceable component of stability and progress' (CGII 1956: 36). Indeed, it is a noteworthy characteristic of small business that it bases its claims to a sympathetic hearing from government, not on threats and agitation, but rather on the crucial role it exercises in the defence of democracy and freedom. Typical of the way it invokes its democratic credentials is the following statement made by the President of the Committee for the Italian *Ceto Medio*:

The *ceto medio* deserves this particular attention [from the state] because it is the centre of life and activity of our nation [and] . . . because it has shown with its wisdom, in more critical moments of our history, to be a fundamental element of equilibrium, free from foolish extremist ambitions, and knows how to bear notable sacrifices to maintain the fundamental basis of democracy. (Comitato d'Intesa Unitaria 1958: 22)

## Conclusion

A major theme running throughout this chapter has been an insistence on the need to 'deconstruct' the *ceti medi* as a politically homogeneous entity. Occupationally and regionally, we found evidence of significant variations in the political tendencies of groups commonly classified as middle class. As far as the small business stratum is concerned, the idea of an anxiety-ridden, status-conscious 'little man', struggling for a space between big unions and big business, and poised for flight into unseemly politics, is one which owes little to solid evidence. One can only suppose that such conceptions flow from a pervasive intellectual disdain towards that 'lower' middle class which appears neither to have reaped the glamorous rewards of capitalist power nor suffered the romantic hardships of wage servitude.

More positively, the profile presented here projects a view of petite capital much at odds with the pathological behaviour conventionally ascribed to it. Expansion and confidence – not frustration and insecurity – best capture the post-war experience of these small economic operators, who have shown themselves to be, on the whole, electorally centrist and politically acquiescent.

It is well to admit, however, that politicians are not immune to intellectual diagnoses, however imperfectly grounded. Since perceptions are not infrequently out of phase with what is objectively the case, we cannot ignore the 'mistake' factor. Thus, in order to save the threat thesis, some might argue that regardless of small capital's actual role in Fascism, it is what the political leadership of the post-war era believed that really counts. The test is whether the behaviour of the state meshes with the perception of danger imputed to its political managers. It is now time to analyse the general features of state support and to see how they affect the general argument made to this point.

# 4

# Patterns of state support I: bountiful but bounded

Even Italy . . . suffers mainly from a political ineptitude that, in its effect upon the society as a whole, is rather less important than ineptitude in Britain's leadership. The Italian state, as such, is in important respects irrelevant to what happens in Italian society

The Hudson Report (1986: 143)

In ways unanticipated a decade ago . . . and without any policy worthy of the name, northern Italy is witnessing the emergence of an embryonic but highly competitive, decentralized economy, one that challenges the long-presumed superiority of industrial mass production.

Katzenstein (1985: 23)

Despite their disagreements over the extent and impact of the state's involvement in the post-war development of small capital, both the danger thesis and the 'three Italies' model view the nature and purpose of state activity in similar terms. According to the latter approach, reviewed in chapter 2, state support has on the whole been negligible. At most the strategy has been to prop up an ailing small business sector in the inhospitable south. But in the flourishing heartlands of the small firm economy where the profusion and vitality of small industry has been most pronounced, the hand of the state has been least visible. For the less discriminating theorists of danger, the state has pursued an encompassing protective strategy to prevent petit bourgeois decline and disaffection. The fact that there is no objective basis to the fear of petit bourgeois discontent does not of course rule out the possibility that such a danger was perceived none the less. But is the behaviour of the state indicative of such a fear?

The task of the present chapter is to consider whether the causal connections implied by these approaches are borne out by the patterning of state support. Since both are informed by a fundamentally similar logic – the instability of small capital determines state support – they can be put to the same test. Pushing that logic to its empirical conclusion, we would expect to find that in the south where economic precariousness and neo-Fascist support have been most pronounced, benefits flowing to small business have been the most generous. Conversely, in the thriving regions of the centre-north, where the electorate has been long 'captured' within subcultural networks by the two major parties, so the resources flowing to the sector should be the least substantial.

Since the only practical means of testing these hypotheses is to quantify state support wherever possible, I shall focus for the most part (but not exclusively) on the financial assistance given to small firms. Above all, I shall attempt to demonstrate three aspects of public intervention, which I refer to as its 'extensiveness', 'intensity', and 'visibility'. Each challenges a basic theme of the 'three Italies' model. Instead of its overall paucity, its concentration in the south and its absence from the third economy, we will see that such assistance has been substantial and nationally focused; that it has been far greater *outside* the south; and that rather than being the centre of a neo-classical capitalism, the third Italy has benefited most from state-sponsored schemes.

Before we undertake that task one point about the scope of the analysis and its organizational rationale should be made clear. To provide an assessment of government assistance in Italy is no easy task. A basic complication is that the terrain of small enterprise is occupied by two distinct categories of economic activity: artisan trades and small industry. One consequence of this distinction is that much assistance available to small firms is dispersed across several agencies, each of which gathers data according to different criteria, for different purposes, covering different periods. This rules out a neat and comprehensive statement of results. I have therefore traced separately the patterns of support for each category of small business. Only then can a cumulative picture emerge. A further complication is the recent administrative innovation. In 1977 the state finally decentralized some of its direct powers in the field of economic development, thus transferring to the regions and communes greater responsibility in administering and initiating schemes for small business development. Thus both the Communists and Christian Democrats are now closely involved at municipal level in the financing of projects, in arranging exhibitions of work and in setting up industrial parks or estates for the sharing of facilities by small industrialists and artisans. For the most part the data therefore cover the period up to 1976. Even if such a task could be accomplished, extending the analysis to the present would not make the slightest difference to the historical thrust of my argument, nor indeed to the fate of the hypotheses to be examined.

## The legal regime of the small firm

To evaluate the Italian state's contribution to the development of the small firm sector, a detailed investigation of the provisions available to artisans and industry was carried out. A content analysis of all the major laws on incentives to industry revealed a copious legislation of support, all privileging firms of small dimensions and all of which was initiated in the 1950s. In fact, in this period, the entire system of public benefits – including ten-year exemptions from income tax, subsidized loans, regional development policy – was structured exclusively for the artisan and small industrial enterprise.[1]

From this analysis, it was clear that firm size has been the major determinant of eligibility for state-provided benefits and that, consequently, through these rules and arrangements, the boundaries of the small business sector have been shaped and an institutional space preserved.

The best illustration of this point is the Artisan Statute, introduced by the Christian Democrat government in 1956 to clarify the boundaries of the category that was to be the subject of special benefits. Unlike the German and French systems, for example, where the artisan qualification is defined on the basis of professional 'lists' of activities, the Italian artisan – or rather, artisan enterprise – is so defined in law, on the basis of numbers employed.[2] Not a professional category, then, but a legal regime, membership of which entitles the owner to a wide variety of benefits, including cheap loans, loan guarantees, lower tax and employers' contributions, welfare benefits at reduced premiums, exemptions from keeping accounts and from bankruptcy proceedings.[3] With such an impressive array of benefits at the artisan's disposal, it is easy to see how the legal classification is itself a very potent stimulus for the small business operator (either potential or existing) to join its ranks.[4] As one student of the artisan economy observes, 'it is not only of statistical curiosity that one who sells pastries from his oven be classified as artisan or shopkeeper, because the more favourable social security and tax treatment reserved for artisans encourages many to join that camp when the occasion presents itself' (Barberis 1980: 11).

Through the 1956 Act then, the Italian state has provided the most fundamental, if little examined, stimulus to the dramatic expansion of the workshop economy. For, as the preceding observations make clear, far from *protecting* the existing artisan world, this legal arrangement effectively opened its doors to a variety of newcomers having little to do with activities of a strictly artisanal nature, resulting in a dramatic increase in the number of artisan firms.

This, then, although a major incentive through which the state has encouraged micro entrepreneurship, is only one of several. In addition to the concessions which lower labour and running costs, protect income and provide welfare protection, post-war governments have also sponsored schemes for collective endeavours such as trade associations, industrial cooperatives and consortiums of small producers. Whether to bulk buy raw materials, to handle marketing and administration, to secure guaranteed loans or to share common facilities, small firms participating in these ventures are offered subsidies, infrastructure and preferential tax treatment. The wider practical significance of these collaborative efforts will be considered in the final chapter.

For a more concrete assessment of the nature and patterning of support which will address this chapter's central concerns, it is time to turn to the main financial incentives. Beginning with artisan enterprise, we shall trace in particular the total amount of credit allocated under the soft loan schemes; the proportion of new and existing firms assisted; and the regional distribution of funds and beneficiary firms.

## Financing artisan enterprise

### The Artisan Fund

The loan scheme, administered by the Cassa per il Credito alle Imprese Artigiane (Artigiancassa), dates from 1947. Although support was limited during these early years – when the state's efforts were directed towards reconstruction, agriculture and public works – the Fund was to receive major impetus in 1952 when its functions were broadened and its endowment enlarged.[5]

Under Law 949 of 1952, Artigiancassa provides ten-year loans at very low rates of interest (between 3 and 5 per cent for most of the period) for setting up, equipping and modernizing workshops. In addition, the Fund discounts medium-term loans, assists in the payment of interest and facilitates loans in the absence of sufficient securities through a government guarantee scheme (covering up to 70 per cent of individual bank loans for investment purposes). The state has also sponsored the formation of credit-guarantee cooperatives among artisan owners, contributing 50 per cent of the total amount pledged by members.

To administer this programme, the Fund draws primarily on public resources from an Endowment Fund, an Interest Payment Fund and a Central Guarantee Fund, outlays for which totalled some 750 billion lire by 1976, a sum which had tripled by 1980![6]

Building on the basic information so far provided, the following section will look more closely at the conditions of the financial incentive, how it has been applied and the extent to which the sector in question has benefited.

### Characteristics and conditions of loans

In addition to the direct subsidy deriving from the reduction of interest, artisan credit is further 'softened' by the practice of discounting loans (by 20 to 30 per cent) repaid before their due date. About one-third of the 370,000 loans made over the period had benefited also from this discounting operation (Appendix I, table A).

With regard to loan values, the maximum amount of each loan was initially set at 5 million lire (up to 10 million in certain cases), a ceiling gradually raised – to 25 million in 1975 – in line with rising costs of installation and equipment. Between 1953 and 1966, for example, the average value of loans granted was 2.6 million lire,[7] whereas for the overall period, it had increased to 6.4 million lire. As Appendix I, table B shows, 85 per cent of all loans granted between 1953 and 1976 were for amounts of up to 10 million lire. However, the substantial value of soft loans is most clearly illustrated by the fact that loan finance covered *c.*64 per cent of total investment requirements.[8]

The attractiveness and importance of the national programme run by Artigiancassa are further underlined by a comparison with a similar loan scheme operated by the Cassa per il Mezzogiorno, the Fund for Southern Development. As one of its minor functions, this agency provides low-interest credit to artisan concerns located in southern Italy. Its contribution, however, has been marginal, not to say exiguous. For instance, whereas the average Artigiancassa loan amounted to 2.6 million lire, the average Cassa loan was barely *one-tenth* that value (Presidency of the Council of Ministers 1971: 56). We can see, then, that in terms of interest rate, discount option, length of repayment periods and overall value, investment loans administered by the Artisan Fund represent a very substantial benefit for artisan enterprise.

Bearing in mind the analytical concerns outlined in the introduction, I propose now to examine the data on both a national and regional basis.

## Results of the loan scheme 1953–1976

### Summary of the main findings

To do justice to the results of the loan scheme, it is necessary to examine these in some detail. However, amidst the mass of information, certain facts will stand out, and are summarized as follows:

1 In just over twenty years, the Fund assisted 300,000 artisan firms with subsidized credit worth 2,388 billion lire, enabling a total investment of 3,722 billion lire, two-fifths of which was spent on *new* workshops.

2 Loan finance covered about 64 per cent of total investment requirements.

3 The proportion of artisans benefiting over the period was just under 30 per cent of the censused universe. Southern firms, however, benefit only marginally. Excluding these from the universe, an estimated 35.5 per cent had received one or more loans by 1976.

4 Viewed in slightly different terms, the number of firms financed between 1953 and 1971 was equivalent to 75 per cent of overall sectoral growth; whilst the number financed between 1961 and 1971 represented 91 per cent of the total increase in artisan units during that period.

5 Both in absolute terms and relative to the size of its artisan sector, the third Italy benefits most from state support: by 1971 it had 41 per cent of the total concerns, but almost 60

per cent of the beneficiaries and more than 57 per cent of the total finance allocated since the beginning of the period.

### 'Extensiveness' of intervention: the national pattern

To assess the importance and impact of artisan finance at a national level, we can consider the number and evolution of loan operations under two aspects: first, in relation to the growth of the artisan sector over time; and second, in relation to the size of the sector at given periods.

*Loan operations in relation to sectoral growth* Over the post-war period the number of firms financed represented a very high percentage of overall sectoral growth. Between 1951 and 1971 the number of artisan concerns increased by 226,700 units. In roughly the same period, about 171,400 firms had received one or more loans. Thus, *the number of firms financed was equivalent to 75 per cent of overall sectoral growth* in the twenty-year period. For the 1961–71 period, the proportion was even higher. The sector grew by 131,200 units whilst the number of firms financed increased by 119,200, which is equivalent to 91 per cent of total sectoral growth for that decade. If we include operations for the 1971–6 period then the number of firms benefiting under the scheme over the entire period was equal to about 74 per cent of the artisanat's post-war growth (Appendix I, table C).[9]

A detailed breakdown of the number of new firms created as a result of the loan incentive is not supplied by Artigiancassa. We do know, however, that at least 31 per cent of the 375,283 loans allocated over the entire period led to the creation of *new* workshops (Appendix I, table D); whilst of the 54 per cent (202,357) granted for machinery and equipment, a good proportion would similarly have led to the establishment of new businesses, because many artisans either lease their workshops or operate from home, and thus require only machinery, raw materials, etc., to begin operations. It is worth noting, under the rubric of type and value of investments sustained by soft loans, that overall investment (including the contribution of subsidized and guaranteed financing of 2,388 billion lire) amounted to 3,722 billion lire. Of this amount, 41 per cent was invested in *new* workshops, whilst machinery and equipment absorbed 46 per cent.

An idea of the relative weight of artisan finance is provided by the President of the General Confederation of Italian Artisans

*Table 4.1   Beneficiary firms as a percentage of the total, 1951, 1961, 1976*

|                     | 1961    | 1971    | 1976[a]   |
|---------------------|---------|---------|-----------|
| Firms censused      | 746,200 | 877,422 | 1,057,500 |
| Firms financed      | 52,107  | 171,389 | 300,500   |
| Percentage of total | 7       | 19.5    | 28.4      |

[a] Estimate based on social security figures from Barberis (1980), less inflationary element.
*Source*: Artigiancassa, *Bilancio* (various years).

(CGIA). Using 1977 figures, Germozzi (1978: 210–11) points out that investments realized through the scheme for that year alone amounted to 1,050 billion lire. This represented 3.1 per cent of total investment in the Italian economy, and led to the creation of 62,435 new jobs. We may therefore agree with his observation that 'craft industry absorbs a very large quantity of resources'.

*Firms financed as a proportion of the total*   We should note also that the scope of artisan finance steadily widened over the period. As table 4.1 shows, the percentage of firms receiving one or more loans reached 7 per cent in 1961, *c.*20 per cent in 1971 and almost 30 per cent in 1976. And the significance of this figure is, if anything, understated because of the much lower percentage of firms financed in the south.

### 'Intensity' and 'visibility' of intervention: the regional patterns

Moving now from the national to the regional distribution of loans, two particularly interesting patterns emerge. The first shows that firms located in the centre–north are consistently favoured over their southern counterparts. Secondly, there is a clear correlation between those areas receiving the largest proportion of loans and funds, and the regions where small firms have flourished and multiplied. Indeed, as will be seen, the third Italy – both in absolute terms and relative to the size of its small business sector – has received the greatest share of loans and investment funds.

*North–south distribution*   As table 4.2 illustrates, the first and third Italies obtained the lion's share of the loans, accounting for more than 90 per cent of the total firms financed and of loan funding in 1976. Moreover, that pattern remained stable throughout the entire

Table 4.2   *Regional distribution of loans and finance (percentages)*

| Area | 1953–61 Loans | 1953–61 Finance | 1953–71 Loans | 1953–71 Finance | 1953–76 Loans | 1953–76 Finance |
|---|---|---|---|---|---|---|
| Centre-north | 87.9 | 90.4 | 91.5 | 93.0 | 91.5 | 90.9 |
| South | 12.1 | 9.6 | 8.5 | 7.0 | 8.5 | 9.1 |
| Total Italy | 100.0 | 100.0 | 100.0 | 100.0 | 100.0 | 100.0 |
| No. (and value[a]) | 52,107 | (112.3) | 212,059 | (811) | 375,283 | (2,387) |

[a] Amounts in billions of lire.
Source: Artigiancassa, *Bilancio* (1965, 1971: table D; 1976: table 2).

period. If we disaggregate the data further to consider the proportion of firms financed within each region, then the concentration of resources *outside* the south is indeed astounding. As table 4.3 shows, while 35.5 per cent of all firms in central-north Italy had obtained at least one loan over the 1953–76 period, the equivalent share in the south was a mere 8 per cent. In terms of the crude north–south division, then, northern artisans are over-whelmingly advantaged, absorbing well over nine-tenths of the total loans and investment funds.

*The third Italy*   When examining the proportion of firms financed in relation to the number of artisan concerns registered in each region, another interesting pattern emerges. It shows that, far from being abandoned to their own devices, micro firms in the third Italy have fared best of all from public support.

The Marche region is a particularly good illustration of this point. For many observers, it is the region most typical of the third Italy, not only because of its small-scale structure (as Appendix I, table E shows, 75 per cent of the manufacturing workforce are employed in small firms), but also because of the recent character of this diffuse industrialization process. The commonplace assumption that such progress, both in the Marche and in the third Italy generally, has 'occurred without the special benefits and assistance of government agencies' (Kogan 1981: 22–3) is quite clearly false.

Whilst the Marche is the favoured example of 'industrialization from below', of Italy's new unbridled liberalism, the records clearly indicate that it has received copious support for its artisan sector. Indeed, the proportion of Marchesian firms benefiting from

Table 4.3   Percentage of firms financed within each region

| | 1953–71 | | | 1953–76[a] | | |
|---|---|---|---|---|---|---|
| Area | Universe | Beneficiary firms | % | Universe | Beneficiary firms | % |
| Centre-north | 640,518 | 155,629 | 24.0 | 772,250 | 274,748 | 35.5 |
| South | 236,904 | 15,770 | 5.0 | 285,250 | 25,752 | 8.0 |
| Total Italy | 877,422 | 171,399 | 19.5 | 1,057,500 | 300,500 | 28.4 |

[a] 1976 figures are estimates, and are based on the assumption that the north–south distribution of firms for 1976 had not changed since 1971.
Source: Artigiancassa, *Bilancio* (various years).

Artigiancassa loans was higher than that of any other region! If one studies the annual regional distribution of loans from the date the Fund began operations up to 1971, the results show that the Marche leads, with 35.4 per cent of its firms obtaining at least one loan. Emilia Romagna ranked second, with 26.7 per cent of its firms financed, followed by Umbria and the Veneto, with 23.3 per cent and 22.1 per cent respectively. In sum, the regions which did best on this dimension all form part of the third Italy (Appendix I, table F).

The particularly favourable situation of firms in the third economy is again confirmed by the information supplied in Appendix I, table G, which sets out the regional distribution of artisan proprietors and of firms financed, as a proportion of the national total in 1971. Where the south has 29.6 per cent of artisan owners, but only 9.2 per cent of the beneficiaries, the proportion is more balanced in the north-west, with 29.7 per cent of the owners and 32.1 per cent of the beneficiaries. Most favoured of all, however, is the centre-north-east which, with 41.2 per cent of total owners, has almost 60 per cent of the beneficiaries.

Finally, if we consider the number of loan operations and amount of finance distributed, then on the basis of the three Italies model, the centre-north-east again emerges as the most favoured region. As a glance at table 4.4 reveals, it accounted for almost two-thirds of all loans granted and 60 per cent of the financial resources allocated up to 1961. For the entire period, the share was in excess of 57 per cent for both loans and funds.

Table 4.4   Distribution of loans and finance in Italy's
'three economies' (percentages)

| | 1961 | | 1971 | | 1976 | |
| Area | Loans | Finance | Loans | Finance | Loans | Finance |
|---|---|---|---|---|---|---|
| North-west | 24.5 | 30.1 | 33.3 | 35.7 | 35.0 | 33.4 |
| Centre-north-east | 63.4 | 60.3 | 58.2 | 57.3 | 57.4 | 57.5 |
| South | 12.1 | 9.6 | 8.5 | 7.0 | 7.6 | 9.1 |
| Total Italy | 100.0 | 100.0 | 100.0 | 100.0 | 100.0 | 100.0 |

*Source*: Artigiancassa, *Bilancio* (1961, 1971: table D; 1976: table 2).

### Concluding remarks on artisan assistance

Both the privileges accruing to artisan status, under the 1956 Act, as well as the more directly quantifiable financial benefits, clearly highlight the generous public support for Italian artisans. The results of the loan scheme, in particular, have underlined how substantial and extensive that assistance has been, reaching almost 30 per cent of the national universe, and an even higher proportion (36 per cent) for that of the centre-north. In sum, from all the evidence presented and summarized at various stages of this analysis, it would appear that the Italian state has played not a marginal, but a central role in the post-war advancement of artisan enterprise. Before discussing the general implications of these findings, a similar analysis is now required for small industry.

## The financial structure for small industry

Turning now to small industry, we can chart a similar pattern of state activity. In particular, three major initiatives of the 1950s have served to consolidate public support for small industry: the special credit system; the law for the industrialization of the south; and the state's subsidy of interest payment.

*The new credit system*   Beginning in 1950, the Italian government introduced a series of legislative measures which, by 1953, brought to completion a new credit system designed to meet the financial needs of small and medium industrial firms (SMI) in setting up, modernizing and equipping new or existing plant.[10]   These measures brought into being a network of Special Credit Institutes (SCIs), banks specializing in the medium- and long-term credit field, operating on a regional and national basis, either owned by the state, or having a semi-public status (Spano 1979). Under this system, the small industry is offered a number of advantages, such as reduced costs of investment borrowing through low interest rates, availability of finance, longer pay-back periods, loan discounts, and in certain circumstances, state guarantees. To fulfil such functions, the SCIs draw the necessary means from an endowment fund, state outlays, bond issues and other sources (Templeman 1981: 221, 244). The first important provision was the 1952 Law 949, which regulates special credit to the SMI and is administered through Mediocredito Centrale.

*The law for industrialization of the south*  The second development of significance for smaller enterprise occurred in the sphere of regional policy. With the Mezzogiorno Act of 1957 (Law 634), the second phase of southern policy was initiated, marking the passage of the Southern Fund's activities from the promotion of agriculture and public works, towards the development of industry. A primary objective of southern policy was to encourage the formation of a local entrepreneurial class and a vast network of small-scale industries (Cafiero and Pizzorno 1962; Amato 1972). The poor results achieved have led to several revisions of southern policy which, as we shall see, pursued the dual and contradictory goals of encouraging large investments whilst simultaneously privileging smaller initiatives.

*The 'state contribution to interest payment'*  The major innovation of the post-war era, introduced in 1959 (Law 623), was a loan programme which dramatically reduced the cost of investment borrowing. This scheme effectively involves a heavily subsidized twenty-year loan. For example, whilst the special interest rate has been set at 3 to 5 per cent, that for normal loans in recent years has been at least three times greater at 15 per cent (Allen and Stevenson 1974: 162). A further aspect of the 1959 law is that it gives the state more direct control over industrial investment, all such subsidies requiring authorization by an interministerial committee, presided over by the Minister for Industry.

The significance of all three developments has been well summarized in a study of the Italian credit structure. As Spano (1979: 267) observes:

This articulated system signals profound changes in the legislation on financial aid to enterprise. Above all, the traditional 'extraordinary' characteristics of past legislation disappear; the appropriation of funds is no longer seen as provisional, but continuous, and the criteria for identifying destinees and types of aid no longer mutable. The grand legislation on incentives of this period establishes institutions specializing in delimited spheres of intervention and provided with renewable sources of funds for their needs.

What the 'grand legislation' of the 1950s also institutionalizes is size discrimination, the characteristic bias towards firms of small dimension which has remained a hallmark of Italian policies over the years. Further discussion of this issue will be reserved for chapters 6 and 7. For the moment, it is sufficient to point out that the schemes to be examined here are not merely 'special' provisions for smaller enterprise. Along with artisan policy, they may be seen as the primary industrial incentives provided by government over the last three decades.

### Characteristics of the major benefits

*National loan schemes (SMI laws)*  In the post-war period, national loan schemes have consistently favoured the smaller firm. Under the 1952 law, the maximum amount of each loan was set at 50 million lire, and although raised in later years to accommodate rising costs of technology, the ceiling has been maintained at a level such that only the very small concerns tend to benefit under this law (Appendix I, table H). As CENSIS (1972: 134) points out in this regard, 'given that loan values for 1953–69 also reflect the devaluation of money which displaces the "trend" towards the highest class of loans, such change does not lead to a substantial increase in the average size of firms to which such finance is directed.' In other words, the loans under this scheme have been destined to the smallest firms.

The second and by far the most important measure in the field of special credit is Law 623 of 1959. Its major attractiveness as an investment incentive consists in the substantially lower interest rates practised (fixed at 3–5 per cent throughout the period), and to the higher value of individual loans. Maximum loan values vary with geographical location and project type. Until the mid-sixties, *new* industries were favoured over existing installations. Up to 500 million lire could be granted for the construction of new plant, but only half that amount for modernizing and extension projects. For investments in the south, the amounts are doubled (see below). In all cases, such loans can involve up to 70 per cent of the capital required for start-ups or modernization of plant.

It is important to stress that average loan values vary considerably between north and south: from an average of 80 million lire in the centre-north to almost twice that amount in the south (Appendix I, table I). This difference provides one indication of the tendency to finance smaller initiatives in the centre and north – a finding which has damaging implications for the danger thesis.

The same tendency is reflected in the proportion of investment expenditure covered by loan finance. Smaller firms, which require much less capital investment than their medium-sized counterparts, obtain a greater proportion of their overall investment needs. Thus, in the centre-north where smaller concerns are financed, loans covered on average 52 per cent of overall capital requirements, compared with only 39 per cent of southern investment (Appendix I, table I).[11]

*Southern laws* In addition to the nationally operated SMI schemes administered by Mediocredito Centrale and the Ministry of Industry, the Cassa Mezzogiorno also provides soft loans for industries locating in the south. The 1957 law provided an incentive package combining tax concessions, capital grants and soft loans to stimulate new small and medium-sized firms. The southern SMI – defined initially as those firms with a fixed investment capital not exceeding 1.5 billion lire – could thus also benefit from regional soft loans, with awards and conditions similar to those specified for southern projects under the 1959 law.

One of the most perplexing characteristics of southern policy[12] is that the various incentives on offer, whilst initially aimed exclusively at smaller enterprise, have been extended to accommodate large-scale projects,[13] whilst at the same time retaining preferential treatment for the smaller firm. As Pugliese (1974: 198) has observed, 'the southern legislation, especially that concerning the Cassa Mezzogiorno has in principle always sought to stimulate the birth of small and medium firms.' Indeed, according to the legislation prior to 1965, large firms setting up in the south were able to benefit only from certain tax advantages (Saba 1969: 87; Graziani 1972: 64).

The eventual but contradictory accommodation of larger initiatives under the umbrella of state support – most notably those of

the state holding corporations – was prompted not only by the failure to galvanize an adequate response from smaller entrepreneurs,
but also by the crisis of small firms throughout the region in the
sixties. The realization that any serious attempt to industrialize the
south would therefore have to involve larger initiatives led to a
revision of southern policy in 1965. Remarkably, however, the
small firm bias was upheld by means of the graduation of benefits.
Whilst larger industry, always *within* certain specified limits, could
now officially enjoy cheap credit and capital grants, such incentives
tended to diminish as the size of the firm increased (Saba 1969: 89;
Pugliese 1974: 209).[14] The reasons for this apparent tension are
discussed in chapters 6 and 7 which set out my argument for state
support. Chapter 7, in particular, shows how the DC encouraged
the development of public corporations in a manner congruent with
its project for small ownership.

## Results of the loan schemes 1952–1976

### *Summary of the main findings*

As in the case of artisan policy, a considerable amount of detail has
been unavoidable in my assessment of the loan schemes. A
summary of the main findings is therefore provided for easy
reference, as follows:

1  Some 80 per cent of all subsidized loans are destined to
   small industry.
2  In real terms, under both SMI provisions, an estimated
   25,000 small firms had benefited from at least 33,000 soft
   loans by the end of 1970.
3  As a proportion of the small manufacturing firms censused
   in 1971, *c.*42.5 in every 100 firms had received subsidized
   loans.
4  At a conservative estimate, the national and regional
   programmes provided some 41,000 loans to small industry
   by 1971. This means that from the inception of the
   programmes roughly 70 loans were granted for every 100
   small industrial concerns in existence at the end of 1971.
5  As a result of these incentives, an estimated 12,000 new
   small enterprises were established over the 1960–70 period,
   which is equivalent to *c.*75 per cent of the global increase in
   the small manufacturing sector in those years.

6   Moving from the national to the regional distribution of loans, we find that under the SMI laws, central and northern firms absorb the lion's share of resources and are the most frequent beneficiaries, with around 90 per cent of total loans and funds allocated.

7   Finally, the third Italy is the most heavily supported area – both in absolute terms and relative to the size of its small business sector – capturing 50 per cent of the loans and funds. Moreover, for every 100 SMI in a given region, the centre-north-east obtained 62 loans, compared with 55 loans in the north-west, but only 38 in the south.

### *'Extensiveness' of intervention: the national pattern*

The general question addressed here is the extent to which the state has contributed to the development of the small industry sector as a whole. The basic approach to this issue is similar to that adopted for artisan trades. In this instance, however, we are dealing with several provisions for which detailed information is lacking. This presents a number of problems, the main one being that none of the existing data sources permits a cumulative picture of results, hence, to a greater extent, the reliance on estimates.[15]

Data are drawn from two main sources, the Mediocredito Centrale (MC) national survey material and official publications. Each has its own peculiar defects.[16] Since the MC survey offers a greater range of information it will provide the basis for analysis, supplemented where possible by the other material.

In 1973 Mediocredito Centrale sent questionnaires to all manufacturing firms which, in principle, were eligible for subsidized credit (for investment or exports). One point we must bear in mind is that small firms were under-represented in the final responses and this leads to an underestimation of their actual share of benefits.[17]

*Beneficiaries of the national SMI laws*   What proportion of firms are assisted? The results of the survey are reported in table 4.5. It shows that of the total firms surveyed, 40 per cent had received at least one SMI loan,[18] and for every 100 such firms, 75.6 were small. Relative to the total number of firms financed, the small sector is therefore the most favoured. Even this figure, however, tends to underestimate the SIs' share, owing to their lower frequency of response in the final sample. Independent data suggest a share in excess of 80 per cent.[19] If we consider as the universe the number of small firms appearing in the survey – excluding those in receipt of

Table 4.5   Size distribution of firms financed at least once under SMI laws, 1973

| Firm size | No. of firms | % |
|---|---|---|
| 11–100 | 6,920 | 75.6 |
| 101–500 | 1,981 | 21.6 |
| 500+ | 254 | 2.8 |
| Total | 9,155 | 100.0 |

*Source*: Mediocredito Centrale (1977: vol. 1, 87, table 42).

disaster loans – then, for every 100 SI, 36.2 firms had received at least one SMI loan as at 1973. This, of course, must be seen as a minimal estimate, for as Mediocredito points out, the vast majority of respondents were those with loans current in 1973. Firms with loans discharged at some earlier date are therefore vastly under-reported. To give one example, where the survey revealed a total of just under 9,500 loans granted under the 1959 law up to 1973, the actual number of operations recorded by the Ministry of Industry between 1960 and 1970 amounted to some 24,000 (Appendix I, table I). Similarly, under the 1952 law, by the end of 1960 alone, a total in excess of 10,000 loans had been granted (Appendix I, table J), compared with the much smaller 1973 survey figure of *c*.3,800 loans.

Building on the available information (detailed in Appendix I, tables I and J), I have estimated that between 1953 and 1970, under both laws just under 33,000 loans were distributed among some 25,000 small firms.[20] As a proportion of the small firms considered eligible for cheap credit in 1973,[21] this means that 61 per cent of the SI universe had benefited from soft loans. On the other hand, if we base our calculations on the 1971 census figure of 58,700 small manufacturing firms, then for every 100 firms, 42.5 had used subsidized credit under the SMI laws. In either case, the significantly high proportion of firms benefiting is impressive.

We turn now to the question of finance. Before discussing the amount of funds flowing to the small sector, it will be useful to have some idea of the importance of the provisions examined. In Confindustria's 1973 Annual Report (CGII 1973: 339), the Committee for Small Industry underlined the 'decisive impulse' provided by the 1959 law, noting that in thirteen years of its operation, the state had subsidized loans totalling 3,406 billion lire,

*Table 4.6  Laws governing soft loans to industry and services and the relevant state outlays for interest subsidies, 1952–76 (amounts in billions of lire)*

| Law year | Number | Sectors of intervention | State outlays for interest subsidies |
|----------|--------|-------------------------|-------------------------------------|
| 1952 | 949 | Small and medium industries (intervention of MC) | n.a. |
| 1952 | 949 | Artisan trades | 707 |
| 1959 | 623 | Small and medium industries | 3,189 |
| 1960 | 1,016 | Small and medium retailers | 145 |
| 1962 | 1 | Naval credit | 591 |
| 1964 | 357 | Vajont catastrophe | 75 |
| 1965 | 717 | Industrialization of south | 2,931 |
| 1965 | 1,179 | Residential construction (SMI) | 2,188[a] |
| 1966 | 614 | Depressed and mountainous areas of centre-north (SMI) | 134[b] |
| 1966 | 1,142 | Natural disasters (SMI) | 160[b] |
| 1967 | 131 | Export credit | 436[b] |
| 1968 | 326 | Hotels and tourism | 122 |

[a] refers to 1952–75.
[b] refers to 1952–70.
*Sources*: CENSIS (1972: table 33); Valli (1976: Appendix).

leading to investments worth 7,880 billion lire and the creation of 878,000 new jobs. The major importance of this scheme is again highlighted in table 4.6 which sets out the state's outlays under various loan schemes. Apart from the prominence of SMI laws in the list, it is interesting to note that the 1959 law for SMI attracted the weightiest financial commitment from the state.

As a statement of overall results, the Bank of Italy calculates that to this programme a sum in excess of 5,400 billion lire had been devoted between 1959 and 1976; and the state had outlaid approximately 3,200 billion lire in interest subsidies (Banca d'Italia 1976). If we include the sums disbursed under the 1952 law, amounting to 1,200 billion lire in 1976 (Banca d'Italia 1976), then the SMI provisions together financed loans worth 6,600 billion lire between 1952 and 1976.

What then is the SI's share of this amount? None of the official sources provide a breakdown of funds outlaid by size of firm, so we

Table 4.7   *Finance obtained under SMI laws, by size of firm, 1973*
*(amounts in millions of lire)*

| Firm size | Finance obtained[a] | |
| | Amount | % |
| --- | --- | --- |
| 11–100 | 584,321 | 37.3 |
| 101–500 | 616,956 | 38.7 |
| 501–1000 | 149,635 | 9.6 |
| 1000+ | 224,942 | 14.4 |
| Total | 1,565,854 | 100.0 |

[a] Note that the amount revealed by the MC survey is the sum obtained by firms in various years, having the purchasing power of those years.
*Source*: Mediocredito Centrale (1977: vol. 1, table 85).

have to rely on the survey material as a guide to the relative distribution of finance.[22]

Table 4.7 shows that small firms obtained 37 per cent of the funds. With only slightly less than its medium-sized counterparts, and a good 13 per cent more than the largest firms (financed in the south), the small sector would therefore seem to enjoy considerable financial support.

Regarding the SI's share of loan funds, there are two points worth emphasizing. First, it is not the absolute size of the loan that is important so much as the share of investment covered by subsidized credit – which, as earlier noted, can in principle be up to 20 per cent greater than that for larger loans. Second, as one study (Capuggi 1981: 48) points out, it is not so much the volume of loans and investments sustained that matters as the rate of capital accumulation, measured by the rate of increase of investment. The study in question concluded that subsidized credit has acted as a strong incentive to invest, particularly in the case of small firms whose investments are designed to raise productivity by economizing on labour. Similarly, the MC survey (Mediocredito Centrale 1977: 59, 63) showed that between 1968 and 1973 (the dates of its first and second inquiries), small firms invested and increased productivity at twice the rate of firms with 101–1500 employees.

*Beneficiaries of southern laws*   Under the laws for industrialization of the south, small firms are again the most frequent recipients of soft loans, accounting for almost three-quarters of the total beneficiaries in the year of the survey (Appendix I, table K). As a proportion of the small manufacturing firms surveyed in the south (2,387), this means that almost 30 in every 100 small firms had received at least one loan.

Nevertheless, the SI's share of subsidized credit under the southern laws was altogether marginal, reflecting the increasing tendency since the 1960s to finance larger investments. Whereas small firms received some 40 per cent of the resources prior to 1960, in the next decade their share had diminished to 13.4 per cent, and by 1973 to a bare 7 per cent (Petriccione 1976: 40).

To summarize the main points to this stage, under both national and regional loan schemes, the vast majority of soft loans – that is, a good 80 per cent – have been destined to small firms. In relation to the amount of finance obtained, however, small industry tends to benefit more from the national schemes, absorbing at least 37 per cent of total credit subsidized under the SMI laws, compared with less than half that proportion under southern laws. As a conservative estimate, in the two decades prior to 1971, the national and regional schemes together had provided at least 41,000 loans for small industry.[23] This means that some 70 loans were granted for every 100 SI's in existence at the end of 1971.[24]

As a result of these incentives, an estimated 12,000 new firms of small size were established over the 1960–70 period.[25] The significance of this figure can be more readily appreciated in relation to the parallel growth of the small manufacturing sector. Between 1961 and 1971 the number of small manufacturing firms rose by 16,000 to 58,700 units. On this basis, the number of new small firms financed under government loan schemes was roughly equivalent to 75 per cent of the global increase in the small firm sector.

### 'Intensity' and 'visibility' of intervention: the regional patterns

Just as in the case of the artisans, the intensity of state support for small industry was much greater in central and northern Italy, and especially so in the 'third' economy. Each pattern is examined in turn.

*North–south distribution*  Under the 1952 scheme benefits have been overwhelmingly concentrated in the centre-north. By 1960 these areas had captured 90 per cent of the loans and almost 90 per cent of the funds (Appendix I, table K). A decade later, as a glance at

Table 4.8   *Regional breakdown of finance granted by*
*Mediocredito Centrale, 1953–1969 (amounts in millions of lire)*

| Region | Amount | % |
|---|---|---|
| Piedmonte/Val d'Aosta | 41,804 | |
| Luguria | 12,224 | |
| Lombardia | 162,635 | |
| Total north-west | 216,663 | 47.6 |
| Trentino-Adige | 29,619 | |
| Friuli-V. Giulia | 27,164 | |
| Venezia | 37,068 | |
| Emelia Romagna | 45,979 | |
| Tuscany | 31,650 | |
| Marche | 15,110 | |
| Umbria | 8,961 | |
| Lazio | 23,702 | |
| Total Centre-north-east | 219,253 | 48.1 |
| Abruzzi and Molise | 1,824 | |
| Campania | 7,453 | |
| Puglia | 1,719 | |
| Basilicata | 216 | |
| Calabria | 1,142 | |
| Sicily | 6,184 | |
| Sardinia | 1,140 | |
| Total South | 19,912 | 4.3 |

*Source*: Banca d'Italia, *Bollettino Economico*, no. 8 (August 1970: 21).

table 4.8 reveals, small firms in this part of the country had gained almost 96 per cent of total finance disbursed by Mediocredito Centrale.

Turning now to the 1959 scheme, whilst data supplied by the Ministry of Industry (Appendix I, table J) do not disaggregate loans allocated according to firm size, we do know that 65 per cent of all such loans went to the centre-north, whilst finance was fairly evenly distributed between north and south. By 1976, however, of all credit subsidized under the 1959 law currently on loan, *the centre-north accounted for almost two-thirds* (Banca d'Italia 1976: table 37).[26]

Table 4.9    *Regional distribution of loans and finance obtained under*
             *SMI laws, 1973 (amounts in millions of lire)*

| Area | 'Regional' SMI | Loans per 100 regional SMI | Total no. | Loans % | Finance Amount | % |
|------|---------------|---------------------------|-----------|---------|---------------|---|
| Centre-north | 18,932 | 58.7 | 11,105 | 91.8 | 1,240,473 | 87 |
| South | 2,683 | 37.7 | 993 | 8.2 | 182,441 | 13 |
| Total | 21,563 | | 12,098 | 100 | 1,422,914 | 100 |

Note: Loans and finance obtained do not tally with the total obtained under SMI
laws, since regional data refer to those firms operating solely within a given region
(hence, 'regional' SMI).
*Source*: Mediocredito Centrale (1977: vol. 3, pts I, II, III).

As an overall guide to the frequency with which small firms in
different regions obtain financial assistance, the survey revealed a
marked disparity between north and south. As table 4.9 shows, of
the loans granted, 91 per cent went to the centre–north, and this
represents a distribution of *c*.59 loans for every 100 eligible firms
surveyed in that area. By contrast, southern enterprises captured a
meagre 9 per cent, and for every 100 such firms in the
Mezzogiorno, only 37.7 loans were distributed. With regard to the
amount of finance obtained, table 4.9 tells a familiar tale: in terms
of actual finance, central and northern firms surged far ahead,
capturing 87 per cent of total funding.[27]

*The third Italy*    The second regional pattern that emerges from
these findings leaves little room to doubt the state's hand in the
industrialization of Italy's so-called third economy. Indeed, far from
being overlooked by state intervention, small firms in Italy's third
economy have obtained, both absolutely and relatively, the greatest
share of the financial benefits in question. In rank order of 'who did
best', table 4.10 shows that the third Italy led the field, with 45 per
cent of the total regional SMI, yet almost 50 per cent of the loans
and finance. The north-west, with 43 per cent of the SMI, gained
just over 42 per cent and 37 per cent of the loans and funds
respectively. By contrast, although the south received finance in
proportion to its share of SMI (destined however to larger-sized
units), nevertheless, its share of the loans (8.2 per cent) was greatly

*Table 4.10   Distribution of loans and finance according to the 'three Italies' model (amounts in millions of lire)*

| Area | Regional SMI no. | % | Loans per 100 SMI no. | Loans no. | % | Finance Amount | % |
|---|---|---|---|---|---|---|---|
| Centre-north-east | 9,709 | 45 | 61.9 | 6,008 | 49.6 | 422,914 | 49.8 |
| North-west | 9,222 | 43 | 55.3 | 5,097 | 42.2 | 531,162 | 37.4 |
| South | 2,632 | 12 | 377 | 993 | 8.2 | 182,441 | 12.8 |
| Total Italy | 21,563 | 100 | 56.0 | 12,098 | 100 | 1,422,914 | 100 |

*Source*: Mediocredito Centrale (1977: vol. 3, pts I, II and III).

disproportionate to the weight of its SMI (12 per cent).

A more meaningful measure of which regions did better, however, is provided in the second column. This tells us what proportion of a given region's SMI has enjoyed investment subsidies. Ranked in descending order, the third Italy leads the field with 62 loans for every 100 SMI, followed by the north–west which gets 55. Comparing these figures with the southern ratio of 38 in every 100, it is clear that the Mezzogiorno once again falls far behind.

From every angle, then, it would seem that small firms in the third economy have benefited every bit as much as, indeed considerably more than, their counterparts elsewhere. Whilst other factors have undoubtedly made this area more propitious than the south for the development of small industry, it seems none the less certain from the patterns traced throughout this survey that the state has lent a very considerable impetus to this process.

## An overall panorama

Having threaded our way through the maze of different schemes for different categories of enterprise, it is now possible to attempt an overview. As set out in figure 4.1, we see that the first and third Italies, although having only 70 per cent of the national firms, accounted for 91 per cent of the artisan beneficiaries and 93 per cent of the finance. In stark contrast, the south, with 30 per cent of the

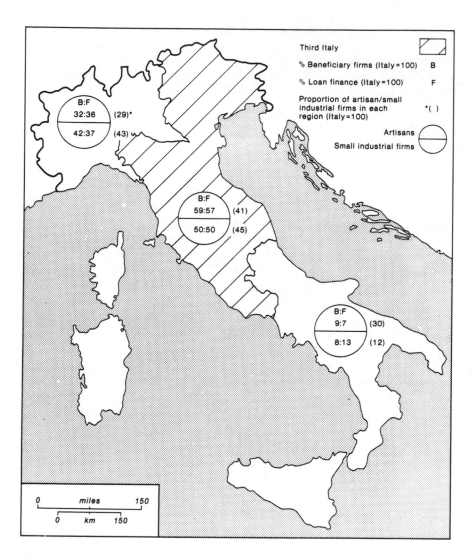

**Figure 4.1**  The territorial patterning of state support

national artisans, has only 9 per cent of the beneficiaries and a mere 7 per cent of the finance.

Similarly with small industry, central and north Italy were far in the lead. Whilst 88 per cent of all small industrial firms were located in these areas, the first and third Italies accounted for 92 per cent of the loan recipients and 87 per cent of the total resources allocated. Again, lagging well behind, the south had only 8 per cent and 13 per cent respectively.

Even more significant is the state's contribution to the artisan economy of the *third* Italy. Whilst accounting for 41 per cent of the total artisan concerns, it received almost 60 per cent of all loans distributed and 57 per cent of the total finance. Glancing again at figure 4.1, a similar story is told for small industry in the third Italy: that is, a share of beneficiaries (50 per cent) and funding (50 per cent) considerably in excess of the relative size of its small firm sector (45 per cent).

## General conclusions

Because of limitations of data, a number of aspects of small business policy must remain insufficiently explored.[28] However, even in the absence of an exhaustive list of benefits, we would still have to conclude that the tangible economic rewards accruing to small business are very extensive. Of even greater significance for the creation and replenishment of micro-capitalist enterprise are the rules and arrangements by which the state, rather than generally encouraging the small firm to expand and grow, has sought to regulate its size and promote proliferation.

The results of this inquiry thus show the importance of extra-economic factors in illuminating a phenomenon which has attracted far more political and theoretical debate than close empirical attention. It amasses sufficient evidence to demonstrate the substantial contribution of the state in promoting Italy's small-scale economy, most strikingly in regions at the centre of Italy's post-war small business boom.

What, then, are the implications of these findings for existing hypotheses? Contrary to the assumptions of the three Italies model, it seems beyond doubt that however much 'market forces' play a part they are by no means the only influences at work in the third Italy, nor for that matter in the industrial triangle. In all respects, small firms in these areas – whether in relation to big capital or to their southern counterparts – benefited most from government support. The evidence has also failed to support the model's assumptions regarding the *nature* of state intervention: resources have not flowed simply to the least developed region to prop up an ailing small business stratum. In this respect, assistance to the small sector can hardly be viewed as 'protectionist'.

In another important respect, the findings also challenge the petit bourgeois 'danger' thesis, because one test of this hypothesis would be the funding of small units in the south where such firms are weakest, where political alliances are more fluid and where neo-Fascism has drawn the bulk of its support. If, therefore, the fear of small business decline and reaction were a major determinant of state support, and if this threat existed in any significant measure only in the south, then we would expect to find most of the small firm beneficiaries concentrated there.

The results show precisely the opposite: not to a declining area, but to the flourishing regions of the centre-north. Importantly, these regions are distinctive not merely for the dynamism and prosperity of their small firm economies, but also for the stability and cohesion of their electorates. Whether in the Catholic-dominated north-east or in the Communist bulwark of central Italy, each major party can count on the traditional allegiance of a solid constituency. Yet it is precisely in these areas that assistance to small business has been greatest. In this light, the government's willingness to promote small capital is not readily explained by the need to buy electoral consensus or to appease a discontented stratum – as in the case, say, of Poujadism or of post-1968 France (cf. Berger 1980: 113–4).

But before we can leave behind such society-centred explanations for state activity and replace them with one consistent with the findings of this chapter, it is necessary to submit the last of our three approaches to critical scrutiny. The activity of post-war governments displays little anxiety about the petite bourgeoisie, but what of the problem of unemployment?

# 5

## Patterns of state support II: beyond employment

For most writers, the fear of *ceti medi* discontent is only one factor in a double-stranded explanation for small firms support. In the second line of argument, the focus shifts from the small employer to labour. Here, the dominant problem no longer concerns the political volatility of small property owners, but the instability of the 'marginal' labour force, due to the insecurity and scarcity of employment. According to this view, politicians protect petite capital for fear of the social explosions that a weakening of the small firm sector might induce.

This chapter considers whether the actions of politicians and the activity of the state are consistent with the 'fear of unemployment' thesis. For reasons indicated in chapter 2, I refer to this as the functionalist argument, of which there are two versions. In the first, and general, version, the so called 'secondary' sector plays a crucial role in the business cycle, absorbing surplus labour in times of economic downturn, containing unemployment levels within tolerable limits and thereby minimizing the potential for social unrest. In order to secure social order, post-war governments have thus been obliged to protect it (Berger 1974; 1980). In the second, more specific, version, these policies are designed not merely to contain surplus labour but to control it (and those who use it) in a manner congenial to the DC's strategy of consensus formation – that is, clientelistically (Pizzorno 1980). Containment of unemployment and clientelistic control of the labour force are thus the two essential themes in the functionalist explanation for the survival-cum-protection of the small sector. Both positions stress the use of the latter for the maintenance of employment (read social order), but differ in their emphasis on how this is achieved. For the 'safety-valve' position, this is accomplished at a national level through provisions aimed generally at sustaining small-scale undertakings.

For the 'clientelistic' variant, it involves a more complex political strategy – pursued at a local level – for the success of which the traditional middle class and the small firm are crucial elements.

Leaving the clientelistic component until last, the present chapter tackles three assumptions at the core of both versions of the functionalist argument:

1   The primacy of labour. Small firms survive by and large because they are used as a safety valve against mass unemployment. But in order to perform this labour-absorptive function they need government protection.
2   Necessity and crisis. Political elites, in turn, fearful of the politically destabilizing consequences entailed by a 'weakening' of this sector, have been obliged to provide support intermittently as the economic situation demands.
3   Economic irrationality. It follows then that there is considerable political, but precious little economic, rationality in these measures: first, because the traditional sector is largely a 'refuge' from unemployment, inefficient and insecurely placed *vis-à-vis* its modern counterpart; second, because keeping it going entails high costs and sacrifices for the economy as a whole.[1]

In order to pinpoint the inadequacies of the functionalist explanation for state activity, three aspects of political action will be examined. First, the assessments and justifications for small business prominent in the early post-war debate, which reveal a measure of economic rationality hitherto ignored by the literature, and which belie any notion of small enterprise as an inefficient survival, useful only as a reservoir for labour. Second, the framing of small business incentives (legislative deliberations and criteria of eligibility), which underline that employment *per se* was not their goal. Third, examples of policy implementation, which show that intervention privileges not the areas or sectors threatened with decline, but those where the prospects for small firm consolidation and replacement tend to be more promising.

As we shall see, the arguments for, the timing, nature and application of, assistance, when considered in combination, reveal a perception and use of the small sector which is far more rooted in the economic, cultural and political context of the time than the idea of a mere cyclical response to the labour problem allows. In anticipating later arguments, this chapter shows that considerations about maintaining or increasing employment form only one aspect of a more general objective in which the *kind* and *context* of that employment are far more important. It will be seen that, far from being 'conjuncturally conditioned and elicited', such measures form part of a more or less coherent interclass ideology and policy to 'deproletarianize' the worker, understood in *two* distinct senses: via labour's individual advancement and transformation into a property owner; and via its personal control in the 'solidaristic' setting of the small establishment.

## Arguments for small business: necessity and preference in political action

In the functionalist analysis, small firms support is not something the political leadership chooses to do, but something it has to do. Political action thus appears as the midwife of necessity: 'protective' measures must be forthcoming if social upheaval is to be avoided. They are the necessary ransom the modern sector and wider society have to pay to avoid something worse. It follows from this argument that, had the problem of containing excess labour not existed, and had the absorptive capacities of the large-scale sector been greater, a small firm policy would in all likelihood never have seen the light of day.

Yet, when we turn to probe the political arguments for small business, we will find two recurrent themes largely unexamined in the literature: one which stresses its economic contribution; the other emphasizing its socially cohesive role in transcending capital–labour antagonism. As implied by the title of this section, discussion of each of these themes will serve to highlight the 'society-centred' deficiencies of the functionalist explanation.

### Small enterprise and economic development

The theme prominent in all the DC's programmes for economic and political reconstruction was the central role envisaged for small enterprise in the country's economy. As the 'Idee Ricostruttive' of 1943 (DC 1968: 4) propounded:

The statistics tell us that in Italy the artisanat, small and medium industry still prevail over big industry of an essentially capitalist and often monopolistic character. It is therefore a criterion of sound realism to promote and reinforce this economic structure of which private initiative and the free market constitute the propulsive elements.

Whilst party programmes are unlikely to give the 'functionalist' reasons for policy choices, we can momentarily suspend such doubts in anticipation of the argument in the following chapter. In that context the significance of the document cited is clearly established: from the very outset, small enterprise was considered not as an inferior proxy for the large, but as an essential instrument for economic development in which the role of large industry was explicitly excluded. Preference and programmatic declaration notwithstanding, Italy's serious balance of payments deficit and the need for foreign exchange were to give export industry, and with it larger enterprise, an important role that the Italian government 'was obliged to recognize and stimulate' (Manghetti 1975: 197). Thus a good part of the funds from the European Recovery Programme was channelled to export industries (machinery, textiles, steel) in the form of loans for primary materials and machinery imports (Romeo 1972: 224–5). Yet this initial policy directive, reiterated in various guises over the years, was to remain a constant point of reference for political action, even as Italy entered its most spectacular phase of economic expansion.

Now, to the analyst of the 1980s, with retrospective knowledge, this small firm orientation poses no great problem of economic rationality. But from the perspective of the early post-war observer with an eye on the international scene and on the concentration efforts of other European states (see chapters 7 and 8), the Italian bias towards micro capitalism must seem grossly out of phase with the general trend. If economic progress and industrial development implied an ever greater concentration of industrial production along Fordist lines, to what extent then could this basic orientation be justified as 'sound realism'? Why, in other words, did the apparent 'brilliance' of Fordism fail to 'blind' the government of the day to the possibilities inherent in a decentralized system of production? question is important because it serves to focus attention on the interplay between economic and technological conditions on one hand, and the prevailing perceptions on the other, which, in the early years of the new republic, made it possible to look to small enterprise as an economically rational proposition, not as an outmoded economic form to be preserved in the service of non-economic objectives.

The first thing to note is the essentially equivocal attitude to

Fordism. Far from being regarded as inevitable or even desirable, its very possibility was the subject of searching debate. In the discussion which took place before the Constituent Assembly between 1946 and 1947, for example, many doubts were raised over the extent and likelihood of future mass markets. These added to the more tangible problem of the country's lack of natural resources. Amongst the industrialists and economic experts invited to speak before the Assembly, opinion was clearly divided between those who saw Italy's future wedded to an economy of mass production, and those who envisaged it developing as a workshop economy of a high order which, lacking in primary materials, could never produce *en masse* (see Prodi 1980).

One further important element which contributed to these uncertainties and worked to enhance the prospects of small enterprise was the technological retardation of Italy's 'giants'. As Prodi (1980: 1007) observes, the country was 'at least a generation and a half behind in modern techniques of production'. Fiat, the acknowledged leader of Italian industry, only began in the 1950s to install assembly lines similar to those which had served America in the thirties. Thus, if small firms were 'backward', the industrial leaders were not spectacularly different.

It is important to note also the positions adopted by various groups on the question of technological progress. Independent craftsmen, for instance, had never adopted a defensive position to exclude modern techniques. On the contrary, in a statement of their grievances in 1930 under the Fascist regime, their leading spokesman argued vehemently that

the craftsmen must be equipped with all the mechanical devices provided by science. . . . We want to compete, we want to be tested against you industrialists, and if there are mechanical devices . . . that will sustain our creativity, our unique inventiveness, if we can utilize what science provides, you must recognize that such devices and machinery have their place in the craftsman's shop. (Cited in Sarti 1971: 85)

Reiterating this progressive orientation in the post-war years, the president of the General Confederation of the Italian Artisanat (Germozzi 1956: 571) observed that for the Italian artisanry there existed no problem of 'defence', beyond that of its traditions and autonomy. The problem was rather one of 'insertion in the contemporary industrial economy' for which the artisan entrepreneur must acquire 'the most recent techniques of production'.

Catholic leaders, for their part – both religious and political – were no prisoners of technological determinism. They not only accepted the need for technical advance, but also insisted that the small firm could and should exploit its benefits. In one of his numerous communications on the subject of private ownership, the Pope wrote in 1944 that, too frequently, technology was merely an instrument for the unlimited expansion of capital: 'Why could it not be used as well to maintain and insure the private property of all? (cited in Camp 1969: 72).

In a similar vein, Christian Democrats in their 1956 report to the special committee responsible for industrial legislation, pointed out that it was wrong to conceive of the artisan concern as one in which the small entrepreneur works only manually with a little family help: 'Even the artisanat is a productive factor with an evolution and development of its own.[2]

The path from this modernizing conception to execution is most clearly traced in the new statutory definition of artisan enterprise (1956), and in the various incentives offered to small concerns generally to update plant and equipment. For the first time, artisans could now legally deploy modern techniques in their workshops – provided that the 'standardized' component of the manufactuting process was limited – as a result of which productivity increased dramatically.[3] In short, technological progress – for the DC, for the Church and for the small firm sector itself – was never regarded as a prerogative of the large factory.

In view of all these considerations – material, technical and cultural – and apart from any questions of preference, it was therefore highly rational for Christian Democrats to argue that small industrial and artisanal production could make a significant contribution to economic development. Using largely national primary materials, such firms would require very little of the scarce foreign exchange; whilst exports of their products would contribute effectively to the balance of payments. Moreover, smaller enterprise would increase the production of consumer goods for domestic consumption and absorb the machinery, tools and products of Italian industry.[4] Typical of the DC's economic arguments for small enterprise was the parliamentary statement made by the Minister for Industry in 1951: 'Artisan industry is one of the greatest resources for the Italian economy . . . enabling a better utilization of our productive capacities and modest resources in primary materials, as well as the conquest of foreign markets for

Italian products with articles of quality and artistic content.'[5]

At an objective level, then, there were sound economic reasons for encouraging small business, increasingly borne out by the statistics on productivity and exports of the early post-war years. In 1961 value added per worker in manufacturing firms with fewer than 100 workers was 23 per cent higher than in units with 100–999 employees, and only 13 per cent less than in the largest units (Fuà 1976: 52). Regarding exports, Conti (1978: 52) has shown that for 1954–5, about 45 per cent of the value of all commodity exports were products of craft-based industry, predominantly those of the clothing, textile, footwear and light mechanical industries in which small firms were then the acknowledged leaders.

The emergent picture then has little resonance with the world of imperatives portrayed in the functionalist account. Following that logic, the primary 'modern' sector was entirely unproblematic. Through preference the ruling party leaned towards large-scale industry for growth and efficiency; but through necessity, it was obliged to favour small capital 'even at the price of retarding industrial development' (Pizzorno 1980: 78; Berger 1980). The evidence thus far indicates precisely the reverse. On this point it is fitting to recall Sabel's historical account of the workshop economy discussed in chapter 1. His general conclusion (1982: 44–5) that 'a different pattern of mechanization based on different markets, rooted in correspondingly different patterns of property rights' might well have prospered is one which the DC would have found little to disagree with.

It could also be argued that what rendered the economic possibilities of small enterprise so 'visible' to the political leadership in the first place, and clinched the arguments in its favour, was rooted not so much in pessimism about Italian industry's prospects in world markets, but in ideological optimism about micro capitalism's capacity to create social cohesion. Whilst reserving a lengthier discussion of this issue for chapters 6 and 7, it will be useful here to look very briefly at some of the ways in which it shapes the more properly 'political' arguments for small business.

### *The social cohesion of a small firm economy*

One of the DC's first and oft-repeated policy objectives was summed up in the phrase 'non: tutti proletari, ma tutti proprietari' ('not: everyone proletarians, but everyone property owners'). The party wanted to 'deproletarianize the worker' and 'remake the *ceto medio*' – curious objectives if one considers the most serious problem as one of mass unemployment; but less curious in the light of the DC's ideological assumptions about the nature of economic activity and of subsequent political developments which intensified worker radicalism and polarized Catholics and Communists.

In this context, small enterprise is not simply an economic possibility or culturally preferred object, but a politically desirable phenomenon. This point is neatly illustrated in the scenario drawn in 1947 by Luigi Einaudi, then Governor of the Bank of Italy, on the impact of technological change on class structure. Like many of his contemporaries, including government advisers,[6] Einaudi saw the industrial sector as an unlikely arena for absorbing the excess agricultural labour force. In an article entitled 'The Future of the *Ceti Medi*' (1947), he argued that the days of the large factory were over. Technological progress, rather than giving rise to further concentrations of labour, would tend to diminish employment possibilities in industry and increase those in the tertiary sector. The interesting feature of this article is not the accuracy of its economic predictions, but its celebration of their structural and political implications. As Einaudi (1947: 1) put it: 'when, after 70 per cent, 75 per cent or more of the population will be engaged in transport, commerce, the professions and the arts, what will be the moral and political attitude of the majority of the population?'

A shrinking industrial labour force ('producers of material goods') was thus to be positively welcomed, for it would be accompanied by an expanding tertiary sector thickly populated by independent 'producers of personal services'. With an eye on the more advanced countries, Einaudi thus reasoned that

in Anglo-Saxon countries where this transformation is more in evidence and where there is no obstruction of industrial capitalism by an antediluvian ideology and by an industrial proletariat called to overthrow it, is not the growing prevalence of producers of services one of the explanations for their greater stability and the scarce importance of revolutionary sentiments?

In short, the key to the dampening of revolutionary sentiments and the basis for greater political stability lay in the further development of the *ceti medi*. By the end of the following decade these transformations were already under way, but to an extent that Einaudi had not foreseen. For, alongside the growth of small commerce and service industries, an increasing number of independent producers, attracted by an expanding market and government provisions, had joined the ranks of industry and the artisanat. Reporting on these developments in a policy statement issued at the DC's Seventh National Congress in 1959, the party noted with great 'satisfaction' that

the Italian social structure is progressively *freeing* many citizens, because the number of people who can live by *independent* or semi-independent labour, *or at least organized in small firms*, is increasing . . . the Italian social structure is moving in a direction that refutes the Marxist hypothesis, that is, in an entirely opposite direction (italics added). (DC 1961: 321)

Both in this context and in Einaudi's analysis, we see then a fundamental political theme of the debate on small business: namely, the implications for social cohesion of the growth of the *ceti medi*. What is at issue in these arguments is not merely or even primarily the absorption of the unemployed, but more precisely, 'the attenuation of labour conflicts'. In a statement before Parliament in 1954,[7] the author of these words, then government spokesman for artisan industry, went on to outline the merits of promoting small firms:

in artisan enterprise as in small industries, conflicts can be more easily composed or remain more or less absorbed by the modest dimensions of the firm and above all by the particular figure of the entrepreneur – personally present as the artisan or small industrialist – who, applying both technique and capital, shares in the work with his dependents who are more like collaborators.

The principle of collaboration, as we shall see in the following chapters, goes to the heart of the demochristian project. For the DC, the small firm not only raises labour from the 'squalor of the proletariat' by transforming its workers into independent workers; it also provides the setting 'where the dignity and employment of the human element are better protected'.[8] Speaking on the 'Possibility and Necessity of the Artisanat' in his report to the DC's 1949 Congress, Rumor underlined the importance of the sector for its wider social effects:

The artisan business helps to form a personal and direct commitment to production; it offers moral satisfaction from labour . . . since it is not based on standardized labour which diminishes the capacity of the worker . . . it is a sector congenial to our people. It is therefore necessary that a party like the DC sees the problem of unemployment also under the profile of artisanal employment which is exquisitely and traditionally Christian. (DC 1959: 248)

It seems clear from these observations that something more fundamental than mere employment is at stake in the maintenance and expansion of the small sector. According to the views presented here, employment in small enterprise is not so much a necessity as a highly desirable alternative to the large factory. So far from being an inferior proxy for large-scale industry, the micro unit is regarded as an economically promising and socially preferable form in its own right. Above all, these arguments suggest that the key to small firms policy lies not in reducing social tensions on the labour market, but in consolidating the kind of economic structure conducive to regime support and social cohesion.

It is time to transpose analysis from the sphere of perceptions to that of practical interventions. The following section presents key examples of the way legislation has been framed and implemented. If the 'needs of employment' were a paramount consideration in small business policy, this should be visible at either or both of these two levels.

## Framing legislation: the primacy of labour?

On the surface, the 'needs of employment' hypothesis has a certain plausibility. Until the late fifties, unemployment remained at a consistently high level, rarely dropping below the 2 million mark, or 10 per cent of the active population. The problem was further exacerbated by the phenomenon of 'under-employment' involving wide sectors of the agricultural labour force which could find only part-time or seasonal work. Whilst the seriousness of the issue is by no means denied, a more pertinent question is surely whether or not the governing party viewed the secondary sector as a dumping ground for labour, and whether, in fact, its policies reflected this. The question is what to look for. On this point the economist's version of the evolution of small business assistance is useful. According to the economist, resource constraints in the early post-war years – the scarcity of capital and abundance of labour – meant that the problem of unemployment had to be tackled through a labour-intensive strategy. Since small firms generally deploy less elaborate technologies, then for a given level of capital investment they would create more work than in large-scale enterprises (see, for example, Graziani 1972: 64).

Thus, if the 'needs of employment' were to be accepted as an adequate explanation, then the legislation should reflect all or at least some of the following conditions: (a) the primacy of job maintenance and creation; (b) the least costly alternative to ensuring this; and finally (c), when these resource constraints no longer apply, that such support – 'conjuncturally conditioned and elicited' – would be withdrawn or significantly reduced.

There is, however, very little evidence that any of these conditions hold. The first point to make is that as the supply of investment capital became more abundant from the mid-fifties onwards, financial incentives to small firms, instead of contracting, became more attractive and substantial. This gradual dilation of financial benefits, moreover, coincided with a period of tendential 'full' employment and the most intense economic expansion of the post-war era!

Second, if the strategy were to secure as many jobs with as little expenditure as possible, why then, particularly when small industry was already so numerically abundant and nationally diffused, promote the birth of *new* initiatives when it was cheaper to *expand* existing plant? As one analyst of Italian development policy remarks, the building of completely new plants is 'invariably more costly than expansion or modernization of preexisting facilities' (Rodgers 1979: 145). Indeed it was precisely the latter option which the employers' organization favoured. Confindustria strongly opposed the creation of new plant, not only because it often involved investment in public enterprise, but also because it was not in the interests of established firms to permit an unlimited increase in new undertakings (see Abrate 1981: 542).

Equally aware of the greater costs involved, the Christian Democrats – both inside and outside Parliament – nevertheless insisted on the need for 'continued and unabated diffusion of industrial initiatives'. Aldo Moro's address to the 1959 National Congress nicely captures that 'decentralizing' spirit:

It is typical of our conception that economic development be considered in both quantitative and qualitative terms; in other words, that it must diffuse throughout the national territory, involve every productive sector and with particular regard to small and medium firms. . . . We therefore must and want to give maximum impulse, always and wherever economically possible and therefore useful, to all those mixed forms of wages and profit, which are precisely those of the productive *ceto medio*. (DC 1961: 265)

With few exceptions, government policy continued to discriminate in favour of new enterprise.

Turning now to the third aspect, to what extent do the conditions governing access to benefits give primacy to the labour factor? As indicated in the previous chapter, the purpose for which loans and grants may be approved are so varied and so broadly defined that any explicit order of precedence is impossible to establish. Typically, the legislation specifies that government will favour initiatives whose capital is autonomously owned by small and medium operators; which utilize local economic resources; which, for the same amount of capital investment, give greater employment; which operate in sectors complementary or subsidiary to those of the state holding companies (Amato 1972: 39–40).

The plurality of objectives, the absence of any explicit order of precedence, the equal admissibility of investments which increase employment and those which improve productivity through labour-saving devices – such a pot-pourri of possibilities certainly does little to bolster the functionalist case.

A comparative contrast provides us with further cause for reflection. Take, for example, French policy. In keeping with its emphasis on scale and concentration, incentives have typically been geared to big business. In the exceptional cases where this orientation has been relaxed (for purposes of regional development), grants have been conditional on the number of jobs actually created. Even here, however, grants are available only for projects *over* a certain size. Thus, whilst giving a fixed contribution for every job created, French policy stipulates a minimum amount of investment and a minimum number of jobs that must be created (Saba 1969: 66–7; Hull 1980: 76, 80). In fact, if that job target is not fulfilled within a specified period, all or part of the award may be clawed back.

In distinction to the French norm, Italian policies have operated on the completely opposite principle. Here, the various loan, grant and tax benefits are not only *not* conditional on job quotas, but also, with few exceptions, Italian policies have always stipulated a *maximum* amount of investment and a *maximum* number of employed, above which firms will not be eligible for support. Thus, to take one of the most striking examples, the ten-year exemption from income tax for new small firms was granted on condition that the enterprise remained within the original limit of 100 workers over that period. It is not too difficult to conclude that the condition not to exceed this limit on pain of losing the right to the exemption conflicts with a law whose primary purpose might be to raise the general level of employment (Guerra 1966: 18).

That small firms have made a significant contribution to industrial employment is not at all in doubt. What is doubtful is the extent to which the employment factor *per se* has determined political action. For, neither as a criterion of investment policy nor as a consideration in the legislative debates has this element been given much prominence.

Much more prominent an issue in the early debates was the size and number of initiatives financed. Thus, when Emilio Colombo, the DC's Minister for Industry, reported to Parliament on the results of the soft loan scheme, the effects on employment were barely discussed. What the ministerial report underlined was the fact that 'initiatives of a really limited size' had been financed and that 'the smaller firms' capital requirements have always been satisfied with absolute priority' (Colombo 1963: 228). Excluding any reference to the number of jobs created as a result of this scheme, Colombo (1963: 173) observed with approval that 'the objective we wanted to achieve – of creating a new class of entrepreneurs, and of giving the possibility of modernizing above all to small businesses – has been realized.'

Especially revealing in this regard were the deliberations involved in the introduction of the government's bill to define artisan enterprise. The centrepiece of the legal definition, it will be recalled, is the specification of a maximum number of persons employed. In this respect, it differs markedly from the system adopted in West Germany whereby the size of the enterprise is at the discretion of its promoter. In that country, artisan business can even be a joint-stock company! In fact, so concentrated has the sector become in the last thirty years that the German artisanat now averages 141 employees per establishment (Barberis 1980: 9).

Yet, of the two distinct courses of action possible – one pursuing the *expansion*, the other the *delimitation*, of the size of artisan enterprise – the DC insisted from the outset that only one option was 'conceivable':

there would be no justification in a policy which facilitated the development of artisan enterprise into an industrial one . . . the latter would be a policy encouraging the death of the artisan. It would not . . . defend the artisanat, but would promote the expansion of firms so that they become medium, if not large.[9]

The adoption of a size-oriented definition was preferable, the government argued in its report, because it would facilitate the multiplication of small firms rather than their expansion. The artisan law is perhaps the clearest example of the rules and arrangements by which an industrial state may seek to control the size of enterprise, as opposed to generally encouraging small firms to grow. Less clear is how that kind of policy can be reconciled with the functionalist argument. For, as the evolution of the German artisanat has shown, fewer and fewer small businesses (entailing a reduction in number by about 50 per cent since 1949) have been perfectly compatible with more and more employment (Barberis 1980: 9; Sauer 1984: 82).

   The Italian artisan law thus provides a prime example of the way in which the limitation of size and the multiplication of enterprise have been important policy objectives in themselves. On these grounds, and on the basis of other evidence examined, it would seem more plausible to argue that the primary consideration in government policy is the *kind* and *context* of employment entailed by units of a certain dimension. From the perspective of policy formation at least, there is little to uphold the functionalist case for employment as a quantitative issue.

## Implementing policy: arresting decline or promoting proliferation?

At the level of implementation, the kind of evidence that might be used to sustain the functionalist claim would involve information on the regional and sectoral funding of small firms. For instance, if as supposed, small firms assistance has evolved primarily to contain the explosive situations feared to result from a *weakening* of the traditional sector, then one ought to be able to identify two particular patterns in the allocation of investment funds to industry. These should show two things: first, greater support for small enterprise in *areas* characterized by higher levels of unemployment and enterprise mortality; and second, greater funding of small firms in *sectors* most vulnerable to market forces, and which employ a high proportion of the labour force.

### The regional pattern

By any criterion we would care to choose – economic, social or political – south Italy would, according to the functionalist logic, be the primary candidate for small firms assistance. It has always had the highest unemployment levels,[10] a relatively limited and fragile productive base highly dependent on public resources and an electorate more volatile than in any other region. Yet, as the previous chapter revealed in some detail, small firms in the Mezzogiorno fared poorly in relation to their north-central counterparts, receiving only a tiny percentage of total financial assistance.

The regional pattern of resource distribution seems particularly damaging to the functionalist case because it shows that the more generous assistance to artisans and small industrialists is associated not with the weakening and decline of the traditional sector – as has occurred in the south – but with its dynamic replacement and expansion.

### The sectoral pattern

To rescue the hypothesis, its proponents would argue that even if the state has done less for southern firms, it is not the relative share that counts but the targets of that assistance. For it is widely believed that the recipients of southern assistance are the ailing, inefficient concerns, unable to compete on the market, yet important for the labour they absorb (Bagnasco 1977; Pizzorno 1980; Chubb 1982).

Which firms fall into this category? The marginal southern firms are conventionally identified as those in the traditional products sectors which have become increasingly vulnerable to competition from northern firms: namely, foodstuffs, clothing and textiles, wood and furniture, footwear and leather products. In fact, the declines registered in southern unemployment and industrial/ artisanal establishments have occurred almost entirely within these sectors. Between 1961 and 1971, for example, the number of establishments in the clothing, wood and shoe industries decreased by 20 per cent, accompanied by an absolute (7 per cent) and relative fall in employment (from 37 per cent to 29 per cent) (Peggio 1975: 54).

In view of these two features – market weakness and significance

Table 5.1    Sectoral composition of loan and grant disbursements
(includes large firms)

| Sector | Loans (%) | Grants (%) | Lire (billions) | Employment variations 1951–61 |
|---|---|---|---|---|
| Chemicals | 40.4 | 23.6 | 2,752.3 | 31,445 |
| Metallurgy | 12.4 | 20.3 | 991.0 | 23,063 |
| Machinery | 9.4 | 16.6 | 760.0 | 46,732 |
| Building materials (stone, clay, glass) | 8.2 | 10.9 | 625.0 | 35,893 |
| Food and tobacco | 7.6 | 12.3 | 604.0 | −52,416 |
| Wood, clothing and shoes/leather | 2.6 | 4.2 | 212.0 | −18,564 |
| All sectors (billions of lire) | 6,172.6 | 1,104.1 | | |
| Total manufacturing employment (1971) | | | | 715,222 |

Source: Cassa per il Mezzogiorno (cited in Rodgers 1979: 117).

for employment – such firms ought to have received substantially greater assistance than those in more stable or expanding sectors, at least according to the 'protectionist' logic. Yet, information on a regional and local basis indicates that the overall tendency has been *not* to finance small firms in the most traditional industries.

Data on credit and grant allocation by the Cassa per il Mezzogiorno for the 1951–74 period show that the sectors in question, despite accounting for 37 per cent of the total workforce in 1961, received only a tiny fraction of the loans (2.6 per cent) and grants (4.2 per cent). By contrast, the light mechanical and building materials industries, which accounted for only 26 per cent of the labour force, received 17.6 per cent of the loans and 27.5 per cent of the grants. With the exception of the food industry, there has been a basic tendency – as shown in table 5.1 – to favour stable and expanding sectors rather than those in crisis and decline.

Whilst these figures confirm that capital-intensive sectors have consumed the bulk of southern funding over the post-war period (notably for public projects in chemicals and steel), what needs to be emphasized in this context is this: the majority of small firms

Table 5.2   *Sectoral distribution of loans and grants, 1960–1969 (Salerno)*

| Sector | Funds allocated (%) | Share of workforce (%) 1960 | 1969 |
|---|---|---|---|
| Canning | 24.6. | 46.4 | 38.5 |
| Foods | 4.4 | 10.5 | 11.8 |
| Wood/furniture | 2.3 | 9.9 | 5.4 |
| Subtotal | 31.3 | 66.8 | 55.7 |
| Textiles/clothing | 17.8 | 8.7 | 11.6 |
| Building materials | 16.3 | 11.3 | 12.3 |
| Machinery | 12.8 | 6.7 | 9.5 |
| Chemicals | 9.8 | 1.8 | 2.1 |
| Tobacco | 9.6 | 1.1 | 5.6 |
| Subtotal | 48.5 | 20.9 | 29.5 |
| Total (millions of lire) | 92,407 | 24,364 | 39,790 |

*Source*: Bonazzi et al. (1972: 113, 115).

which have been sustained by state intervention are not those in the so-called traditional and declining sectors. On the contrary, the tendency has been to favour firms in the more stable or expanding industries involving the mechanical and building-related trades.

The southern pattern of allocation thus calls into question one of the most widely held assumptions in the literature: namely, that the state supports the most fragile concerns to protect employment. Further evidence in support of the tendency identified is provided in two studies of southern entrepreneurship in the provinces of Salerno and Catania. Both document the relative neglect and decline of 'traditional' products industries employing higher shares of labour, in favour of modern goods sectors which depend on local markets.

The relevant findings can be summarized thus: small firms in the most traditional sectors, despite employing a higher proportion of the workforce, received only a marginal share of investment funds. By the end of the period examined, employment in these firms had fallen absolutely and relatively. Conversely, firms in more stable or expanding sectors were more generously funded, despite their initially low incidence on overall employment.

*Table 5.3   Sectoral distribution of loans and grants, 1947–1973 (Catania)*

| Industries grouped by technological content | Resources allocated % | Share of workforce | |
|---|---|---|---|
| | | 1951 | 1971 |
| Traditional (mature) – foods, clothing, wood, shoes, etc. | 28.7 | 67.2 | 39.6 |
| Modern (medium-low) – mechanical, non-ferrous, metals/building materials | 65.3 | 25.3 | 41.4 |
| Modern (high-tech.) – paper, rubber, plastics, chemicals | 6.0 | 7.5 | 19.0 |
| Total (millions of lire) | 82,950 | 23,916 | 29,347 |

*Source*: Catanzaro (1979: 200).

Information from the Salerno study (Bonazzi et al. 1972) is reported in table 5.2. Note that, with the exception of textiles and clothing, the traditional sectors – which employed two-thirds of the labour force in 1961 – received less than one-third of the total grants and credit over the 1960–9 period. On the other hand, almost 50 per cent of the resources went to industries which accounted for only 21 per cent of the workforce.[11]

Similar findings are reported in the Catania study (Catanzaro 1979), and are set out in table 5.3. Observe, once again, that the 'traditional products' sector – which ought to have received most resources since it employed over two-thirds of the workforce in 1951 – obtained an altogether marginal share for its overall weight. Notable also is the absolute and relative decline of employment in these industries over the twenty-year period. As in the Salerno case, the large majority of resources went to firms in sectors least important for their contribution to employment: the 'modern goods' industries, with only 25 per cent of the manufacturing population in 1951, obtained over two-thirds of total finance. In contrast with the declines registered elsewhere, employment in these sectors had expanded considerably by 1971.

Another feature highlighted by the sectoral data, and already evident in the Cassa figures for the region, is that the relatively more privileged enterprises – those with a proportion of funding far in excess of their employment shares – tended to be found in the light mechanical and building materials industries. The author of the Catania study, noting this discrepancy of treatment among small firms, concludes that the state has been a 'protagonist', not a passive spectator of southern development, encouraging precisely those sectors which could benefit from its public expenditure programmes and the local construction industry (Catanzaro 1979: 207).

The evidence assembled here suggests that in Italy's most economically depressed region, the state pursues a dual strategy of assistance. This is characterized on one hand by substantial support for public enterprise in heavy industry (especially chemicals and steel);[12] and, on the other, by a tendency to privilege small firms in sectors which are more closely integrated with the local economy. The allocation of investment funds has thus operated in a selective manner, tending to favour not the weakest firms most destined to extinction from outside competition, but those which receive a strong impulse from local and public sector activities, and thus with correspondingly better chances for survival.

In view of this distinction, the 'needs of employment' argument surely needs qualification. For it is difficult to reconcile the available evidence with the claim that the government's small firms strategy has to do with doling out largesse to protect the ailing and uncompetitive, their significance for labour absorption notwithstanding. Contrary also to another commonplace of the literature, it is not at all clear from the regional and sectoral information that the management of financial incentives flies in the face of economic rationality. Rather, if the southern data illuminate any clear overall tendency, it is this: among the potential recipients of state aid, governments, disposing of a limited amount of resources, have sought to back not the lame ducks, but those in sectors with apparently better chances for survival and replacement – in particular, initiatives which, because they can be stimulated by local demand and public works expenditure, are not at a competitive disadvantage.[13] If one adds to this the observations made earlier for the regional pattern of support, then an even stronger case for the 'rationality' of small firm support can be made.

Having examined the arguments for small business, the criteria and the management of assistance, one is led to conclude that support for petite enterprise has depended only in small part on its importance for employment. The artisan law provided a key example of the way the limitation of size and the multiplication of enterprise have themselves been important objectives. In a similar manner, the data on funding indicated that in so far as the state seeks to prevent the 'decline' of the traditional sector, it does so less by bolstering the most fragile and precarious concerns than by encouraging those in areas and sectors where the prospects for survival and proliferation are more promising.

I have sought to emphasize the economic logic apparent in the arguments and application of small business policy, not because it has been the prime mover of state activity but in order to stress the seriousness with which the DC viewed small business: not as a museum piece to be preserved for socially costly ends; but as a viable and preferred alternative to a concentrated industrial structure. The significance of this logic is that it undermines the notion of 'social pressures' at the core of the functionalist account. In so doing, it paves the way for a more explicitly state-centred argument in the following chapters.

### Clientelism and firm size

In the clientelistic version of the employment hypothesis, identified chiefly with the work of Pizzorno (1980), necessity and preference are intertwined: on one hand, the DC was 'obliged to favour' the small producers to avoid social tensions; but on the other hand, it also wanted to protect the small sector for its crucial role in the clientelistic strategy preferred and adopted by the governing party. What made the small firm sector so important, then, was not merely its capacity to sustain employment, but its function in the DC's strategy of individualistic exchange and mediation. According to Pizzorno (1980: 83) this required an alliance with the small producers in the common task of controlling social tensions. In so far as the need for work and for financial support can be turned to political advantage, the small sector becomes a resource in the hands of local politicians who seek to place personnel clientelistically in exchange for credit given. In the granting of credit then, 'The criterion is not the maximization of productive efficiency, but rather the solidity of the bond of recognition established and the type of service to be rendered for that given fraction of the political class. In other words, to the economic credit corresponds a political debt' (1980: 86–7). Thus, in return for maintaining existing employment levels or for taking on to the payroll extra workers 'recommended' by local politicians, the small employer is offered 'as a reward . . . participation in the political benefits of a protected entrepreneurship' (1980: 89).

Now the achievement of Pizzorno's argument is to have drawn attention to the processes underlying the emergence of a new sub-political category of public functionaries who manage the outflow of all manner of resources. By extending the activities of the state in the economic arena, and by directly placing its own loyal functionaries in key positions controlling access to special credit, the power of commercial licensing and the allocation of public spending, the DC has widened its hold over both the state apparatuses and local society.

What Pizzorno's essay fails to explain, however, is why it is that the economy of small producers should be the most fertile terrain for the exercise and success of clientelistic practices, why political pressures for labour absorption should be more effective in small, rather than in large, units. In other words, what is the necessary connection between such a strategy and firm size?

Central to Pizzorno's argument is the notion that support for the secondary sector was designed to further a strategy of 'individualistic consensus'. This implies that the DC is not interested in the simple delivery of benefits to supporters via standardized procedures. Rather, it seeks to allocate resources on a discriminatory basis in order to forge solid bonds of reciprocal obligation. Whilst such transactions no doubt serve to strengthen the position of individual politicians within the party, it is not at all clear that the discrimination of small firm beneficiaries would be politically more rewarding for the party as a whole.

However, leaving aside this problem and assuming for the moment that the crucial issue has been to maximize political obligations, whilst simultaneously responding to demands for stable work, it is still difficult to see why this would entail favouring firms of a small dimension. It is by now well documented that clientelistic mediation and exchange are fundamental principles of Italian social organization, operating at all institutional levels and involving all social classes.

At the level of economic enterprise, for example, it is both logically and empirically the case that large firms not only offer greater opportunities for political exchange, but are also more likely to be the object of that practice. As the economist Graziani (1978: 203), writes:

Everyone knows that the large installations in the Mezzogiorno take on their personnel in a strictly clientelistic manner . . . the local political class, by controlling the hiring of personnel, substantially controls the entire political life of the region. And this is much easier through the large plant . . . than through a multiplicity of small firms which exist in a more independent labour market.

Such installations are typically those of the state holding companies. Largely responsible for the concentration of heavy industry in the south, they 'are more open to political manipulation from Rome than are the large private companies, particularly on the question of the location of investment and who gets jobs' (Wade 1979: 214). Even within the private sector, it is the medium or large firm which most frequently bears the brunt of political pressure to maintain its workforce or to hire politically 'recommended' personnel. A study of relations between local entrepreneurs and politicians in Salerno showed that the frequency of 'political contacts' increased with the size of the firm. As a proportion of the universe, 24 firms in every 100 experienced political pressure of a general nature to prevent dismissals or increase employment; whilst 39 out of every 100 firms received requests to take on to their payrolls specifically 'recommended' workers. However, if one excludes the small firms from these calculations, the proportions increase to 40 per cent and 60 per cent respectively. As the authors of the study (Bonazzi et al. 1972: 229, 386) remark:

It is perfectly comprehensible that such pressure increases with the size of firm because the larger the size, the more opportunities to employ manpower. . . . [Conversely] . . . the prospect of medium or large industries going under, with the consequent dismissal of labour, social tensions and political complications, is always a sufficient deterrent to call forth rescue operations.

If, as this example shows, clientelism is not a size-related phenomenon, but applies equally, indeed more frequently, to the large firm, what then is left of the notion that the small sector is especially functional for the DC's consensus strategy? Given the pervasiveness of clientelism and its lesser relevance for small enterprise *vis-à-vis* the large, the supportive measures in question cannot be reduced to this category of explanation.

## Conclusion

However much the problems of employment and consensus may be important to an understanding of political action in contemporary Italy, their resolution, as this chapter has shown, does not necessitate a policy in favour of *small* enterprise. If we consider that this policy has been expansionary both in its orientation and its effects – that it has sought to promote rather than simply prop up – then it would appear that the nature and patterning of support are consistent with a different explanation from the ones so far considered.

The more generous flow of resources to areas and sectors with greater potential for the growth of small firms suggests that it is the overall structural significance of the small entrepreneurial stratum that counts. For this reason, government support should be related not to the specific political pressures and problems of vote-getting or appeasement or employment, but to a more fundamental concern: that of maintaining a particular social structure in which economic independence and the 'collaborative' character of small, craft-based enterprise feature not as objects for preservation, but as models for imitation. For the development of that argument, we must turn to the next chapter.

# 6

# The social project

## Introduction

The prevailing explanations of state assistance, as we have seen, focus on short-term themes – the need to protect jobs, to obtain votes, and to appease an uneasy stratum – all of which are inferred from the presumed vulnerability of the small firm sector as a whole. Consistently society-centred, these 'protectionist' positions assume that the political leadership has merely maintained the existing, 'reacting' favourably to small business 'when the road ahead looks bumpy', thereby averting the eruptions and agitations that could ensue from petit bourgeois radicalization and mass unemployment. In this view, certain crucial aspects of government policy – namely, measures to propagate small units throughout the economy, and, more importantly, schemes that *exclude* big business – can have no place and make no sense.

My explanation of the state's relation to small capital departs from these positions in one crucial respect. It emphasizes the independent nature of government action, moving the focus beyond the short term to a broader, long-term objective. The latter involves a concern to strengthen certain organizational forms and social identities which, in the Christian Democratic conception, promote 'solidarism' at the expense of class solidarity. Such a focus implies that small firms support has a deeper, structural base than hitherto apparent from the literature. Electoral and employment criteria form only one subordinate part of this conception. More important is the social structural balance, the cohesion and collaborative context for employment that the existence of a substantial small firm sector provides.

Since this and the following chapter comprise two closely interwoven strands of my argument, it is essential to say something about the fit between the two. Together, they present the necessary elements for an explanation of state assistance, which links substantive political action to an ideologically based social project and to the political challenges and power struggles which helped carry it forward. Thus, with reference to the ideological orientations of Christian Democracy and to the political problems of the late 1940s and 1950s, I argue that the promotion of small enterprise in post-war Italy has been the outcome of two variables: the historically based preferences of the ruling party, namely, Christian Democracy's ideology of small ownership; and the politicized nature and anti-system orientation of the labour movement. In this chapter I therefore propose to examine how the choice for a small-scale productive structure was *shaped* ideologically and – in the following chapter – reinforced politically.

Before plunging directly into that analysis it is important to briefly clarify the meaning and place of the 'ideological' in my argument. Since the term has been used in so many diverse ways it will conjure up many different expectations and no doubt a good deal of sociological disbelief. I therefore refer the reader to the note section.[1] It will become apparent, however, that I am using the term to indicate a set of cultural preferences formed historically by Catholic–Communist divisions and reinvigorated by the rise of a politicized labour movement.

The crucial point to bear in mind is that the main purpose of examining ideology is to show that state elites pursued their own interests. It matters not one whit to my argument whether these interests were selfish, moral or utopian. They were all three. What matters is that these objectives, although forged out of historic divisions, were defined independently of contemporary power struggles and taken up in economic programmes. My argument therefore departs radically from the established understandings examined earlier, in so far as it shows that the DC had a social project. This project positively valued the petite bourgeoisie, sought to create more of them and thereby generalize for all society the ideals of economic independence: the small firm, the skilled craftsman.

Thus, although my explanation is double-stranded, I shall nevertheless in this chapter establish a case for the independent explanatory importance of ideological preferences (as state-defined objectives), drawing on temporal and cross-national comparisons. The task is two fold: to elucidate the core ideological components of the demochristian project as it was shaped *before* the party's immersion in the world of power struggles; and to test their relevance for practical outcomes, by showing how the DC's economic programmes for small business are deducible neither from class interests nor from economic structure. The following chapter complements this analysis by showing that the state could have acted otherwise and that the social project in question, whilst carried forward by a particular cycle of political conflicts and configurations, nevertheless remains in force after their dissolution.

### The middle class core of demochristian ideology

Extolling the virtues of small business has long been an intermittent pastime of conservative parties. Few however have ventured beyond electoral slogans. And even fewer could match their Italian counterpart for historical consistency. Indeed, throughout its evolution from nineteenth-century social movement to post-war mass party, Christian Democracy displayed a striking constancy of objectives in its proposal to 'abolish the proletariat' and 'extend the class of small property owners'. Indeed, when turning to examine the nature of its 'interclass' appeal, we will find that the new Catholic party emerged on the post-Fascist scene as the bearer of a middle-class project. By appealing to all those who have, *or aspire to have*, property, the means for their own livelihood,[2] the DC sought to define and to mobilize an essentially middle class collectivity.

In emphasizing the role of small property, the DC was heir not only to the principles espoused by its predecessors – the fledgling Christian Democrats of 1894 and Luigi Sturzo's Popular Party (PPI) of 1919 – but also to the very problem that had eventually urged Catholics into the political arena: the struggle to win the proletariat from socialism (Sturzo 1923; Scoppola 1963; De Rosa 1966).[3] This 'great labour question', as Leo XIII defined it in the *Rerum Novarum* of 1891, 'cannot be solved save by assuming as a principle that private ownership must be held sacred and inviolable. The law, therefore, should favour ownership, and its policy should be to induce as many as possible of the people to become owners' (cited in Camp 1969: 84). In effect, the proletariat could be redeemed not *qua* worker, but by conversion to something else, by 'restoring' all those means of production indispensable for conducting one's own livelihood: land for the peasant, tools for the artisan, machinery and equipment for the entrepreneur. Thus, at the heart of all Catholic programmes, the solutions brought to bear on the labour problem centred typically on property diffusion – from profit-sharing schemes (the 'just wage') to land reform.[4]

Such solutions meshed with the traditional Catholic preference for a society of producer–owners (Webster 1960: 67). This tendency, insisted the PPI leader, was not to be viewed as a nostalgic opposition to large industry, for that, he admitted, would be 'a backward conception of two centuries'. Rather, emphasized Sturzo (1923: 11), the economic base at the centre of the demochristian conception was simply the 'natural counterpart' to that of socialism. Where the latter, especially the German variety, had given expression to 'the proletarian movement of large industry', 'In like manner, the Christian Social movement has theorized and represented the constitutive elements of the middle class . . . the economic currents of agriculture, the crafts and small industry . . . supported by a mingling of middle-class groups and urban professional people.' As Sturzo defined it, then, the Catholic movement's 'fundamental and distinctive' character consisted in its aim to suppress the class struggle by recognizing this independent middle class as 'the legal, economic and political base of society' (1923: 11).

## The DC project: a property-owning democracy

The middle class contours of the solidaristic state, as outlined by Sturzo, were again etched firmly in the proposals that De Gasperi and fellow Christian Democrats had successively elaborated during and after the fall of Fascism.[5] What must be emphasized, however, is that the middle class nature of the demochristian project derived not simply from the character of the collectivity it sought to mobilize, but from the methods envisaged for giving the working class a stake in the new democracy.

### *Deproletarianization*

These schemes rotated around the principle that the proletarian – whether on the land or in industry – 'must be eliminated' (*Il Programma* 1944; *Idee* 1943; *Programma di Milano* 1943). Thus, the DC's 1946 proposals for the new Constitution (DC 1968: 245) announced:

Our ultimate aim is the elimination of wage labour and the consequent servitude of the proletariat, favouring access of labour to ownership . . . in this we differ from communism and liberalism which maintain capital distinct from labour: liberalism leaving it to the capitalist, communism attributing it to the state. None of the two systems *effect a coincidence between capital and labour in the same hands.* [Italics added]

Maximum freedom and social justice would be achieved not through collective projects for 'levelling downwards', nor by allowing market forces to prevail, but by encouraging those lowest in the social hierarchy to rise gradually to the ranks of property owner (*Idee* 1943: 4–5). The labour reform programme was thus precisely the opposite of socialism. Rather than making everyone a wage earner by eliminating private property, the party wanted to generalize the property institution. Capital and labour, the DC emphasized at the 1946 Congress, 'must be brought closer together' in a way that capital would not be a 'parasitic oppressor', nor labour a 'rebellious slave'. In the party's words, it wanted to 'deproletarianize the workers' and 'remake the *ceto medio*, by inducing as many as possible to become property owners (DC 1968: 246).

The concrete proposals to bring about these objectives differed according to economic sector. In agriculture, on the basis of the principle that the 'proletariat of the land must disappear', a land reform was to be gradually implemented 'to allow the constitution of a healthy class of small independent farmers' (*Idee* 1943: 5; *Il Programma* 1944: 30). In industry, two courses of action were envisaged. That most favoured was 'to make the worker the owner-entrepreneur', for which purpose the artisanal and cooperative forms of production were considered ideal, 'both being forms typically suited . . . to transforming the worker from the victim of the will or errors of others into someone responsible for the major decisions affecting his future' (*Riforme* 1946: 18).

Where this option was not possible, and where for technical reasons large concentrations of workers would be required, then the party would have to have 'recourse to surrogate means', typically, through schemes for worker participation in the administration and profits of the firm (*Riforme* 1946: 7).[6] Here, the state would encourage those companies which enabled their workers to have a stake in the running and capital of the enterprise, thus 'raising wage-earners to a level of independence and responsibility as co-owners' (*Codice* 1943: 327; *Idee* 1943: 4; *Programma di Milano* 1944: 10; *Il Programma* 1946: 28).

It is worth pointing out that all of these proposals, excepting those for worker participation, have been put into operation. The land reform eliminated the latifundia but because of the dramatic reaction was never applied on a universal scale (see chapter 7). Of all proposals, however, those for workers' participation in management councils were to have least resonance. As Barucci (1978: 88) writes, 'The fears of the industrial world, the criticisms of experts, the cold reception [the scheme] received among trade unionists, soon squashed the idea of their institutionalized presence.' Significantly, the only steps ventured in this direction have occurred in the state sector (see Montalenti 1978: 75–81).

Central to these proposals was the assumption that workers in large-scale industry were exposed to particular hardships, and that these resulted not simply from low wages, but from a productive arrangement whose anonymity and far-reaching division of labour denied the full development of human faculties and personal skills. For the Christian Democrats then, the current regime of industrial management suppressed such attributes both by depersonalizing labour and by rendering the worker 'extraneous to all those decisions which affect his livelihood, serenity and future':

In short, the worker does not like the enterprises in which he works because, either denying him sufficient bread, or requiring of him depersonalized labour, they impede him from giving full proof of self . . . and from realizing all the talents he possesses for his own perfection and for the advancement of society. (*Riforme* 1946: 5)

To be a collaborator rather than an agitator required a sense of dignity and responsibility; and for Christian Democracy there could be no productive form more respondent to the dignity of individuals and more suited to develop in them a sense of responsibility than the small-scale business. Thus, setting out their 'Principles for a Christian Social Order' in the *Codice di Camoldoli* (1943–4: 321–2), Christian Democrats, in collaboration with economic experts and Catholic theologians, designated as the ideal productive arrangement the artisan business and agricultural family enterprise. For, in contrast to other economic forms, they managed to combine the requirements of technical efficiency with those of the worker's development as a person.

Viewed from this perspective, the deproletarianizing potential of small property had a dual significance, briefly alluded to in the previous chapter. For its diffusion would reduce the number of proletarians, not only by transforming them into owners, but also by better protecting the 'human dignity' of those employed in small units. The *ceto medio* as we have seen were not just those who worked on their own account. They were most frequently employers. For Christian Democrats, however, what mattered was that artisans, small industrialists, commercial retailers, farmers and professionals were all engaged *directly* in the production process, and therefore 'not regrouped in complex capitalistic forms'.[7] As one party spokesman expressed it at a conference for the *ceti medi,*

The *ceto medio* is made up not only of autonomous or independent workers, but also entrepreneurs. . . . The small economic operators who provide capital for the firm and generally have a managerial or even working role certainly belong to the *ceto medio*. But those entrepreneurs who have a living standard which is rich or superior or capitalist are not part of the *ceto medio*. (Rubinacci 1958: 39)

Such distinctions derive not from any anti–capitalist attitude, but from the fact that for Christian Democracy the small producer was the very symbol of the integral society: he was both employer and labourer; he worked alongside his assistants and related to them in a highly personal way. Consequently, in the small firm, the organization of work was 'more human', the worker's dignity 'better protected', the sense of responsibility and collaboration more keenly developed. In short, where the large firm promoted class solidarity, the smaller unit fostered solidarism, thus transcending the capital–labour split.[8]

### Anti-monopoly

In conjunction with these proposals for property creation, the state would also have to intervene to combat those 'parasitic' and 'antisocial' forms of property – from the latifundia to the large industrial and financial concentrations. 'The state', it was argued, 'must eliminate those industrial and financial concentrations that are artificial creations of economic imperialism; and modify the laws that have up to now encouraged the centralization of the means of production in the hands of a few' (*Idee* 1943: 4; *Consiglio Nazionale* 1945: 192).

Social justice thus entailed pushing back the frontiers of all those capitalistic or monopolistic concentrations 'that are not really inevitable through the force of things or for technical reasons' (*Idee*

1943). This anti-monopoly component of DC ideology derives from the Catholic idea of the 'third way', the notion that the concentration of ownership – whether in the hands of the state (collectivism), or of private groups (liberalism) – 'prevents the diffusion of small private property and endangers the development of a free people' (*Il Programma* 1944: 28). It is worth noting that this anti-monopoly orientation – which, as the following chapter shows, would become increasingly prominent under Fanfani's leadership in the fifties – was based not on any objective assessment of the Italian market or economic structure, but on the assumed attributes of scale. Whether monopolistic or not, the *large* enterprise was almost invariably cast in that role. Christian Democrats, in other words, tended to identify big business *tout court* with the monopolies, with obvious consequences for the allocation of state benefits. I shall develop this point in the following chapter when discussing the exclusion of big capital from state assistance.

In the demochristian vision of the new social order, the battle for deproletarianization and against capital concentration formed part of a seamless web of objectives for a decentralized economy in which property was diffused and ownership personal, conflict defused and control more effective. Thus, the centrepiece of the 'New Social Economy' was the economically independent middle class:

Wherever the natural tendency to constitute property with the fruits of one's own labour, free initiative and competition between single firms exercize a function useful to the common good, the state will limit itself to protect, promote and integrate. . . . In Italy, this is the vast area of small and medium industry, of small and medium commerce: it is therefore the case of the majority of Italian families and businesses. Here, the State will intervene to encourage and consolidate small property and the small business, with fiscal and legal provisions . . . and with the organization of small credit; but above all by defending this free area against the monopolistic tendencies of big industry and the imperialistic ambitions of capitalist plutocracy. (*Il Programma* 1944: 27; cf. also *Idee* 1943: 4)

For the Christian Democrats, then, the notion of a property-owning democracy implied above all an economic system which enabled wide access to individual enterprise and, consequently, a considerable amount of state intervention to secure it. Compared with that espoused by the British Conservatives, which entailed pushing back the frontiers of the state, the contrast could not be more dramatic. In fact, in spite of a superficially similar 'rhetoric', the Tory idea of a property-owning democracy carried none of the policy implications of the Italian conception. As Gamble has shown, it merely identified something already in existence. For the Tories, property-owning democrats were all those able or willing to fend for themselves. They were 'middle class', not by virtue of their economic autonomy, but because of their independence from the state. Thus, the self-employed Marshall family whose photo adorned the 1949 policy document, 'The Right Road for Britain', embodied the Conservative ideal, not because they were *economically* independent, but because they were typical of those 'who neither demand state help nor need state interference, but only ask to be able to do a fair day's work for a fair day's pay, and to accumulate steadily sufficient property to enable them to be independent' (Gamble 1974: 58). In the British context then, the 'property-owning democracy' was at most a rhetorical device to oppose 'nationalization' (Harris 1972: 107), a convenient slogan for the advocates of *laissez-faire* and self-help. As Gamble (1974: 59) remarks, 'The slogan, a property-owning democracy, did not concern policy. It identified what already existed . . . [all] those who were prepared to save and collect a small amount of property, yet remain independent of the state.'

This sturdy individualism of the self-help variety is, however, peripheral to the demochristian understanding, in which independence is first and foremost of an *economic* nature. On this point, the following statement, issued by the Papacy on the occasion of a study conference (ICAS 1951) on the *'Classe Medie'*, is both representative and explicit:

The precise character of this [middle] class is economic independence, on the basis of which it is possible for it to secure social stability and the production of goods, forming thus a happy harmony between personal labour and private property. With his own effort and labour the man of the middle class conserves his autonomy and his dignity without having to beg for his means of subsistence.

In the party's ultimate goal to create 'a society of worker owners in order to be really a society of free men' (see Barucci 1978: 70), 'independence' is thus essentially the freedom achieved from capital subservience and wage dependence. In the words of the DC Minister for Industry, Giuseppe Togni, to become part of the middle class was 'to free oneself with dignity, on one hand from the servitude of collectivist myths, and on the other, from the tyrannical sovereignty of the employer'.[9]

Clearly, then, the idea of a property-owning democracy contained in the slogan *Non: tutti proletari, ma tutti proprietari* was no mere rhetorical frill or idealization of the existing, but a policy to be enacted. For how else could the DC hope to combat collectivism and champion freedom, if not by affirming its commitment in word and deed to small property and individual enterprise?

By now, enough has been said on the nature of the DC's fundamental goals and the presumptions and perceptions which underpinned its decision to build on the small-scale characteristics of the Italian economy. My chief purpose has been to isolate and evidence the ideological core of small firm support, as manifested in the DC's founding documents. Later discussion will of course draw on less conspicuous sources of 'ideological production', and will attempt to relate these to operative policy and, in chapter 7, to an analysis of the wider political context. However, the documents examined have a special importance in so far as they predate the onset of electoral contests, the Cold War and the crystallization of class alignments which, from 1947 onwards, saw a hostile and excluded labour movement pitted against an anti-communist majority. Such developments were to give the *ceti medi* an increasingly pivotal role in the dominant bloc. But whatever interpretation we may reserve for subsequent events, the essential starting-point for the DC, as these documents show, was not to build support against, but amongst, the working class. Either way, the state's 'use' of the micro-capitalist sector, as I shall argue in the following chapter, is not readily explained by the push and pull of political conflict *per se*. Reference to the presuppositions and preferences of its central political managers is, in other words, crucial to an understanding of how subsequent state activity was shaped.

## The case for ideology

To give some preliminary support to this assertion, it is useful to consider two ways in which the role of 'ideology' can be denied. Now it may be argued that the DC merely wooed the small business sector because it wanted support from a middle class constituency which in Italy had considerable electoral weight. This statement can be broken down into two propositions, each of which I shall examine separately. The first is that a large middle class constituency or substantial small firm sector can be expected to solicit a correspondingly substantial response from the state. The test is whether the state has acted similarly in other countries with comparably large sectors of small business. The second proposition is that small firm support can be accounted for in terms of the economic interests it served. The test here is whether the relevant provisions aimed to preserve the status quo or to alter or modify existing arrangements in some way.

### The structural argument

The structural case for small firm support, based on the notion that a substantial secondary sector calls forth a correspondingly significant response from the state, can be refuted by comparative analysis. Both for its population size and occupational structure (1951 data), France is perhaps ideally suited for this purpose. If we take as a measure of the highly dispersed pattern of business ownership, the number of 'employers and own account workers' (or their proportional weight in the active population), then the differences between Italy and France – as indicated in chapter 2 – are indeed minimal.

Despite this structural similarity, French policy could not have been more different. As all the literature on economic policy has shown, French governments since the end of the war have pushed for greater scale and concentration, 'fighting the prewar attitude that equated the development of small and medium-sized firms with the social and economic welfare of French society' (Sheahan 1963: 43; cf. also Denton 1968: 82ff; Lauber 1981). For the French administrative elite, the experience of the formidable German war economy reinforced the Fordist view that France's industrial future, indeed its national prowess, lay with the giant industrial complex. Given this premise, any effort to assist the small firm to adapt to the new techniques and requirements of production could only be regarded as pointless. Thus, whereas Italian governments helped small firms to modernize, the French emphasis was on phasing them out (Lauber 1981: 232; Shonfield 1965: 148).

Hence, whilst the Italians set up Special Credit Institutes and tax schemes to expand their class of small entrepreneurs, the French moved in an entirely opposite direction, providing similar facilities to foster mergers and increase the size of plants 'so that mass production methods could be employed. The effects of these big business measures, most vigorously endorsed under Gaullism, and the attendant neglect of 'areas of native strength where small and medium-sized firms could have been successful' (Lauber 1981: 232), were already evident before the major wave of concentration in the late sixties (see Coffey 1973: 31). Chapter 7 will return to the theme of European concentration policies when comparing the Italian response and the continuing impact of the DC's small firm bias.

Perhaps the most important thing to note for France is that the rules of the game established in the post-war era placed a premium on absolute size. Under these conditions, the most that could be done by small business and its spokesmen was to opt for a defensive strategy in the interests of *preserving – but not increasing –* smaller units.

The structural test can be similarly applied to Germany. Today of course, with its highly concentrated economic structure, Germany does not lend itself as readily to comparison. Yet, thirty years ago, despite the ravages of the German war economy, it too possessed a not insignificant small business sector. Whilst only some 16 per cent of the active population were independently employed in 1972, in 1950 that proportion was twice as great (31.6 per cent) (Bergmann and Muller-Jentsch 1975: 238). Indeed, in the early fifties, non-agricultural 'employers and own account workers' numbered slightly in excess of 2 million in Germany, Italy and France (Hilderbrand 1965: table 65). Moreover, in the *Handwerk* sector (which includes services, trades and manufacturing), Germany's 860,000 small businesses reached levels similar to those of Italy and France (Barberis 1980: 9).

From the perspective of numbers, then, Germany's small business sector was comparably substantial at the beginning of the period. However, the German treatment of small enterprise differs markedly from both the Italian and the French. Seeking neither the *multiplication* nor the *elimination* of smaller concerns, German policy stressed the concern for *equilibrium*.

Whilst that emphasis derives from the 'competition' principle of the 'social market economy', the policy itself was initially shaped by popular fears that economic power was becoming too concentrated. For, in spite of earlier attempts by the Allied forces to break up some of the larger industrial combines, with a view to eliminating one threat to peace, by 1952 a reconcentration effort was under way as the process of 'mergers, the expansion of large firms and the elimination of smaller ones' accelerated (Braunthal 1965: 249). To take but one aspect of this trend, the number of plants employing over 1,000 workers rose dramatically between 1954 and 1961, from 708 to 1,045 – an increase of 208 per cent which brought German industry close to British levels of concentration (1,206 giant plants) (Ray 1966: 65).

Yet it was perhaps a different and more visible aspect of this process that most stirred up the public. The successful pressure by industrial groups upon the German government, for its own reasons anxious to reverse Allied policy (see chapter 8), allowed giants like Krupp and Thyssen to reconstitute their corporate structures; and it was above all against this type of concentration movement that parties, trade unions, independent entrepreneurs and tradesmen united in protest (Braunthal 1965: 249). As a result, the CDU government in 1957 formally inaugurated its *Mittelstandspolitik*, declaring that:

for political and cultural reasons it is absolutely necessary that we have a sound middle stratum. We do not want the people to be divided into a small class of economic overlords and a vast mass of dependents through the ever-increasing concentration of the economy into large firms. We require independent medium and small units in the crafts, trade business, and in agriculture. (Cited in Denton 1968: 62)

The important difference, however, is that unlike the Italian emphasis on middle class *expansion*, the keynote of German policy is the maintenance of *balance*. As Denton (1968: 63) observes,

The policy itself is defined as one of constantly examining past, present and future legislation in order to ensure that any unnecessary harmful consequences for the small and medium-sized firm can be prevented, removed or modified. If this is impossible, 'the federal government intervenes in favour of small and medium-sized firms and *restores the balance* through special measures of assistance'. [Italics added]

As part of this 'balancing' act, the CDU/CSU governments have been outspoken advocates of large-scale industry whilst simultaneously stipulating a role for smaller units; and, at a practical level, have sponsored concentration whilst launching measures of assistance to smaller concerns (see Irving 1979: 157; Peacock 1980: para 4.27). Indeed, German legislation actually 'encouraged concentration by granting tax benefits to firms that merged their subsidiaries' in the very period that the *Mittelstandspolitik* was launched (Braunthal 1965: 252).

That the CDU government sought to maintain the small business stratum, 'but not to foster it too much' (Denton 1968: 62) is perhaps best explained in terms of its commitment to the principles of the 'social market economy'. For nothing in that policy entailed a commitment to the 'small' enterprise. It simply meant a competitive framework. The small firm was at most one among several *means* of maintaining it (cartel policy, at least in theory, being another). Indeed, the 'social market's' chief exponent, Ludwig Erhard, was no 'advocate of a petty capitalism' and strongly opposed deconcentration (Berghahn 1984: 189). Consequently, once the terms of competition appeared to have altered, so the federal government came out explicitly in favour of big business. Thus, for example, in 1967 it announced that

The Common Market and the trend to world-wide economic integration have created new premises for competition. Larger markets demand in many ways larger and more efficient company units . . . The Federal government is concerned to remove obstacles which stand in the way of concentration of enterprises now blocked by cartel law, so that the development of firms of optimum size will not be hindered. (Cited in Kuster 1974: 79)

Apart from the fact that the cartel law had been so watered down by the amendments of the Federation of German Industry as to be virtually useless (see Smith 1983: 23, 271ff; Braunthal 1965: 246), the government's sponsorship of concentration was all the more remarkable in view of the already large average size of German plants (Peacock 1980: para 2.57). As a result of this endorsement, the pace of concentration visibly accelerated from the mid-sixties onwards. Thus by 1970 the top 100 enterprises had increased their 1950 share of industrial turnover from about one-third to over one-half. But by 1980 the top fifty alone accounted for half of all industrial turnover (Smith 1983: 287).[10]

The general point that emerges from these observations is not that small business has been ignored or discriminated against, as in the case of French policy, but rather that it has played a subordinate role to the wider competitive principles of the so-called social market economy. As we shall see in chapter 8, it seems doubtful that the Christian Democratic government in Germany was ever committed at the outset to the extension of small property. Whilst further research would be required to establish this, we can at least mention three reasons why, in practice, German legislation has not privileged smaller units as a model for that economy.

First, to a much greater extent than has been the case in Italy, the German Christian Democrats have depended on big business as a major source of financial support. As a result, close ties have been established and big business has wielded considerably more power in CDU circles (see Braunthal 1965: 97–101; 112–118). As chapter 7 shows, however, large private capital in Italy has been much more of an outsider *vis-à-vis* the dominant party, for the DC has sought instead an independent footing through the expansion of the public sector.

The second reason for the CDU's distinctly different policy orientation may very well lie with the protectionist stance of small business in that country. In effect, that stance demonstrates a greater concern to restrict access, to exclude competition from newcomers, rather than with big business encroachments. Such long-standing traditions (see Winkler 1976), so far from being overturned by the post-war legislation, have been considerably strengthened, a point to which I shall return.

The more general and perhaps most important reason, discussed in a wider comparative setting in chapter 8, has to do with the way the German state, for geopolitical reasons, has historically endorsed and encouraged industrial giantism.

These brief comparative examples are not meant to explain the configuration of policies in other European countries. To do that would require a more lengthy investigation (the task of chapter 8) which, although important, is not strictly relevant to the logic of my argument. For what I have sought to show up to this point is not that 'ideology' is the operative variable, but that structure is not the determining factor. From the comparative material presented, it cannot be concluded that structural resources determine government policies or the direction of state activity. As I shall argue in the following chapter with reference to France, whether and how the state will use the small firm sector depends not only – or even primarily – on the 'problems' it has to resolve, but on the assumptions, goals and perceptions with which relevant political elites face those problems.

### Economic interests

Another way of denying the role of ideological preferences would be to show that the relevant provisions were merely aimed at satisfying the economic interests of a particular class from whom the government sought consensus. There is of course always a complex relationship between interest and ideology; nevertheless I shall try to disprove the interests hypothesis by showing how certain ideological principles are at work in the realm of practical policy. Although the examples could be multiplied, I shall focus on two particular aspects of small business policy, the artisan law and retail trade licensing. Both exemplify the DC's 'expansionary', anti-closure orientation and its endeavour to both shape and satisfy workers' aspirations for individual advancement.

*Artisan legislation*   It would be difficult to deny that Italian artisans enjoy a privileged existence. Although most frequently employers of labour, they are taxed at the same rate as their workers and receive equivalent family allowances. They pay lighter social security contributions than other employers and are exempted from those for their apprentices. They benefit from a generous health and pension scheme, subsidized by the state. They receive technical and marketing assistance from various government agencies; and, not least, they have access to low-cost investment and running capital, again, publicly subsidized and guaranteed. Comparative research on government policies in the sixties indicates that nowhere else in Europe was the micro enterprise so copiously provided for, nor government so conspicuously active on its behalf (MEC 1962; Ministero dell'Industria 1963).

It would be superficial, however, to conclude from this that artisan policy represents a simple defence of the category's interests. To appreciate why this is so, let us recall that an essential component of the DC's interclass ideology was that wage earners be given a chance to become independent. For, just as it was 'the major ambition of every father who belongs to the poorest class . . . to be able to realize with his efforts and labours the passage of his son from the proletariat to the middle class,[11] so it was the essential hope of the proletariat to escape from the working class: 'It is in contradiction with all sociological laws to insist that the industrial system based on wage labour, as it once was on universal slavery is a normal and definitive regime, up to the point of removing even the worker's *hope of rising in status* (italics added).[12] Importantly, if the independent middle class was to provide a model of 'individualistic mobilization' to set against collective struggle, then its sheer existence and protection would not suffice. For what mattered, as a DC spokesman put it to his small business audience, was the extent to which the *ceto medio* exerted a powerful attraction for upward mobility: 'It is this force of attraction that demonstrates to us that even he who is lowliest understands that social justice is achieved not by bringing every one down by an absurd levelling, but by seeking to rise by degrees, as much as possible' (Lucifredi 1958: 82).

To release the desired pattern of social action, policy thus had to emphasize the 'propulsive' role of the *ceto medio*, so that 'all those workers to whom Marxist policies of levelling downwards have created the false impression that the *ceto medio* is a *closed caste of useless people*, will look to the future with greater *hope*' (Togni 1958: 31) (italics added). For the DC then, an open and expanding middle class was an essential condition not only for reducing the number of proletarians, but for keeping alive that all-important element of Catholic ideology, hope.

The path from conception to practice is most clearly traced through the government's introduction of the Artisan Act. It will be recalled that, far from protecting acquired positions, this law effectively opened the doors to all manner of newcomers, all eager to exploit the special benefits offered to the artisan. The most important thing to be stressed in this context, however, is not the benefits available to the Italian artisan, but rather the mode of access to that status. For, alone in Europe, the Italian system excludes 'credentialism'. The prospective Italian artisan requires no certification of expertise, thus ensuring ease of entry to the sector. By contrast, the restrictive German *Handwerksordnung* of 1953 specified obligatory training and qualifications for those wishing to so establish themselves (Denton 1968; Barberis 1980: 9). Such measures, as indicated earlier, underwrite the protectionist traditions of German craftsmen and are clearly aimed at keeping down the numbers of new entries to the sector in question.

Reversing the logic of the German premium on professionalism, which imposed stringent conditions of entry but no size limitation, Italian policy sought saturation rather than stability of existing interests. Not surprisingly, then, 'professionalism' was to become a key issue for the Italian artisanat in the 1970s. The major Catholic-affiliated organization for the artisanat, the CGIA, consistently and unsuccessfully argued for a 'certificate of professional capacity', pointing out that the Italian artisanat merely wanted what already 'exists in other EEC countries, to combat abuses and improvization . . . a criterion of efficiency to overcome the levelling of the sector and to combat the threat of proletarianization' (Germozzi 1972: 5). In putting the case for credentialism, the

President pointed out the idiosyncracies of Italian policy. All other countries, he argued, had resolved 'the problem of professional qualification' with reforms that require a licence to exercise a given occupation. If in France, 'where *abusivismo* is severely punished', all workshops must display their 'artisan' or 'master artisan' credentials, why should it not be so for Italy? And if in Germany 'no trade can be exercised' without the requisite examination and registration, why should not similar controls exist for the Italian artisanat? (Germozzi 1974: 26).

It was with the aim of forestalling precisely such exclusionary demands that Christian Democrats appealed to the class of small entrepreneurs as the 'propulsive' force, open to all those who seek to avoid or escape from the 'squalor of the proletariat' (Rubinacci 1958: 45). Addressing an assembly of the *ceti medi* in 1958, the DC Minister for Industry, Togni (1958: 31), offered the following advice:

We must not consider ourselves other than as a way of entry . . . towards the improvement of our conditions. We of the *ceto medio* are not and could never be a caste. We do not want to and could never be a category, if not in the sense that this is the category of all those who free themselves from outdated conceptions of class exclusivism in social life. . . . We are not a category in the sense of Marxist closure; we do not want to be a class . . . because the real class distinguishes merit and effort wherever it is found, the sense of discipline and responsibility, wherever they reside in labour.

The *ceto medio* was not to be simply a static 'third force' between capital and labour, but 'the point of fusion and encounter of various social sectors' (Foresi 1958: 55). Its tasks were to attract and inspire others to 'raise themselves to a position like that of the *ceto medio* . . . so that gradually the condition of life of the *ceto medio* becomes the condition of life of Italian citizens in general' (Rubinacci 1958: 45, 44).

In other words, if the quest for independence – the Italian dream of 'il mettersi in proprio'[13] – was to act as a demobilizing incentive, it required for its effectiveness an 'open' middle class, able to accommodate, not poised to exclude, potential newcomers to its ranks.

A measure of the seriousness with which the government viewed this relationship between *ceto medio* and social mobility is afforded by a series of studies commissioned by the Ministry of Industry, under the tenure of Emilio Colombo. The studies were based on a survey of 50,000 artisan proprietors, conducted in 1960. Such an initiative may not, to the outside observer, seem especially significant; but for Italy, an empirical inquiry of this nature was then a most rare event.

Although the terms of reference of the inquiry were quite broad, significantly, they included an assessment of the artisanat's role in promoting upward mobility. Hence it was a finding of some importance to discover that 24 per cent of the owners surveyed had previously been wage earners, the grand majority in manufacturing industry. And if those without previous paid employment are included, the figure rises to 95 per cent (see Lasorsa's report in Ministero del'Industria 1963: 465).[14] On the basis of this and other information, the studies confirmed that the sector's 'contribution to social pacification' – considered in terms of social ascent – was considerable (see reports by Gasparini and De Falco in Ministero dell'Industria 1962/3: 81, 149).

By confirming also the artisanat's contribution both to economic progress and to the Italian population's 'desire for autonomy' (1962/63: 25, 150) these studies also served to vindicate the thrust of government policy towards encouraging 'new men' (women were not included) and 'new initiatives'. As Aldo Moro had announced at the 1959 Congress – with reference to recent small business provisions – it was not the working class that the DC intended to enlarge, but the class of small entrepreneurs, by 'bringing to it broad sections of the proletariat' (DC 1961: 265). With these measures, argued the party secretary, the DC was not simply flouting the common conviction that there was no place for small enterprise in an advanced industrial society. It was reaffirming the solidity of its guiding principle: *Non: tutti proletari, ma tutti proprietari.*

*Commercial licensing*  Although shopkeepers are of peripheral concern to this study, commercial licensing policy affords an especially interesting case for our present purposes. It is unfailingly invoked in the literature as the classical example of state protection of small business interests, yet even here some qualification is in order.

From one perspective, commercial policy is clearly protectionist: the licensing of supermarkets and large department stores has been severely restricted. For example, according to one study, both Italy and West Germany had only one 'self-service' outlet in 1949. By 1966, however, Germany counted 63,000 outlets, compared with a

Table 6.1 *Number of inhabitants served per retail outlet (1971)*

| Country | No. |
| --- | --- |
| Italy | 67 |
| France | 101 |
| UK | 108 |
| West Germany | 128 |
| Switzerland | 138 |

*Source*: INDIS 1972: *Rapporto sullo stato della distribuzione* Milan, p.30.

modest 2,000 in Italy (Ravalli 1967: 64). From another perspective, however, retail licensing policy is clearly a further manifestation of the 'diffusion' principle. Between 1951 and 1971, the number of censused retail outlets grew from 500,000 to 807,000. To put this datum in perspective, in 1951 there was one retail outlet for every 95 inhabitants, but one for every 67 Italians by 1971 (Ariotti 1974: 525).

Comparatively viewed, the atomized nature of Italy's distributive network, as set out in table 6.1, is striking. In practical terms, these figures illustrate not so much the protectionist nature of the government's policy, but the extreme facility with which it has handed out licences to small traders. In fact, in taking this line, Christian Democrat-led governments actually reversed one of the first measures introduced by the Fascist regime, which imposed restrictive licensing arrangements in order to reinforce the position of established retailers (Sylos Labini 1972: 403).

But to what extent are 'established positions' the object of a policy which has deliberately pursued the line of 'the more the better', leading to the rampant inflation of commercial activities? Various writers have argued that the commercial licence represents a 'privilege' which, in tying the small trader to the local political elite, provides an essential mechanism of patronage for obtaining electoral consensus. According to one commentator, 'The commercial licence represents the tutelage of a vassal; it is a feudalistic investiture of a few square meters of territory, by which to insure the shopkeeper "forever" from competition. It is the creation of a small monopoly . . . in sum, a reward to the good and faithful servant from the holders of local power' (cited in Chubb 1982: 18).

Yet, it is difficult to see what sense of privilege or insurance of survival could be derived from the licence so *freely* available. As

Ariotti (1974: 533) rightly observes, 'when the distributive network dilates, the importance of the licence and attendant privileges diminish', and as Chubb (1982: 122) herself acknowledges in a study of patronage in Palermo, in the highly dispersed distributive network of that city, 'The average shopkeeper leads a very precarious existence indeed, the mean life span of retail shops being only five years.'

Again, like the artisans, shopkeepers have begun to feel the effects of saturation, of the DC's policy of proliferation. In 1971, for the first time, national legislation was passed to defend the interests of the *existing* commercial class. In theory, at least, the opening of new retail outlets and the granting of new licences would from then on be dependent upon the number of shops already in existence in a given area, and upon the demonstration of certain 'professional' capacities.

What the 1971 Act should call to our attention is not its protectionist consequences but the underlying conditions and government measures which gave rise to it. Nor was this the first time that shopkeepers had called for a halt to liberal licensing. As early as 1960, the Confederation at its annual General Assembly complained that the sector was becoming too overcrowded and called on the government to tighten up entry regulations. At the same venue, Colombo (1963: 672), as Minister for Industry and Commerce, rejected these appeals, insisting that the problem was a temporary one resulting from the displacement of agricultural labour which industry momentarily could not absorb. It would be resolved by further industrial development, not by restricting the number of shops. Cautioning his audience, Colombo (1963: 692) outlined the options acceptable to the government:

With regard to your specific problems . . . it is necessary above all to be very prudent about prohibitions, restrictions, impediments. When there are difficulties within a sector, whether temporary or structural, the government prefers to help operators to resolve the basic problems, rather than to adopt interventions that lead to a crystallization of the situation . . . thus, we prefer to help out with credit facilities.

To the *commercianti* complaint that there were an excessive number of shopkeepers for existing retail business capacity, Colombo (1963: 693, 689–90) thus responded that 'The evolution of the general economic situation is . . . creating premises for a more balanced development of commercial activity that will enable us to avoid recourse to restrictive measures which are contrary – I have said many times – to the letter and spirit of the Constitution.'

## Conclusion

When viewed alongside the other evidence presented here, such resistance to 'exclusionary' pressures lends support to the central argument of this chapter: that government action on behalf of small enterprise is deducible not from the interests, needs or demands of particular socio-economic groupings but from the independent goals, ideals and interests of the ruling party. Drawing on examples from retail and artisan trades, our analysis has sought to show how the DC, adopting an anti-closure stance, looked to the *ceto medio* not as a class to be defended so much as a model to be extended.

Questions of political calculation aside, was there not then something 'moral' about this project, in the appeal to small producers not to close ranks like their German neighbours had done? From the state, they might justifiably expect some 'protection' against 'monopolistic' interests. But they should not expect it against those who sought to enter the *ceti medi*. Thus the political leadership appealed to economic operators to share economic space for the good of society as a whole. 'Don't be a caste!', they enjoined. 'Don't be exclusionary: be a model for emulation!' Hence the refusal to recognize *inter alia* the demand for credentialism.

And was this project not also 'ideological' in the way it invested small enterprise and its owner-promoters with a high moral significance: as a place where the 'dignity' of labour could be restored; as a positive social force whose task it was to mobilize others to similar pursuits? However utopian the ultimate aim of turning proletarians into property owners, small business assistance could thus be upheld in the interests of both workers and *ceti medi*. By improving the prospects for the small entrepreneur, an alternative to the assembly-line system would be provided and, importantly, the worker's 'hope of rising in status' kept alive. In other words, the 'demobilizing dream' of quitting the factory and setting up independently would survive best if the small sector could be seen to offer a real point of entry.[15] For this reason, Christian Democrats have viewed small business measures as a clear enactment of interclass principles, defined in interviews as 'not just supporting the *ceti medi* in acquired positions', but also opening 'the doors to those who seek through their own capacities, the means for their own social ascent'.[16] The fact that the DC firmly rejected the 'acquired position' strategy does suggest that it was attempting to give its claim to rule a moral basis, far beyond the narrow protectionism of established interests.

What needs to be added to these observations, however, is the important but exceedingly banal point that groups so obviously interest-centred as politicians and state elites are rarely if ever impelled by disinterested, society-enhancing ideals. But whether the DC's behaviour was consistent with moral considerations or material interests is of no relevance to my argument. It clearly liked the petite bourgeoisie and devalued the proletariat. It assumed, more or less correctly, that many workers wished to become and could be made into small business operators; that independence had a society-wide resonance (in a culture with long-standing peasant traditions of self-sufficiency); and that the quest for independence and the possibilities for dynamic entrepreneurship did not cancel each other out. In short, it envisaged a workshop economy of a high order, not bereft of towering factories and giant corporations, but one in which these might be contained, kept within limits. For reasons indicated in the preceding chapter, that vision was in part sustained by a belief (validated as it turns out) that many things could be produced in ways that did not require the centralization of production. Thus, the emergent 'party of government' assessed the possibilities in terms of these presuppositions and came up with a programme that could feed its 'interclass' aims. In so doing, it advanced a project complete with moral, utopian and selfish interests.

What the preceding analysis amounts to then is a substantiation of independent goal formulation. And as Skocpol (1985: 9) reminds us, 'Unless [this] occurs, there is little need to talk about states as important actors.' Nevertheless, this tells but half the story. As previous points have anticipated, the social structure the DC sought to strengthen and reinvigorate was one that would at once support democracy, sustain social cohesion and secure the DC's own position at the political centre. To see how that project was carried forward, we must turn to the political struggles and power challenges of the time.

# 7

# The internal challenge

The temptation for most analysts has been to assume conversion to the doctrine of scale and then to seek out the 'constraints' which pushed government action in another direction. The basis for this approach has been the conviction that concentration means efficiency and modernization, and any measure which impedes or retards this process – such as the reinforcement of the secondary sector – thereby falls outside the realm of economic rationality. Consequently, it must be explicable in terms of socio-political necessities (of the kind analysed in chapters 3 and 5).

The argument I have been advancing attempts to reverse the logic of this position. As a preliminary step towards this task, I sought to show in the previous chapter how the public priorities in economic policy – described and analysed at length in chapter 4 – were related to historically based preferences for certain authority and ownership structures which could create social cohesion by transcending the capital–labour divide. To complete my argument, I shall now attempt to spell out those features of the Italian political environment which 'pushed' government action in the very direction it proposed to follow, by placing a premium on the political support and class collaboration that a substantial small sector could provide.

Overall the chapter makes two central points. The first is that domestic political struggles gave an important stimulus to the social project. The source of the political problem, however, is not the petite bourgeoisie, as others have most frequently claimed, but the working class. In particular, organized labour is a destabilizing factor because it cannot be integrated within the state and industrial system. The way the state resolves or responds to that problem, however, is not determined by or reducible to the nature of the problem itself. To read off state activity from the objective structure of constraints and opportunities is one thing. To argue that the logic of the situation favoured a certain course of action is quite another. The second major point then is a theoretical one: far from becoming superfluous the independent interests of state actors have a central explanatory status.

To advance this argument it is necessary to tackle three main tasks that society-centred approaches fail to consider. First, if political challenges obliged the Italian government to reinforce small capital, why did France, confronted with similar problems, respond so differently? Second, why – in view of the extensive and exclusive nature of incentives policy – was it politically strategic not only to extend the secondary sector, but also to exclude big business? The explanandum, in other words, is not simply assistance to smaller enterprise, but an industrial incentives programme which, in distinction to European practice and with few noteworthy exceptions, has explicitly excluded large enterprise. The major exception, to be discussed later, has been with regard to the public corporation whose expansion went hand in hand with that of the small firm sector. Finally, if societal threats and pressures explain everything, why did a small business strategy continue to prevail even after the political problem had subsided?

Addressing these issues will open out a much wider window on to state autonomy. Most generally, it will be seen that the state could have acted otherwise, that its activities were not hostage to the need to avoid punishment or to curry favour. In particular, it will be shown how, in carving out a power base of its own, the dominant party 'used' the public enterprise sector in a manner congruent with its small firm strategy. Finally, the analysis suggests that in so far as policy elites were at all 'obliged' to privilege small capital, this is because they became captive to the very programmatic commitments and system of public constructs by which they divided the entrepreneurial universe in distinctive ways.

## The nature of the political problem

Because of well-documented characteristics associated with enterprise size, it can be generally stated that the small firm is no seed-bed of radical politics.[1] We may therefore expect that wherever support for the far left is .strong, the political militancy of labour high and capital–labour antagonism intense, then the small firm sector will provide an important pillar of political stability and of support for the moderate or conservative forces. Our first task is to consider the extent to which these conditions prevailed in Italy in the period in question and to assess their relationship to the advance of small capital.

## Working class support and the left

A party which defined itself as 'of the centre moving towards the left', the DC aspired to forge a broad alliance of workers, peasants and *ceti medi*. By 1947, it was clear that the foundation of the new consensus would have to rest on a more exclusive social bloc having only the most tenuous links with the working class movement. In the first place, not even the promise of reform had managed to dim the attractions of the left: in the institutional referendum of the previous year, when Italians voted for the Republic and elected deputies to the Constituent Assembly, two-fifths of the electorate – largely industrial and agricultural workers – had displayed their allegiance to the Communists (19 per cent) and the Socialists (21 per cent). In the second place, international ties and internal pressures were to preclude any share in power. The mounting tensions of the Cold War, the PCI's insistent allegiance to the Soviet Union, the threat of subversion and the massive pressures from the Church – all worked to precipitate the expulsion of the PCI and its Socialist allies from the government and with it the loss of consensus for the new state from broad segments of the working class.

Yet, despite this loss, the Christian Democrats actually strengthened their 1946 position (35 per cent), always capturing in excess of 40 per cent of the total vote. Indeed, the essentially conservative nature of majority sentiment manifested itself in successive contests, always providing enough support to enable the major party to form governing coalitions that effectively excluded the Social–Communist left, without relying on the Monarchist–Neo-Fascist right.

By contrast, the combined strength of the left, due to earlier defections within the Socialist camp, declined between 1946 and 1958, averaging around 36 per cent of the total vote. The Communist share, however, thanks largely to new supporters in the south where it had previously been marginal, increased to almost 23 per cent. The Communist advance, in other words, did not take place in the most industrialized region of the country, but among the unemployed and landless peasantry in the rural south. Unlike the north and centre, where the Catholic and Socialist presence was well established, the southern electorate, loosely organized within clientelistic networks, was still under the control of the local notables, and therefore electorally 'available'. For this reason, many writers have pointed out that the Mezzogiorno was the most vital terrain on which the DC had to stem the advance of the PCI and broaden its own political base.

One could of course go on to make a more detailed dissection of the electoral map, but even the most subtle territorial and temporal analysis would not enable one to link small firm policy to purely electoral exigencies. In the first place, it would be too superficial to tie such measures to electoral outcomes. They were well under way before the first real progress of the PCI (1953), and they became even more substantial after the electoral fortunes of that party had suffered an arrest (1958). In the second place, there is no neat connection between the increasing strength of the PCI and the kind of industrial policy pursued. For the PCI's major electoral gains took place in the Mezzogiorno, the one area of the country in which the DC eventually pursued a big business strategy, by encouraging the location of large industrial installations.

The general point of these observations is that the strength of the Communist presence – even in combination with Socialist support – was not sufficiently great to threaten the survival of the DC or to prevent the formation of centrist governments. What deserves to be emphasized is that in the most industrialized regions of Lombardy and Piedmont, the DC still drew twice as many supporters as the PCI between 1948 and 1963 (Galli and Prandi 1970: 333ff). Whilst such observations do not diminish the fact of Communist support and thus of an antagonistic working class isolated from political participation, they do however, from a purely electoral perspective, serve to loosen up those objective constraints within which the ruling party could realistically hope to move. The point is an important one and I shall return to it when considering striking parallels with France. Let us now turn to examine the second component of the 'working class threat'.

### Trade unionism and political mobilization

If political stability seemed threatened by support for anti-system forces, what sharpened that sense of precariousness was the presence of a highly mobilized, politically militant labour move-ment, under the control of the Communist-affiliated trade union, CGIL. It is by now well documented that, for historical, structural and contingent reasons, Italian trade unionism was in the main politically motivated.[2] The CGIL, always the most powerful and until 1950 the sole representative of labour, acted as 'spokesman of the general interests of the workers as a class, whether employed or unemployed, and not as an association for the defence of the specific interests of its members' (Salvati 1972a:205). Conceived as a 'transmission belt' for the PCI,[3] the Confederation thus tended to channel the militancy of its rank and file away from narrow work-place grievances towards more broadly defined political objectives consonant with party strategy. As the leader of CGIL reasoned, there could be no legitimate distinction between economic and political collective action, the strike being 'the simplest and highest means the workers have for demonstrating their own will against a political fact which, in their judgment, may damage society or the working classes' (Di Vittorio 1955: 35). Accordingly, as Hine writes of France and Italy of the forties and early fifties, 'Trade unionism was orientated not so much at bargaining situations as at political targets, and undertaken in the name of non-negotiable ends – or at least ends negotiable with the political authority rather than the employer' (1976: 186).

This does not mean that contractual objectives were absent, simply that they were not accorded the primacy that they assumed in later years when party–trade union ties were loosened. Once the left were removed from the government arena, the CGIL became increasingly a vehicle for attack against the government and the institutions of the state. Despite, and in part because of, labour's weak economic position, the political strike predominated. Collective action against the cost of living and against economic and foreign policy was frequent and between 1947 and 1954 the weight of 'non-contractual' conflict remained very high, in certain years accounting for some 50 per cent of work hours lost by strike activity.[4] Massive political purges took place throughout industry and the state intervened wherever possible to disperse collective protests. Government sought on several occasions, through the legislative process, to prevent or limit trade union action; and inside and outside the labour movement the debate turned around the question of the 'pathological' nature of conflict and, consequently, the concern not with how to institutionalize it so much as how to put a stop to it (Zaninelli 1981: 434–6).

One could point out that the strategy of sensitizing the political framework functioned as a compensatory device for bargaining weakness, that it played into the hands of the capitalist class and that it ultimately exhausted the enthusiasm for collective action.[5]

But this should not distract us from the central issue that in those years the Italian government faced a highly mobilized working class, economically weak but organizationally strong enough to threaten the stability of the political system. For the DC leadership, the trade union thus represented 'the principal force of Communism'. As such, the problem was not how to incorporate, but rather how to defeat, organized labour and the class-based solidarity which nourished it.

We have thus far discussed two aspects of the historical context germane to the political logic of a small firm strategy. But before we can draw any sensible conclusions we must add one further element to the analysis.

### Capital and labour

It should be clear from what has been said so far that for labour, the route of economic integration was equally impassable. Whilst denouncing those 'political strikes which have nothing to do with the sphere of production and labour, but seek to represent – in the intentions of the promoters – a reaction of workers to certain events of a political character and to general circumstances',[6] Italian employers nevertheless did nothing to foster a more industrially focused traded unionism. On the question of participation, Confindustria at the outset rejected any measures which might have given the workers effective deliberative powers. On wage-related matters, the employers' Confederation took the line of conceding as little as possible, not only in the reconstruction period when it was generally recognized that greater sacrifices were required, but also in the following years when productivity and profit levels soared (Saba 1981). In general, management had no need of economic inducements whilst they were able to exploit an extremely unfavourable labour market and the internal divisions within the trade union movement.

The Christian Democrats for their part looked with increasing concern at the behaviour of employers towards their workers. In the documents emanating from the central organs of the party, references were made in the early years of the Republic to the disorder provoked by the 'antisocial selfishness of certain capitalist strata', and employers were criticized for attempting to escape their social responsibilities (DC 1968: 285). At the 1949 Congress, these sporadic criticisms had developed into a polemic against the industrialists for their 'disinterest towards that process of social osmosis through which the workers acquire a more direct participation in the productive process' (DC 1959: 236, 247). A bitter exchange subsequently took place between the head of Confindustria and the leader of the trade union wing within the DC, the one accused of violating labour laws and installing an economic dictatorship; the other of 'preaching class hatred'.[7]

In response to these hostilities and disclosures, DC leaders issued a directive in 1953 that the party should 'dedicate itself' forthwith to the 'task of persuasion' in order to elicit 'a more evolved social consciousness from the industrial class', and to urge its support for 'those unions which rejected political and Marxist prejudices' (DC 1968: 650ff; cf. also 1976: 53). At the 1953 reunion at which this resolution was made and which was held to discuss 'problems of productive activity', it was pointed out that production depended not only on market conditions, 'but also and in significant measure on industrial order within the enterprise and the atmosphere in which work is conducted . . . where the greatest possible and effective equilibrium between factors of production must be realized' (DC 1968: 650). Obstacles to that equilibrium, it was argued, derived as much from 'the imposition of the employer's will' over his workers as from deliberate political manipulations to increase the worker's hostility. The regressive attitudes of employers were therefore equally responsible for stirring up class antagonism and for pushing workers into the arms of the PCI. It was therefore necessary that the employer 'be animated by a sense of *socialità*, so as to recognize in the employee a person of equal dignity and rights'. Above all, the party had to convince the economic operators 'that a business, especially when it reaches a notable size, involves aspects of social and public order that it is not permissible to ignore' (DC 1968: 650).

In short, employers had to be made aware that through their actions they were not simply hindering economic progress, but fuelling support for communism. As part of this task of enlightenment, De Gasperi in 1953 (1969: 223) outlined the problem to his party colleagues in Milan. Why, he posited, do workers vote Communist, despite the many efforts by government to improve conditions in the sphere of social services?

On one hand, it is because of [the PCI's] mass propaganda efforts and, on the other, it is the fault of employers who have no relationship of trust with their workers. Workers no longer tolerate being treated as inferiors, even when they receive benefits. They see themselves as collaborators and must be treated as such. Many acts of largesse and welfare by some employers are destroyed by other high-handed gestures, by a despising take-it-or-leave-it tone, by an anachronistic paternalism.

If unrealistic to suppose that the large complex could replicate the social relations in force in the small plant, based on collaboration and trust, it was nevertheless possible and necessary for employers 'to consult workers on technical questions' and 'to take an interest in their social and family problems'. But such changes could not be wrought overnight. Whilst the 'bitterness of the ideological class struggle' and the 'anachronistic attitudes' of the capitalist class reinforced each other, it was no use looking to the large private concerns for that social solidarism deemed so essential to economic and political progress.[8]

It was against this background of employer rigidity that the call for a withdrawal of public enterprise from Confindustria, initiated by the DC's trade union wing, gained increasing support within the party. As we shall see when examining the problem of DC autonomy, the party took the unprecedented and bitterly opposed step of establishing a wholly independent employers' association. Intersind thus became the terrain for enacting an advanced system of industrial relations, involving plant level bargaining and forms of worker participation and, ultimately, 'wages and conditions of work far superior to those in the private sector' (Allen and Stevenson 1974: 257).[9]

## Challenge and response: some interim conclusions

Having examined three closely related aspects of the central political issue – referred to in Catholic circles as the labour question – let me now try to formulate some conclusions. How to depoliticize trade unionism and promote class collaboration, how to stem the advance of communism and increase consensus for the state – such were the concerns that dominated Christian Democrat-led governments of the fifties.[10] Under these conditions, it would appear that the micro-capitalist sector and the role of small ownership take on a crucial structural importance.

A policy privileging the development of independent initiatives made good political sense for two reasons. In the first instance, the diffusion of small business would reinforce the class structure of the 'solidaristic' state, and at the same time expand what the party saw as its social base of consensus. Second, by dispersing labour among a myriad of small firms, chances for collective action would be minimized and conflict defused. The small sector thus offered the ruling party much more than a means for securing political support. Above all, it provided a solidaristic alternative to set against the solidarity of class.[11]

By concentrating on the 'secondary' sector, the DC could broaden its ties with the working class and at the same time steer 'a median line' between the needs of 'production and manual labour' which 'whilst defending the weakest, does not create a permanent antagonism between factors of production'. This much is clear from De Gasperi's report to the 1954 Party Congress (DC 1976: 11–14), in which he emphasizes the 'decisive importance of the *ceti medi*' both for the party's own equilibrium[12] and for that of the nation as a whole:

It seems to me that as a result of the Italian social structure, an alignment detrimentally formed around the conflict of interests and crystallized in the dialectics of class struggle is contrary to the real vitality of the Italian nation. It is naturally obvious and legitimate that on the trade union terrain wage earners and employers often find themselves in conflict with employers.

But this dialectical trade union position cannot become the synthesis of a party's electoral policy, at least if it does not adhere to the Marxist conception of the organization of state and economy. . . . it is therefore too simple to synthesize our policy with the generic phrase, 'elevation of the wage earner'. . . . Thus our analysis brings us back to our principles of social solidarism.

In other words, it was necessary to strengthen the network of small and medium enterprise where the diverse interests of 'production and labour' could be reconciled.

It cannot be denied then that the consolidation of small capital served the political interests of the Christian Democrats. Is it possible, however, to put forward the stronger thesis that the nature of the political problem required a small firm strategy? It has been argued, for example, that the presence of antagonistic forces – neither politically demobilized nor economically integrated – impedes the total opening of the political system. A relatively closed political system, in turn, requires the political elite to renounce a 'dynamic and modernizing' strategy because, in order to acquire a certain autonomy, it has to build up the very social categories which impede that progress (Provasi 1976: 30–1, 34).

We need not at this stage make any assumptions about 'modernization' in Italy. If the argument were to have any plausibility it ought to withstand the comparative test. France of the forties and fifties provides an almost ideal case for comparison, revealing many striking parallels with Italy, both in economic structure and in political relations. First, it had a substantial small firms sector. Second, the political exclusion of large segments of the working class, the politicization and bargaining weakness of the unions were problems common to both the Italians and the French (Hine 1976). And, finally, France had to contend with an even larger Communist presence at least until the late fifties. Moreover, the French conservative forces experienced far greater difficulties in forming stable governments which excluded the radical left. This contrast has been well drawn in a study of French and Italian political elites (Field and Higley 1978). Field and Higley point out that in Italy 'in election after election in the fifties and sixties an anti-Communist majority repeatedly demonstrated its existence.' In France, on the other hand, until the advent of De Gaulle in 1958, 'there was no clear demonstration of a reliable, relatively conservative electoral majority' (1978: 303–4).

If anything, then, the initially greater level of political instability in France, coupled with an equally uncompromising stance towards the left, ought to have precluded a big business strategy in that country. Yet, despite the similarity of conditions, there was no corresponding drive to increase the chances for small capital. Very much to the contrary, the Fourth Republic broke radically with pre-war political economy, as the new planning authorities set about pushing French industry out of its artisanal mould (Sheahan 1963: chapter 14; McArthur and Scott 1969: 208, 215; Zysman 1977: 62). As Suleiman (1975: 26) writes, 'Nowhere has the change in the state's attitude been more radical and nowhere has it represented a sharper break with the past than in its desire to encourage the development of large industrial enterprises.' Far from seeking the multiplication or even the reinforcement of small entrepreneurship, the long-term goal of French policy has been to phase it out in favour of a more concentrated industrial structure.

Looking at the similarities of both national experiences, it would seem then that 'political problems' are far from explaining the whole of it. Clearly the different courses of action possible in two politically (and economically) similar contexts tend to loosen the bond of social constraints and tighten that of state interests, which brings us back to the objectives and presuppositions of state elites.

For the DC, the political diseconomies of scale evident in the large plant underlined the inadequacies of the impersonal contract. What was necessary were 'new social relations' in which 'the worker would see in his own principal not an enemy, but an older brother' to whom he could turn when necessary, rather than being 'constrained to run to the Communist Party local headquarters or labour office'.[13] The deproletarianizing potential of the small firm could thus be realized not merely in the economic sense of providing a 'human model for social elevation', but also in the political sense of transcending the capital–labour divide. As one prominent Christian Democrat, Mario Scelba (CGII 1956: 275), put it to his audience of small industrialists at their first national conference held in 1956:

if here a Christian Democrat may express his own opinion, I must say that small industry is the nearest . . . to the ideal plans [*impostazioni*] of the DC, because in small industry is realized that human contact between employer and worker which can constitute a powerful contribution to the formation of a real democratic society. If there is something to regret about large industrial complexes on the social level, it is precisely that they do not have this human contact. . . . A democratic society . . . can and must draw strength from an organization like that of small industry.

Scelba's statement is of course no isolated view. The ideology of personalism is itself enshrined in all the official and working definitions of small enterprise, in which the entrepreneur is at once owner and manager, contributing both capital and technique, thus working alongside his or her workers on a day-to-day basis. As studies of small Italian enterprise confirm, this high visibility and personal involvement implies in turn that the employer is not just a manifestation of authority or the enforcer of impersonal rules, but someone on whom moral pressures can be brought to bear. For this and other reasons, the class of small entrepreneurs are far more likely to constitute a point of reference than a conflict group.[14]

In view of these observations, it is not difficult to point to the political rationality of a small firm policy, or to conclude that the wider political struggle placed a premium on the cohesive characteristics associated with the small firm sector; but why this should be recognized and acted upon in Italy and not in France is not readily explained by recourse to those political processes themselves. The politics of conflict and worker exclusion may have propelled the Italian political elite in a certain direction, but that path was one already traced out in the ruling party's project for individual advancement and social solidarism, in its programmatic goals of deproletarianizing the worker and curbing capitalistic concentration.

In so far as one might distinguish the French and Italian approaches to industrial organization in more general terms, it would seem that on the French side, the technocratic elite, for reasons elaborated in the following chapter, conceived industrial organization as a means of furthering the political power of France as a nation; and to that end promoted the concentration of private capital (see Hoffman 1963: 53; Zysman 1977: 62). By contrast, in the Italian context, industrial organization was viewed as a means of strengthening the political framework and the power of Christian Democracy. To this end, small business and – as we shall see – the public enterprise sector became the two key pillars, the former providing its social and moral force, the latter its power base.

Thus far we have examined that part of the political context relevant to an understanding of small business assistance: namely, the problem of political and economic integration of the working class. By way of elucidating the *exclusive* nature of state assistance to industry, it is now necessary to foreground that other economic subject, big capital, specifically its relation to the problem of DC autonomy.

## Christian democracy and big business

It has been observed of the Italian economy that it possesses not one but two striking features. For, hand in hand with the numerical expansion of small business, there has developed at least until recently an ever-increasing presence of public enterprise, particularly of the 'state holding' variety. That the two phenomena are in some sense linked is a possibility I shall presently explore. But first, we must look briefly at the weight of state-controlled industrial enterprise and its evolving importance in the post-war economy.

The state holding sector refers to all the joint stock companies for which the government is the controlling or sole shareholder. In 1972 there were six holding groups, comprising some 350 firms in total, employing in excess of half a million workers (Allen and Stevenson 1974: 217–18). Not included in this category of state enterprise are the public utilities – like the postal and railway services which central government has always managed, the government-owned credit institutions; and the originally private enterprises, now nationalized, such as the tobacco and electricity industries.

Within the state participation system, IRI (lstituto per la Ricostruzione Industriale), ENI (Ente Nazionale Idrocarburi) and EFIM (Ente Partecipazione e Finanziamento Industria Manifatturiera) are the largest concerns. IRI's interests span the shipping, engineering, metallurgical, shipbuilding and electronics industries, telecommunications, banking and air transport. ENI's holdings extend over oil and natural gas, including their exploration, production, refining and marketing at home and abroad, subsequently expanded to engineering, petrochemicals, textiles and certain service industries. The youngest, EFIM, also has operating companies in engineering (see Podbielski 1974).

As a result of considerable post-war expansion, the public corporations not only dominate in the banking, transport and communications fields, but are also responsible for major proportions of the industrial sector. These range from over two-thirds of iron and steel production, all of hydrocarbons, the bulk of shipbuilding and about one-quarter of other engineering production.[15] As the following figures illustrate, the sector's growth both in employment and investment has been especially rapid since the 1960s:

|      | *Employment* *(1953 = 100)* | *Investment* *(1955 = 100)* |
|------|------------|------------|
| 1960 | 115        | 218        |
| 1971 | 195        | 994        |

The predominance of these holding companies in capital intensive sectors, however, has meant a less impressive growth in employment (Allen and Stevenson 1974: 217–18). Thus, whilst accounting for 31 per cent of total gross fixed industrial investment in 1972 (Podbielski 1974: 149), their share of industrial employment was little more than 8 per cent. Another way of assessing the economic significance of public enterprise is to compare its share of output, employment and investment with that of big business. In a sample of the 150 largest manufacturing firms, the percentage of the public sector increased over the period 1963–72 from 19 to 24 per cent of total output, from 28 to 35 per cent of invested capital and from 20 to 24 per cent of employment (Alzona 1975). Indeed, it was estimated that by the late seventies, the public groups accounted for 30 per cent of all workers employed in the large industrial companies (those employing more than 500 persons) (Sasso 1978: 277).

In the southern economy, the state-controlled firms have played an especially important role. In accordance with regional development policy, legislation of the late fifties required that at least 60 per cent of their new industrial investments and 40 per cent of their total investments be located in the Mezzogiorno. Consequently, between 1957 and 1972, the annual average investments of such firms (mainly in steel, machinery, cement, petroleum and petro-chemicals) accounted for more than 40 per cent of total industrial investments located in the south (Rodgers 1979: 35). Thus, by way of summarizing their role in the Italian economy, the public groups have not only acted as guardians of the capital-intensive sector of industry, but have also assumed primary responsibility for the industrialization of the south (Shonfield 1974; Rodgers 1979: 34).

The various problems and objectives which have spurred this expansion, such as the development of key industries, rescuing ailing companies and counteracting the growth of foreign producers and investors in local markets (Shonfield 1974: 285), are not factors peculiar to Italy. What seems, however, 'in certain respects unique' is the way Italian governments have responded to such problems. For, as one noted student and critic of the public enterprise system points out, rather than strengthening private enterprise by promoting mergers, concentration and acquisitions, the Italian approach has consisted in 'a continuous expansion of the public sector' (Prodi 1974: 52). In short, 'Mergers have been relatively infrequent, public enterprise and state-owned financial institutions have been dominant' (1974: 54).

To my knowledge it has never been suggested in the literature that there might be some sort of relationship between these two striking characteristics of the Italian economy. Perhaps that would attribute too much coherence and design to public policies which for the past twenty years have seemed to many remarkable only for their lack of unity and direction. Closer inspection, however, might warrant a different conclusion. For, if the state, which controls the outflow of industrial investment capital,[16] tends for whatever reason to favour only those private initiatives *beneath* a certain size threshold (Saba 1969), then in order to meet those problems normally requiring large-scale undertakings and huge injections of capital, it is likely that the state itself will have to step in to fill that gap.

It would seem then that there is some logical relationship between the government's small firm policy and its use of public enterprise. This connection, I would argue, flows from a more or less explicit stance towards the big business component of the private sector, and can be described as one which – through the manoeuvre of financial assistance and the development of public enterprise – has generally sought to discourage the concentration of private capital. The position is one already implicit in the logic of an incentive system designed to privilege smaller initiatives. But to understand why it was so exclusively oriented, why public enterprise was given greater economic space and why the accommodation of big capital in the private sphere has been the exception rather than the norm, it is necessary to examine two sets of factors which have conditioned relations between big business and the Christian Democrats. The first has to do with political exigencies: the DC's marginal institutional presence and the limitations this posed on its ability to push through policy goals. The second factor concerns a strong component of its ideology which tended to identify scale with monopoly, understood as the power to subvert the political process. I shall discuss each of these in turn.

### Constraints on policy and the bid for autonomy

When the DC came to power in 1948, it was heavily dependent on sources of support outside the party's direct control. 'This implied a heavy mortgage over its policy' (Galli 1968: 61). Its outstanding electoral victory had been obtained with the massive backing of the Church, with the financial assistance of big business and with the clientelistic support of the southern notables (landowners and professional strata): in short, groups which expected a thoroughly conservative policy from the DC.

As the fierce reaction to the land reform demonstrated,[17] the major party had therefore either to abandon its 'interclass' objectives or to acquire greater organizational and financial independence. As several studies have argued, the DC would not have been able to pursue its programmatic goals whilst subject to the constraints imposed by the agrarian bloc, by the employers and, indeed, by the Catholic flanking organizations. The so-called 'occupation' of the state and subsequent 'colonization' of the economy flowed from these exigencies (Pizzorno 1980; Cassano 1980: 250). In taking the latter path, the DC began from the early fifties onwards to systematically enlarge the public sector of the economy, utilizing the state machinery to consolidate an institutional and social presence. Loyal party men were thus placed in key positions of power, notably in the banking and credit institutions, in the reform and welfare agencies and in public and semi-public enterprise (Cazzola 1979). A key component of this strategy, the state holding corporations like ENI and IRI, provided the DC with both an independent financial base and a powerful tool of economic policy.

Despite the close personal ties between the political and industrial leaders De Gasperi and Costa, relations between the ruling party and Confindustria had never been cosy. For a few brief years, prior to the death of De Gasperi and to the DC's establishment of alternative sources of funding, Confindustria could count on a well-disposed party leader and on the appointment to key posts in the bureaucracy of personnel sympathetic to its interests. But it had never established a *parentela* (insider) relationship with the DC, which from 1953 onwards was to be the real basis for exerting any effective influence over policy-making.

The first signs of division within the dominant coalition began to surface as soon as the threat of subversion from their common adversary subsided. In the early fifties, the constrictions of the Confindustria embrace were most clearly felt in the sphere of alliance policy and in the employer's handling of the labour problem. To convey an idea of the brittle partnership that existed even in an era when relations between industrialists and government were supposedly at their 'best', I shall briefly discuss each issue.

In the first place, Confindustria opposed government spending on social welfare programmes. The best way to defeat communism, it insisted, was not through measures of a popular nature, but through the installation of a strong right-wing government. Above all, organized business wished to curb what it perceived as the DC's 'demagogic' tendencies, by enlisting the aid of Catholic Action. Thus, in 1951 Costa wrote to the leader of that organization pointing out the DC's deficiencies as a governing party:[18]

Christian Democracy has not been in its policy either democratic or Christian. The thrust of demochristian policy has been opportunism, not hesitating to exploit for this purpose the low sentiments of man.

The economic problems of our country are serious and one cannot expect them all to be resolved in the best way; neither can one expect a perfect economic policy from those who have not sufficient preparation; but one can expect economic policy to be conducted with sincerity . . . and with that minimum of courage that is often necessary to recognize the truth.

Insisting that the DC was wrong to reject collaboration with the Monarchists and neo-Fascists, Confindustria to that end intensified its support for Catholic Action in an endeavour to steer the party rightward.

In the second place, organized business had remained deaf to pleas for a more progressive approach to industrial relations, refusing participative schemes, shunning its legal and social responsibilities and thereby adding fuel to the class war. Many prominent Christian Democrats – largely associated with the centre-left-wing factions and trade union circles – together with leading members of the Church had therefore begun to campaign in the provincial press throughout the country, attacking employers for their evasion of statutory obligations and for installing an oppressive regime in the factories (Abrate 1981: 498–9).

The intensity of this campaign was sufficient to prompt Confindustria to seek the intervention of the Vatican to put a stop to it. In one of many such epistolary exchanges, the Confederation writing in 1950 (Abrate 1981: 500) denounced the party to the Secretary of State to the Vatican for inciting the workers against the industrialists so as to compete with the Communists, adding however that such acts had implications 'far more dangerous than those of the Communists because originating from sources held to be worthy of the faith':

The policy of many democratic men . . . and that of many *aclisti*[19] is aimed at removing healthy energies and capital from industry, which is the only possible source of greater employment, because no one is disposed to run risks disproportionate to the benefits and no one likes being labelled as a starver of the people.

In reality, the employers had rejected even the most moderate and collaborative forms of trade unionism, which the DC–affiliated CISL offered through proposals for productivity bargaining at enterprise level (La Palombara 1963).

For this reason, Catholic trade unionists and the nascent left within the DC were the staunchest advocates of state enterprise, defending both its expansion and its detachment from the private employer's association (see Romagnoli 1970; Maraffi 1980: 519). Despite intense and unabated opposition from big business, the creation of a completely separate organization went ahead. Following the establishment of Intersind in 1956, both DC trade unionists and the state as employer were thus able to distance themselves from the repressive policies of Confindustria and to take the initiative in updating industrial relations procedures (Hine 1976: 194).

On both issues, then, that of industrial relations and that of party independence, the development of the public enterprise sector offered a crucial means for disengagement from organized business, enabling the DC to pursue its 'modernizing' objectives in a more autonomous way and, importantly, without opening to the left and without increasing the economic and political weight of private capital.

From 1953–4 onwards, under the leadership of Fanfani, the balance of power within the party gradually shifted leftwards as the relatively more radical Catholic trade unionists and younger intellectuals exercised greater weight within the party (La Palombara 1963: 10). The DC would subsequently pursue an aggressive interventionist strategy, upsetting the balance between public and private, political and economic spheres. Organized business, in its turn, would respond *inter alia* with the Confintesa venture in an abortive attempt to enter directly into politics. Consisting of an alliance between the three employer confederations in agriculture, commerce and industry, the aim of Confintesa was to channel the massive financial aid of the industrialists and Confindustria towards the Liberal Party and to encourage businessmen to stand for local and national elections.

That the entrepreneurial class should consider it necessary to take this course of action clearly demonstrates the extent to which the DC was both able and willing to take an independent line. As La Palombara concluded on the basis of interviews with bureaucrats, trade union leaders and politicians,

To a considerable degree, the industrial Confederation has become an outsider as far as the DC is concerned, scarcely different in its party influence from some of the left-wing groups and obviously the victim in administrative circles of power thrusts that are based on a *parentela* relationship. It may well be that Confindustria is now trying to re-establish the relationship to the DC under the Costa presidency. *The*

*current and critical difference is that the DC no longer needs Confindustria funds.*
(1964: 318)

Thus, having earlier hedged its bets by backing several parties responsive to its interests, followed by a withdrawal of financial support for the DC in the 1953 elections as a form of protest, the employers' confederation now found its financial clout emasculated – hence its desparate and disastrous efforts on behalf of the Liberal Party. By way of concluding these observations, let us simply note La Palombara's (1964: 210) statement that, whilst Confindustria is not by any means weak or helpless, 'Those in Italy who blandly speak or write about the overbearing political power of the industrial confederation are well advised to examine in detail the outcome of elections as well as of the major pieces of legislation on which Confindustria assumed a strong position.'

The creation of ENI and the enlargement of IRI's activities, the establishment of a new Ministry of State Shareholdings and of a separate state employers' association were among the more conspicuous initiatives of the 1950s contested by big business. There can be no doubt that through such measures the DC gained access to vital resources and established a power base of its own. But as writers of various political persuasions have pointed out, the underlying project was far more ambitious than that of simply occupying power (Peggio 1973; Cassano 1980; Maraffi 1980). As these writers have documented, initiatives of this kind formed part of an explicitly formulated strategy designed to break the hold of private monopolies, to equip Italian industry for international competition and to institutionalize class conflict. As such, they were designed to assist the process of accumulation, not to weaken it. Nevertheless, big business bitterly resisted all such moves, demanding that the state corporations withdraw from sectors 'where private initiative, in its full efficiency, had the sacrosanct right to see its risks and efforts protected and defended against damaging competition, above all from the State itself'.[20] For Confindustria, the state's 'invasion' of the economic sphere was construed as an attempt on the part of the major party to assert the primacy of political over economic power. Party statements themselves explicitly affirmed this objective, making clear that the expansion of state-controlled industry was not only a condition for the autonomy of the DC itself, but also, consistent with its anti-monopoly ideology, a means for checking the power of large private economic concentrations.[21]

*Ideology and economic identities: 'public' champions, 'small' heroes, 'large'*
*monopolies*

The first major step in the post-war expansion of state industry was the 1953 Act of Parliament which established ENI as a powerful agency responsible for the exploration, development and supply of natural gas and petroleum products to the national economy. As Provasi (1976: 166–71) has documented, this Act dealt 'an unprecedented blow' to those large private holdings which had held a monopoly over energy sources. It also initiated a vigorous phase of state entrepreneurship under the Fanfani and Moro governments, when the state holdings were called on 'to fulfil unambiguous anti-monopolistic objectives' – breaking into the field of chemicals, fertilizers, cement and steel where previously private groups had dominated (Shonfield 1974: 282; Prodi 1974: 60; Peggio 1973: 54–5).

In his speech to the Senate in 1953, DC Finance Minister Vanoni makes clear that the purpose of the ENI bill is to remove an important resource from the control of powerful private groups and thereby provide the government with an effective anti-monopoly instrument with which to diffuse the benefits of economic development and, in particular, to secure the growth of small and medium industries. 'Those who have responsibility for policy direction of this country could not escape this question: what would have happened to the Italian economy and society if these discoveries [of natural gas] had been abandoned to so-called private initiative?' Going by past experience, Vanoni argued, if the government had not taken charge in this field, it would soon have been the object of private monopolies:

And if you bear in mind that certain of these groups could also have been consumers of gas, in competition with other small and medium firms constrained to acquire it at market prices . . . you will immediately see that the problem is not simply one of enjoying some tens of billions of profits, but of the necessity to secure for medium and small firms through-out our country the possibilities of development and coexistence . . .

It is, in other words, the problem of giving or negating a basis for the development of monopolistic organizations to the detriment of the conditions of existence of the medium and small firms. This has been the prime reason which has led the Government to consider with great seriousness, concern and prudence the problem arising from the fortunate discoveries of natural gas.

Vanoni's statement (cited in Provasi 1976: 160–2) is of interest not only for the way it links the cause of state entrepreneurship with that of smaller firms, but above all as an example of the tendency among Christian Democrats generally to identify big business *tout court* with the monopolies. Although the examples could be multiplied, three typical statements selected from different contexts will serve to illustrate this point. All deal with aspects of policy regarding small enterprise.

The first set of statements are taken from Committee reports in the Senate and Chamber of Deputies in support of a bill to improve medium-term credit facilities for small and medium industrial firms. The Industry Committee, having examined the bill in the Chamber of Deputies, expressed its opinion that

The bill proposed by Senator Luigi Sturzo merits our lively attention and sympathy because it favours the development of that small and medium industry to which the legislator has frequently and justly given his preference and cooperation. . . . *initiatives which in contrast to plutocratic organisms emerge among the most courageous categories* . . . whose strength – *based on numerical diffusion rather than on the single concentration of power* – supports national economic progress no less than that of larger industries. [Italics added][22]

In a similar vein, the government's report to the Senate declared that

[The *small and medium industries*] represent the most vital part of the country because they represent the concrete enhancement of private initiative . . . If we manage therefore to strongly support *private initiative* in the commercial and industrial field we will combat most effectively the *monopolistic concentrations* which in given circumstances can be and are dangerous. [Italics added][22]

The final example is drawn from a speech by the DC Minister for Industry, Emilio Colombo, delivered at an international study conference in 1960 on 'technological progress and Italian companies'. In that context, Colombo – one of the most powerful post-war leaders of the right-wing *dorotei* faction – explained why the Italian government was intensifying its financial support for small business. Larger firms which had greater capacities for self-financing were able to keep abreast with technological developments more readily than smaller firms which would have to turn to external sources of credit at greater cost, thus putting them in an unfavourable position with regard to larger firms.

The democratic orientation of a country's economy poses the problem of having adequate instruments so as to avoid a situation in which the advantages of technical progress benefit only certain sectors of production.
   If because of different capacities for self-financing the difference in production costs increases between firms of diverse size, then such phenomena may ultimately bring about *the elimination of small and medium productive units, and the concentration of production in units of large size*, with all the subsequent damage that would result. These and other considerations . . . explain why technical progress requires an attentive policy capable of making available adequate instruments to diffuse as widely as possible the beneficial effects of such progress, *to avoid the emergence on the market of monopolistic or dominant positions.* (Colombo 1963: 63–7) [Italics added]

   As we saw in chapter 6, the equation of scale with monopoly was also a dominant motif in the DC's programmatic documents which stressed the need to counteract the 'monopolistic tendencies of big industry' that 'endanger the development of a free people' (*Il Programma* 1944). On the question of what precisely constituted a monopoly, one study of the political debate of the reconstruction period concludes that none of the parties had anything but the vaguest notion. Sometimes it alluded to a dominant position in the market; but for the most part its significance was explicitly political, referring to 'an economic overlord capable of subverting government policy and the democratic process' (Barucci 1978: 682–3). Invariably, as these examples indicate, the term monopoly was applied to all those private firms which fell outside the small and medium-sized universe.
   Identified as the 'healthy', free and dynamic element of the economy, the small firm thus figured as the natural beneficiary of state support. By contrast, the large enterprise was cast as monopolistic in tendency, lacking in social responsibility and potentially subversive of freedom.[24] It had to be watched. This could be done, argued Fanfani at the 1956 Congress, 'if the State knows how to fulfil its functions in two particular areas: that regarding enterprises under its ownership; and that pertaining to the control of industrial enterprise size' (DC 1976: 83). In other words, whether directly as entrepreneur, or indirectly via the control of credit, prices and taxes, it was the state's role to impede the formation of monopolies and the concentration of economic power

'harmful to the efficiency of our system, to the progress of our economy, to the liberty of our democracy'. Since there is no evidence that this anti-monopoly orientation was forced on the Christian Democrats from below (that is, from small business), one can only assume it to be the combined product of traditional sentiments generally, and the specific goals of party autonomy earlier outlined.

The extent to which these measures were effective or to which the DC gained supremacy over economic forces need not concern us here. In this context, what matters for our purposes is the way certain assumptions and outlooks are cast into public form; and how these public constructions of economic identities, rendered authoritative by the state, have consequences for the allocation of rewards and opportunities. For, if in the demochristian vision of the entrepreneurial universe, large firms were considered actually or potentially 'monopolistic', then they could not be legitimately included among the beneficiaries of direct state support.

On the other hand, we have seen that the strategy which took shape in the fifties was to develop an institutional presence in order to gain a degree of independence from private sources of economic power. Consequently, the adoption of measures which might have facilitated the concentration of private capital would have been incompatible with the DC's political objectives.

In this section, I have examined the preferential treatment of small firms from a different perspective – that of the relations between ruling party and big business. It was argued here that the exclusion of large firms from state assistance could be explained in terms of the political strategies and ideological orientations of the dominant party. To illuminate this problem, my discussion focused on key factors behind the expansion of public enterprise. It was shown that in initiating this process, the DC sought to create an autonomous power base with which to offset the pressures of big capital and other private interest groups; to advance a new model of industrial relations; and to secure an anti-monopoly instrument aimed at reducing the power of large private groups and modernizing Italian industry.

Throughout the chapter, I have thus tried to show the interplay of societal pressures and state objectives – of the problems and challenges emanating from civil society and the projects and interests of state elites – and have leaned decisively in favour of the explanatory power of the latter. In other words, I have argued the case for the pull of state-defined goals in a context in which the push of social pressures was also very much in evidence. It is now time to follow through this argument by showing how governments acted in a very different political (and economic) context. For, if preferential treatment for smaller enterprise were simply a product of the contingencies of Italian politics, then we would expect to find significant changes in policy, consequent to the lifting of constraints and the establishment of a new balance of power.

## Against the trend: state and enterprise in the concentration era

The sixties furnish a particularly good setting for conducting the kind of test I have indicated. At the beginning of the decade, Italy was already on the eve of opening to the left, having experienced substantial political, social and economic change. Moreover, it was in this period that European governments, stimulated by foreign competition and inspired by the Galbraithian belief that the industrial future lay with the giant concern, gave a decisive boost to industrial concentration, promoting wave after wave of mergers and the enlargement of home industries.

These internal and international developments, as will be shown, had only a mild influence on government policies. In fact, aid to small business in the 1960s and 1970s (as discussed in chapter 4) was if anything far superior in kind and quantity to that of the previous decade. Continuity, not decline, of assistance is thus the keynote of post-war policies. The contrast with France is again instructive. For in that country, Berger has shown that shifts in policy towards the 'traditional sector' are linked to the changing social base of Gaullism. Thus, the phasing out process of small business began to be reversed only in the 1970s as the Gaullists attracted fewer salaried voters, and, one might add, as the disillusion of the small business stratum spilled over into violent protest (Berger 1977: 30). Turning to Italy, however, Berger correctly concludes that despite changing social coalitions, 'In Italy, the impact of shifts in the bases of support of the DC cannot be similarly traced through shifts in policy' (1980: 118).

Indeed, in spite of substantial change – in political alliances, economic conditions and cultural models – all of which paved the way for a more receptive attitude towards large industry and the advantages of scale, the basic policy concern is not the continuity of support for smaller enterprise, but rather in which measure and under what conditions can the promotion of large-scale undertakings be 'justified'. It is in relation to these characteristics of the Italian context that I understand and propose to substantiate the 'legacy effect' of Christian Democracy's small business ideology, and ultimately its impact in moderating the quest for scale in Italy.

### New terms of the 'social question': from class struggle to uneven development

A combination of political processes, maturing towards the end of the fifties, gradually laid the foundation for a different approach to economic development and social integration, embodied in the centre-left formula. As international tensions eased and as the Socialists dissolved their alliance pact with the Communists, the moderate left gained a new respectability. The accession to the Papacy of John XXIII (denounced in later years by Italian conservatives as the 'red' Pope), also added plausibility to calls for a Catholic–Socialist coalition, which by 1959 the DC secretary-general, Aldo Moro, had forecast as an 'historical inevitability'.

Concurrently with these trends, the trade union movement underwent several important developments. The politically oriented militancy of the earlier years had disappeared; ties between unions and parties loosened; and gradually, aided by the international thaw, divisions within the labour movement attenuated. Towards the end of the decade, economic growth and an improving labour market held out increasing opportunities for an industrially focused action. As Hine (1976: 189) writes, all of these developments 'had the effect of elevating the economic and business functions of trade unionism, and de-emphasizing its political aspects'. In the eyes of the ruling party, the trade union thus acquired new legitimacy. Considered now as the 'forces of economic development', trade unions are praised for their 'valid contribution in excluding destructive and deforming politics from their action and in protecting workers' rights, thereby encouraging the democratic maturity of workers and broadening popular consensus for the democratic state'.[25]

Finally, to these political transformations we can add those within the economic sphere. A generally buoyant economy and the particularly brilliant results being achieved by the state holdings in the capital-intensive sector of industry helped strengthen the conviction that government now had both the means and opportunity for dealing a decisive blow to the Communists. In a dynamic and extensive public sector, DC intellectuals saw a primary instrument for economic planning which would lay the basis for a new social contract and for the correction of regional imbalances.

At the first of three study conferences held at San Pellegrino between 1961 and 1963, party intellectuals thus pressed the case for a more 'rational and efficient state structure' which would guide and direct the 'new tendencies of the modern world'. Deruralization, mass migration northwards to the industrial triangle, the increasing income gap between north and south, plus the tendency for organizations – productive and associational – 'to increase in scale and number' – all indicated the need for a fresh approach towards big industry and the world of organized labour. What was required, argued the main speakers, was a democratic plan through which to incorporate the workers and new middle class, and at the same time to ensure a more efficient allocation of resources in those areas hitherto on the margins of industrial development. In short, argued the sociologist Achille Ardigo, the DC had to 'ride and tiger' of industrialization in order to come to terms with the increasing scale of organization.[26]

Within Catholic circles, it seemed clear then that large enterprise now offered increasing prospects for class collaboration. Church and party statements confidently affirmed that the age-old 'social question' had been superseded. The problem of class struggle had given way to the less destructive issue of uneven development. Regional imbalances, not class inequalities, defined the 'new terms of the social question.' In view of this displacement, Papal pronouncements in the 1961 Encyclical *Mater et Magistra* were even prepared to concede that 'deproletarianization' – giving the worker a chance to become a property owner – might have less urgency, especially now that the dignity and rights of labour could be secured by means other than that of private property (see Camp 1969: 108; Vito 1961).

All of the processes that I have briefly outlined helped pave the way for a new political deal – technocratically inspired and reformist-oriented – under the centre-left umbrella. That economic planning remained little more than a series of intellectual exercises, in Fanfani's words, 'a book of dreams',[27] or that little was achieved in the way of reforms need not concern us here. What matters for our purposes are the political and social transformations themselves and how they affected the government's stance towards enterprises of diverse size.

For if the old constraints no longer applied and if, as current economic thinking implied, the internationalization of markets required firms of optimum size, then it was surely no longer realistic to exclude large-scale initiatives from access to state assistance. After all, the more industrially mature of Italy's European partners were promoting industrial giantism to increase national competitiveness. French governments, obsessed since the fifties with adequacy of scale, gave selective favours only to the most dynamic of the larger companies in each sector (Sheahan 1963: 248; Suleiman 1975). And as we have seen also in Germany – second only to Britain in degree of concentration – federal governments considerably boosted the rate of mergers and acquisitions through both direct and indirect measures (Kuster 1974: 79).

What then of Italy? Before answering this, it is important to emphasize that without necessarily adopting extreme measures, the consolidation of Italy's highly dispersed industrial structure was still well within the bounds of political possibility: for example, by giving financial support *independently* of size, and by withdrawing it to discourage *new* entries. Neither of these measures, however, was contemplated. If anything, Italian governments sought to facilitate the process of enterprise formation by introducing a loan guarantee scheme for the smallest category of firms (in addition to loan subsidies already on offer). Moreover, size restrictions were *generally* maintained, even as the faith in bigness acquired new followers. The one exception – although even here the ambiguities are significant – regards regional policy for the industrialization of the south. We will examine these and other attempts to accommodate the new trends for it is here that the changes are as significant as the continuities.

### Modernization Italian style

In common with other ruling parties and elites in Western Europe, Italian governments of the 1960s placed industrial modernization and efficiency at the centre of their policy concerns. For most governments, this meant larger company units. In the Italian context, however, the equation of efficiency with scale was less readily assumed. A study by the prestigious government advisory body, CNEL (National Council for Economy and Labour) (1961: 9) had already concluded in 1961 that economies of scale could be found 'at diverse levels of enterprise size', and that small industrial firms generally have 'autonomous possibilities of progress' in numerous branches of production, ranging from the traditional consumer goods areas to the more technologically sophisticated sectors of electronics, engineering, etc.

Even the first Five-Year Plan approved in 1967 – regarded as a major piece of Italian technocratic thinking, embodying a commitment to the new philosophy of efficiency – was far from explicit on the subject of scale and concentration (Benedetti 1979: 259ff). In the section on industry, for example, the plan announced that

The efficiency of the industrial system must be pursued *on one hand* via the enlargement of enterprise dimensions in sectors of 'impulse' [that is, heavy industry sectors where the public presence is strong or paramount]; and *on the other hand*, via the introduction of advanced technologies in firms of small and medium size. (cited in D'Antonio 1968: 1009) [Italics added]

With regard to the artisan economy, the plan was even more explicit:

The artisanat will maintain in our country's economy a significant economic and social position of its own . . . not only because it consists of more than one million 100 businesses but also because it has demonstrated its capacities to adapt to the exigencies of modern productive activity . . . The artisan economy must therefore be regarded as a dynamic, autonomous and modern force.[28]

As already stated, however, the relationship of planning to operative policy has remained largely fortuitous. Its interest here lies purely in the way the document restates one central goal of small firm support pursued under the pre-centre-left ministry of Colombo. As outlined by Lasorsa, DC junior minister for Industry and the Artisanat, the explicit aim of the government's efficiency drive was to update the technologies used by smaller enterprise. Thus, artisans and small industrialists would be encouraged not so much to grow large as 'to adopt on a small scale those technologies and processes which have been widely diffused in industrial complexes of more or less vast dimensions' (see Lasorsa's report in Ministero dell'Industria 1963: 83; cf. also Colombo 1963: 636–7). The contrast with the Gaullist faith in bigness could not be more striking, for it will be recalled that under that regime 'instead of helping small firms to modernize, the emphasis was on phasing them out' (Lauber 1981: 232)

Christian Democrats tended to justify this focus on the basis of two largely divergent assumptions. The first, as represented in Finance Minister Tambroni's policy statement to the 1959 Congress, was that large industry would seek to escape trade union burdens and improve productivity by increasing its capital investments. The more this trend continued, 'the more the small and very small firm would be constrained to compress wages to remain competitive'. If, therefore, the survival of small industry came to depend on a low wage regime, this phenomenon could ultimately 'threaten the unity of the state' by playing into the hands of the Communists who were seeking to unite small entrepreneurs and their workers against large industry in a strategy of broadening working class alliances. 'Of this, friends', the minister warned his colleagues, 'the Communists are aware, and on this they watch attentively' (DC 1961: 483–4).

Pre-empting or eliminating 'dualism', however, was but one objective. The conclusion more commonly drawn was that, lacking the assistance to modernize, smaller firms would be progressively eliminated and the Italian economy would become more concentrated. In parliamentary reports, ministerial statements and political speeches, Christian Democrats thus viewed the technological modernization of small industry as a preventative measure against the concentration of production in units of large size.[29]

In short, the national assistance schemes for industry continued through the sixties and seventies to privilege smaller units and to exclude the large firms from state subsidies. In practice, however, the situation is somewhat more complicated. Although the extent of the phenomenon is unknown, commentators have reported several cases where, in order to gain access to SMI benefits, big firms have subdivided their investment projects into several pieces, creating fictitious legal entities which fit within the prescribed limits of the law (Prodi 1974: 62). Whereas critics have been quick to denounce such practices as 'corrupt', it is not difficult to see that such violations of the statutory norms are themselves presupposed by a supportive structure whose essential premise is the privileging of small-scale initiatives. Perhaps of greater significance than the 'corruption' are the structural consequences of such a system. For if, in order to obtain a share of the SMI benefits, big business has been obliged to 'decentralize' its investments, then it would seem that the Italian system of incentives has provided an added stimulus to the deconcentration of industry in that country: additional, that is, to the trade union 'rigidities' most frequently cited.

As another example of the Italian government's ambivalent endorsement of the European faith in bigness, consider the merger law of 1965. Introduced under the Socialist ministry of Tremelloni, responsible for Finance, the 1965 Act gave temporary tax concessions for company mergers 'to render optimal business dimensions' in the new phase of international competition.[30] As in most such matters, the bill reflects a typical compromise between the coalition partners, each with a different vision – 'dichotomous' for the Socialists, 'pluralistic' for the Christian Democrats – of the social structure that they sought to govern.[31] Thus, while on one hand the scope of the bill was to encourage firms to reach optimum size, on the other hand, it seemed more concerned to impose conditions so that this might not happen. For example, the law stipulated that the tax concessions would be granted for mergers between companies – not individually owned firms – on condition that such operations resulted in one productive cycle, did not give rise to a dominant market position, and did not normally exceed a total invested capital of *one* billion lire. Since a medium-sized firm was conventionally defined as one with a maximum of 500 employed and *three* billion lire of invested capital (six in the south), it is clear that the amount of capital specified would allow for only a relatively small, low-capitalized undertaking. By adding the disincentive that mergers exceeding this figure would have to obtain a special decree from the Minister for Industry, the tax measure clearly did not represent a concerted effort to facilitate the process of concentration.

One writer, whose sympathies clearly lie with the Gaullist approach, concludes from his examination of those cases requiring the ministerial decree that although government was aware of the limited possibilities of this provision, the concession was refused whenever it was felt a dominant position might have resulted (Benedetti 1979: 264). Of even greater significance, argues Benedetti, is that despite its limited effects, the 1965 Act 'has remained an isolated case, in that it has not been accompanied or followed by other provisions intended to demonstrate a decisive will of Government to proceed in the direction undertaken'.

At the risk of belabouring the point, it is nevertheless worth noting that the same contradictions and ambiguities towards scale and concentration apply to the legislation for industrialization of the Mezzogiorno. It will be recalled that this is the one area of the country in which the DC *has* pursued a big business strategy – initially, by requiring public enterprise to invest there; belatedly, by loosening the conditions of eligibility for grants and loans to accommodate large northern investors.[32] The latter move was taken in response to the crisis of the southern economy and to the state's failure to solicit the formation of an extensive and dynamic network of small industries (Graziani 1972: 65, 74). In view of the special problems of the south, what is surprising then is not that the state should finance big capital, but that this should be so constrained by the old rules of the game.[33] The convoluted and equivocal manner in which large industry was granted access to state assistance tells a story that amply reinforces the theme we have been tracing. Extensively and thoroughly documented, Saba's (1969: 141) verdict conveys the point of that tale in a nutshell: 'It is senseless to encourage firms so that they might realize economies of scale, on condition however that they do so without increasing too much their scale of production.'

Elaborating on this 'typical contradiction', Saba observes that on one hand, it is widely admitted that rapid industrialization of the south cannot take place without large, vertically integrated complexes. On the other hand, however, the political leadership fears that 'the large enterpreneurial groups will escape the state's control, or even dominate and condition it. Thus, to concede incentives to the Italian oligopolies appears, at the moment of formulating the legislation on incentives, clearly anti–democratic' (1969: 8).

The presence of a large Communist Party in the wings, ever eager – as we saw in chapter 3 – to prove the DC a big business wolf in sheep's clothing, has no doubt helped to condition the terms of support to big capital. But the categories with which the ruling party has construed the entrepreneurial universe have made that process possible. For within the framework of identities constructed, the act of granting advantages to the large installation could not easily be separated from that of courting the 'monopolies'. However much, in private, individual politicians actually may have made such distinctions, it is not the private convictions which matter. It is the public constructs which count. For, to borrow a formulation of Du Preez (1980), once such a system of constructs has been established and become the investment of a party, it tends to acquire a reality of its own and to impose its own constraints.

## Conclusion

The fact that a small business strategy prevailed even after the waning of the internal challenge points to two possible conclusions, each of which can be reconciled with the state-centric focus of my argument: first, that the challenge itself was only a proximate determinant.

Although political constraints and antagonistic class relations in the fifties gave some structural basis to the state's use of the small-scale sector and to its exclusion of big capital, they were not the primary determinants of the decision to strengthen and expand micro capitalism. Indeed, the political exclusion of wide segments of the working class coupled, as it was in France, with a vigorous promotion of industrial concentration, demonstrated that the mere existence of similar 'problems' is a poor predictor of policy outcomes.

The second point, which the final stage of my analysis emphasized, is that willingly or otherwise, political agents became captive of their own ideological constructs. To this extent the legacy of the DC's small firm bias and the rules of the game thereby set in motion have played an important part in moderating the quest for scale and in directing the modernization drive along a particular path. But the more general point of this excursion into the sixties, and indeed of the chapter as a whole, is that in order to explain the direction traced by state activity, it is necessary to consider the projects and interests of relevant state elites as much as the configuration of power relations and domestic struggles which gave them impetus.

This and preceding chapters have shown how Italy's unusual economic structure was shaped by the state. But this would seem to imply that only micro capitalism is a political creation. The following chapter buries that possibility by indicating that if Italy was distinctive at all, it was not because the state *intervened* to shape capitalist development but because it did so in a *very particular way*. It suggests, in other words, that the industrial concentration we have seen elsewhere in Europe is itself a state creation. This in turn has one important implication: that societies can to some extent choose between different strategies of capitalist development. It is in this light that I explore in the conclusion how exportable the Italian model might be to other nations.

# PART II

# The Creative State
# in Retrospect and Prospect

# 8

# Giantism and geopolitics

## Introduction

The preceding analysis has opened up a new puzzle: if successful capitalism need not come in a big business package and economic development does not preclude the existence of extensive micro-capitalist production, why then is it so comparatively rare? The main argument thus far implies that the key to that puzzle lies with the state. More particularly, I have shown that in post-war Italy micro capitalism flourished because of an unusually 'sympathetic' state, one whose project-oriented managers remained more attentive to the internal rumblings of class politics than to the external pressures of international rivalry. But it is possible and necessary to extend this point. In this chapter I attempt to show that a similar state-centred perspective applies to the formation of big business economies. This time, however, geopolitics, which was of minor importance to the Italian state, must be central to that analysis.

We must begin though by anticipating, and discarding one of, two possible conclusions. Up to this point, my analysis has demonstrated how, for reasons of its own, a state can regulate the market to advance a distinctive form of capitalism. Now if this were the whole story, we might be led to a conclusion with somewhat narrow theoretical implications: where small capital triumphs it is because of a correspondingly greater regulation on its behalf; conversely, where it suffers overall decline, this is because market forces have been allowed to prevail. We might, then, happily write off the Italian experience as a special instance of politics triumphant over market. Accordingly, the classical rule could be reinstated, with one qualification: provided states do not interfere with market forces, big business capitalism will prevail.

But this is clearly not the full-blown tale. Cross-national

comparisons have led us some way beyond that point to reveal the makings of a more complex 'plot'. As we saw in the two preceding chapters, states in other European settings have not been neutral bystanders. On the contrary, just as Italian governments have promoted economic dispersion, so other national authorities have typically sponsored concentration. That comparative scenario points us towards a much bolder conclusion whose theoretical ramifications are far more serious. In short, the suggestion is that bigness, no less than smallness, is in significant part a political creation. From this perspective, politics does not so much 'triumph over' economic forces. It enters into their overall configuration.

The present chapter attempts to make two general points. The first is that states, not markets *per se*, have generalized the impulse to scale and concentration. Clearly, this does not imply that *all* instances of concentration are state induced: rather, my aim is to exploit the disagreements and uncertainties among economists that concentration is continuous or inevitable (see Samuels and Morrish 1984: 20ff) and to suggest that even the most 'mature' of capitalism's creations owes considerably more to the rationalizing[1] and regulatory activities of states than existing theories allow.

The second major point is that the substitution of large-scale capitalism for small has typically gone hand in hand with the state's response to crises generated by external challenges. The attempt to mediate and manage pressures of interstate competition both military and economic has, at critical moments this century, spurred states to centralize production facilities, foster Fordist arrangements and eliminate small undertakings. Whether in seeking to protect, enhance or recuperate their own powers within the international political system, national authorities have thus pushed into prominence a set of concentration policies, extending the tracks that capitalist activity would follow, blocking or shortening others which traced out alternative paths. The argument therefore introduces a hitherto neglected geopolitical dimension into the analysis of recent capitalist development.[2] As Mann (1980) has shown, geopolitics has been central to the way capitalism developed historically within national political units. This chapter suggests that the form in which capitalism has typically come to predominate nationally may also be linked to the competitive activities of nation-states.[3]

Since it is enormously difficult to separate out, let alone measure, the state's contribution to the formation of big business economies – in reality a highly complex process – the question is how best to proceed. Here, timing is of key importance. At what point is it sensible to speak of the generalized supremacy of big business? Significantly, the answer is: not before the First World War. I therefore justify 1914–18 as the great divide, arguing that significant advances in this direction issued from the confrontation of national economies in two major wars. In some cases, however, as will be seen for France and to some extent Germany, the war factor encompassed more than the construction of managed economies. It also impinged via state responses to the circumstances of defeat.

I therefore begin by describing very generally two principal phases in the replacement process spanning the period 1914 to the 1970s. Phase one covers very broadly the impact of the world wars. It considers how the establishment of war economies helped reshape national industrial structures. The second phase of rationalizing activity, after 1945, marks a transition in the nature of states and their international environment. Whereas prior to 1945, the most persistent sources of external threat have been primarily military, since then, the nature of modern militarism plus the increasing internationalization of capitalist economies have rendered interstate rivalries more directly economic. Analysis of interstate competition is therefore still necessary to explain the promotion of giantism, although in less militaristic, more narrowly economic, terms.

Phases one and two therefore sketch a general argument relating geopolitical–military factors to the consolidation of big business economies. To illustrate these general themes, the final section focuses on differentiated instances of the replacement process in which the state took the lead in Britain, West Germany and France. As we will see, the effects of war and the pace of concentration were unevenly distributed. In Germany and the UK, for example, the substitution of large for small business was well advanced between the wars. In France, that transformation dates largely from 1945. Thus, rather than providing a chronology or survey, my discussion breaks into the overall period, singling out moments of particular significance in each national setting. Finally, I consider the significance of the American experience for the overall argument.

## Interstate competition and capitalist concentration

### *Phase one: the role of total war*

This section argues that the period punctuated by two major wars marks a decisive shift in the development of nineteenth-century capitalism and in the relationship between the state and national capital. Whereas prior to the Great War, European economies were highly dispersed, craft methods widely diffused and state–industry intervention limited, by the end of the war spectacular changes in all three spheres were apparent. The significance of war is not that it suddenly issues in the ascendance of big business or the eclipse of small production. The uneven pace of that process does not admit easy generalization. Nevertheless, one generalization can be risked. In no European country was a critical turning-point reached prior to 1914. It is true that the mass production factory and the giant corporation had begun to emerge before 1914. But the war helped to generalize the trend and to place it under state sponsorship. The significance of that date is that it heralded a wholly new form of international violence – full-scale, protracted, mass mobilization warfare. In that first great struggle for national survival, war issued in a clash not just of national armies but of state-managed and state-organized economies. As a consequence, differences in state capacities, structures and traditions rapidly dissolved as each national authority set about organizing the nation as one giant commercial and industrial enterprise (McNeill 1983: 326–7). Twentieth-century war – the most intense expression of interstate competition – can thus be seen as a key chapter in the rationalization of capitalist enterprise.

The case for treating 1914–18 as a 'great divide' is based on the three related points mentioned earlier. First, in the decade prior to the Great War, national economies were still widely decentralized at both plant and ownership level. Small firms colonized numerous sectors of industry and employed a very large share of the industrial workforce. Consider first the French figures.[4] In 1906 France's small establishments (1–100 workers) employed three-quarters of the industrial labour force, the bulk of which was concentrated in tiny undertakings with fewer than twenty personnel (Levy-Leboyer 1976: table 10). On these indications we can safely assume that giantism in the Gallic economy had made little headway by the eve of the First World War.

What of Germany, that formidable industrial power and birthplace of the giant combine? Even here, the figures for 1907 are sobering. Although truly gargantuan in some branches of industry, Germany's largest enterprises (with more than 1,000 employees) accounted for only 5 per cent of all industrial employment.[5] At the other end of the scale, the statistics leave no doubt as to the transnational character of petite industry. With 57 per cent of the personnel, firms with fewer than fifty employees absorbed the bulk of industry's labour force, while the tiniest concerns still accounted for close on 40 per cent (Hardach 1980: 219). It should also be noted that these figures exclude one-person establishments which made up 17 per cent of the industrial workforce. Either way, the overall pre-war picture is one of economic dispersion, not concentration.

Turning to Britain, we encounter greater difficulty since comprehensive data on the size-structure of industry is not available prior to the 1935 Census of Production. Nevertheless, two points seem beyond dispute. First, although much of the independent artisanry had collapsed by the end of the nineteenth century, British capital for the most part remained small, decentralized and familial right up until 1914 (Payne 1967: 525–6; Kemp 1969: 185). Indeed the typically small-scale nature of manufacturing enterprise in the industrial first-comer has posed a traditional puzzle for economic historians. Britain it seems, much closer to France in this respect, tended to specialize in commodities which were unsuited to large-scale production (Payne 1967: 525). Outside a handful of industries – especially food-processing, cotton and certain engineering sectors producing armaments and warships under government patronage – it appears that giant enterprise was uncommon.

The second point on which there is considerable agreement concerns the timing of capitalist transformation in Britain, the so-called 'rise of the corporate economy'. As Hannah (1983: 139) concludes, a clear general trend in this direction can be discerned only in the wake of the Great War:

wherever quantitative assessment of trends in these developments is possible, the case for a clear shift in industrial practices in the 1920s is overwhelming. In the statistics of mergers, in concentration and overseas acquisitions . . . structural changes were occurring at an unprecedentedly high rate . . . paralleled by statistics on mass production at the plant level.

Precise calculations here are impossible, but extrapolating from the trends reported by the Bolton Committee (Bolton 1971: 58–60), we can be reasonably certain that prior to the outbreak of war a good half of the industrial labour force (excluding 'own account' workers) worked in smaller firms.[6]

These observations on the relatively decentralized nature of the pre-war economy are reinforced by a further distinctive feature, the limited presence of mass production. Outside America (to which I return much later), the mass manufacturers of standardized goods had made little headway before the sudden emergency of the First World War (McNeill 1983: 330–1; Milward 1984: 18). Even the manufacture of automobiles – that giant symbol of the modern Fordist economy – remained more a matter of craft methods than mass assembly. But when the European states entered into battle, 'thereupon jigs and dyes and automated assembly lines came rapidly into their own' (McNeill 1983).

It seems doubtful that markets alone – in the absence of international pressures and intense state involvement – would have called forth the momentous transformations introduced by the war economy when military items were required in quantities so vast as to demand a mass production response. As McNeill (1983: 331) has remarked, it is to the demands of militarism, not industrialism, that we owe the enormous industrial transformations of the twentieth century, 'changes pioneered in near-panic circumstances when more and more shells, gunpowder and machine guns suddenly became the price of survival as a sovereign state'.

Assessing the material changes wrought by the war economies (including that of the Second World War) on patterns of ownership is clearly a hazardous exercise. This is partly because most national statistics measure establishments rather than enterprises and partly owing to the fact that the census dates are rarely coincident with the temporal boundaries of the wars. None the less, wherever appropriate time series data are available, a strong pattern emerges. In virtually every single case – including Germany, France, Japan, the USA and the UK – one can glimpse in the relative shares of employment major shifts from small- to large-scale production. Such shifts tend to be most strikingly concentrated within the time span of the two major wars.[7] By contrast, the inter-war pattern is one of overall stability, occasionally marked by the resurgence of petite capital, as in Germany and Japan.[8]

Turning now to the third point, these transformations were not simply incidental by-products of the war effort, but very closely related to the concentration policies adopted by national governments. Where small capital was mobilized not via direct incorporation into larger units, but via cooperative mechanisms (as in Germany, for example, in the First World War), the micro sector held its own. By contrast, in Britain, where smaller units in both wars were either excluded or (in some industries) encouraged to consolidate facilities, the purgative effects of war tended to be more marked (Grunberg 1941; Allen 1951).

The more important point to be made here is that the establishment of war economies expanded the scope of government intervention much more profoundly than in any previous time and carried forward lasting changes in the relationship between state and industry.[9] As hostilities intensified, governments became the chief customers of industry, instituting policies to mobilize the resources of the entire nation. The imperatives of coordinating and regulating the national effort enormously favoured the growth of industrial giants as did the massive scale of government orders for standard items. Where shortfalls occurred in certain industries, wartime agencies stepped in to fill the breach, financing the creation of huge plants from the ground up. In others, concentration schemes were introduced for the merging of facilities and labour.

Of much more enduring significance for government's relation to the industrial economy, however, was the lesson drawn from the first all-embracing contest. Industrialized warfare dramatized for all the belligerent powers the new relationship between militarism and industrialism. This went far beyond the nineteenth-century notion of a small empire of armaments and defence-related industries able to deliver military might. The clash of 1914–18 and its more formidable successor drove home and reinscribed the message that national survival now turned on the industrial economy as a whole and, above all, the state's ability to tap into that giant resource. In practical terms, this meant the capacity to centralize and coordinate supply, to standardize and concentrate production. Invincibility in the trenches and invulnerability in the market-place were thus coupled in a way that privileged giantism as a superior economic form whose inevitable ascendance governments must seek to encourage. As Pearton (1982: 181), generalizing for all the wartime participants, has aptly observed in this regard, 'What happened during the years of attempted recovery and even before the Depression, was that the relationship between the state and industry which, before the war, had been devised for weapons production, was extended more generally throughout industry as a whole.'

It is difficult to systematize the economic effects of international struggle for these impinged in varied ways in different national settings. What can be generally stated is that critical events like the two world wars are crucial for explaining the 'logic' of capitalist development. On each occasion, states became central managers of their economies, sponsoring mass production methods, centralizing production and, in some cases, deliberately combing out small capital. The forms of cooperation that twentieth-century war established between industry and the state, the concentration of resources required to conduct it, the manufacturing responses it invited, even the national defeat and humiliation it brought about – all generated a momentum for change that could not be halted with the peace. In many instances the wars fuelled government-backed movements for national regeneration, seeking rationalization, efficiency and growth. With varying success and encountering more or less resistance, state elites thus set about extending to the industrial economy as a whole the giant structures associated with state power.

### Phase two: from militarism to industrialism

The wars marked a turning-point in the development of twentieth-century capitalism. But they were not the closing chapters. Since the Second World War, the concentration of capital at both plant and ownership level has proceeded apace and governments in virtually all European countries have actively intervened to assist that process. The aptly named 'merger mania' of the sixties, when governments set about creating national goliaths to fend off the American challenge, was certainly the most visible if not the first expression of state-sponsored giantism after 1945.

In this section,[10] I attempt to relate these rationalizing activities to changes which have helped to displace traditional power rivalry from primarily military to primarily economic competition. After 1945, interstate competition still remains central to the logic of industrial giantism, but this is less militaristic and more directly economic than hitherto. Broadly speaking, two changes relevant to the relations of government to national capital have taken place since the end of the last war. There has been a change in the nature of militarism which has rendered warfare ineffective as a tool of state competition. And there has been a transformation in the nature of the international economy which has made national capital, the material base of sovereignty, more vulnerable to external forces. Together, these changes imply that industrialism is now the most important basis of state power, breaking finally the equation of prosperity with military strength.

Let us take first the military changes. The whole point can be made very baldly by stating that ever since Hiroshima and Nagasaki, war between the great powers is no longer a rational, accepted tool of state policy. The nature of modern warfare has demilitarized great power rivalry in the sense that it rules out force and conquest as effective instruments of geopolitical strategy. It is possible to emphasize this point by noting that the relationship between militarism and industrialism that was so decisively revealed in the First World War, when military power depended on the mobilization of entire industrial economies, is now less direct. To a large extent, militarism has become uncoupled from industrialism. To say this is not to deny that militarism is still a core feature of the modern world. But the equation of prosperity with military hegemony – at least outside the United States – is no longer true for western capitalist states as a whole (Mann 1987a: 69). West Germany and Japan are of course the outstanding examples of this disjunction.

One consequence of this uncoupling is that industrialism has become the *sine qua non* of international position and domestic legitimacy, a point well made by Poggi (1978: 134) who observes that 'once the experience of two World Wars and the terrifying prospect of nuclear disaster made the pursuit of old-fashioned power politics among Western States an unacceptably disturbing proposition, the pursuit not of power abroad but of prosperity at home became the chief justification for the state's existence and the lodestar of its operations (at least outwardly).' When imperial expansion and military aggression are no longer realistic options for collective enrichment or national aggrandizement, states are compelled to seek new means. Participation in economic expansion, as opposed to imperial or military glory, thus appears ever more vital. From this perspective, commerce figures not as an antidote to war, in the sense reasoned by early thinkers, but as an indispensable means to avoid it. Modern militarism thereby makes industrialism, ever increasing economic growth, the necessary price of domestic peace and international effectiveness.

This development has a very direct bearing on the state's aggrandizing activities *vis-à-vis* its national capital but it needs to be seen in conjunction with another major transformation. Since 1945, but especially from the late sixties onwards, the economies within the western bloc of capitalist states have become increasingly integrated internally. This has created a much more genuinely internationalized economy than hitherto, a key feature of which is the ability of national capital to trade internationally and to operate internationally through foreign direct investment.

The significance of both developments for the state's relation to economic activity can be highlighted by way of historical contrast. Prior to 1945, states were primarily political units. They could control and regulate markets within national boundaries and expand their markets and territorial dominion externally through military power (Vogler 1985: 66). Today, however, these options are effectively blocked by the twin processes of demilitarization and internationalization previously described. Their combined effect has been twofold. The first has been to make the state increasingly important as an economic actor in its own right, compelled to act in the international arena in order 'to maximize the world surplus in its own favour', and at home to increase the competitiveness of its national capital. As a result, and this is the second consequence of the changes discussed, states now look to big business, not Big Berthas, as the crucial vehicles of competitive strength, both to defend markets at home and to win them abroad. Both developments then give some structural underpinning to the state's increasing involvement generally in the economic–industrial process and in particular, to its interest in creating new economic groupings of international significance.

Nevertheless, they are far from explaining the whole of it. This is so for two reasons. First, not all nations responded to the pull of industrialism and the push of internationalization in the same way or with the same vigour. As the Italian case serves to remind us, international pressures did not impose one model of capitalism, one recipe for economic success. Despite the impact of the international economy, it still left some space for political choice among capitalist forms. There is one further point to consider here. The drive into foreign markets – evident only from the late sixties onwards – certainly intensified the push to concentration. But it did not *initiate* that process. French and German state elites, as we will see, were sponsoring concentration at least a decade earlier, long before these economic pressures could have been felt.

What then accounts for the consistent preference for generosity of organizational size? The contrast with Italy is instructive. In all three countries considered here – Britain, France and Germany – the rationalizing energies of states were mobilized in direct response to crises precipitated by external pressures. But these pressures were not directly economic. As discussed in the following section, all three powers suffered a dramatic slide in international position, induced either by the experience of occupation and defeat, as in the case of France and Germany, or by the collapse of empire following the Suez crisis, in the case of Britain. For France and Germany, the external failures and threats revealed as a direct result of the conflicts of 1939–45 provided a spur to industrial recovery and to an emphasis on giantism that was at first lacking in victorious Britain. But the Suez confrontation in 1956 similarly served to focus state attention on reorganizing the nation's productive base.

As a contrasting case, the Italian experience may serve to reinforce this point. Italy suffered no similar externally induced crisis. Somewhat ironically, it was the only belligerent nation to emerge as it had entered the war: as 'the least of the Great Powers' and, it should be added, a power eager to play the client role to its superpower patron. True it suffered defeat. But it was not their international weaknesses that the Italians held up for political scrutiny. It was the age-old internal divisions which the collapse of Fascism had unleashed and revealed. One must also recall here that in its short history as a nation-state, the most compelling challenges to state power have been mounted from within, not from outside the nation-state. Thus, whereas the French, for example, twice the victim of a stronger industrial power, defined their failures in primarily economic-external terms, the Italians perceived their weaknesses as predominantly political and domestic. For the latter, this meant a focusing of political energies not on external weakness but on the more pressing problem of internal social cohesion. The fact that Italy lacked a compelling sense of national decline suggests that it was just such a perception that elsewhere translated into a concern with international position and equated industrial strength with big business battalions.

The details of this argument have still to be worked out. Before turning to that material, let me briefly restate the main points of this section. I have suggested that the combination of three developments – the uncoupling of militarism from industrialism, changes in power relations within the interstate system and the internationalization of markets – all helped to galvanize political efforts on behalf of giantism. If behind this generalized drive for big business capitalism lies an enduring concern with place in the world, this is no longer conducted openly as a struggle of sovereign states disputing international precedence. It now takes the form of a competition of national economies contesting world markets.

## National variations on the geopolitical theme:
## France, Germany, Britain

What follows is an attempt to highlight the general points made in previous sections with illustrative material from France, Germany and Britain. The analysis is deliberately circumscribed: material has been selected with the aim of illustrating key moments in the replacement process. Thus, discussion of the French experience focuses for the most part on phase two, whereas for Germany and Britain, more attention is paid to the creation of war economies in phase one. The analytical issues are the same for each national case: what are the relations between the state and capitalist transformation? How is that relationship linked to international forces, in particular to the relations between states?

### *France*

To trace the links between international relations, state intervention and capitalist transformation in France, we can largely confine our analysis to the period since 1945. The main reason for so circumscribing our focus is simple. In contrast to the developments in Germany and Britain, France's small business sector was still very extensive at the end of the Second World War. Its submergence and replacement by the rise of a mass production economy are thus relatively recent transformations, dating largely from 1945.

This is not to suggest that the wars had no impact. Very much to the contrary. Between 1906 and 1954, for example, France's largest establishments (with at least 500 wage earners) more than doubled their share of the industrial workforce, from 12 to 25 per cent. At the same time, the progressive expulsion of one-person under-takings was very marked, declining from 27 to 6 per cent of the labour force. Much of this movement into and out of the respective sectors was concentrated within the periods covered by the two major wars. None the less, despite the virtual disappearance of self-employed artisans and the severe contraction of micro units (with fewer than five workers), the French, like the Italians, inherited a substantial small firm sector in 1945, still employing more than half the country's industrial labour (Levy-Leboyer 1976: table 10).

What happened in subsequent decades, however, set French capitalism on a quite different path from the Italian model. With the avowed aim of dealing a death blow to petite production, the officials of the *économie concertée* embarked on a set of policies designed to rationalize the national economy. Eventually, with bold precision, they would even specify their vision of the new industrial order. It entailed the creation of an economy in which 10 per cent of the firms would produce 80 per cent of the output (Shonfield 1965: 141).

The nature and impact of these policies have already been indicated in earlier chapters. Two points, however, are worth emphasizing. The policy of concentration was pursued right through the 1950s into the following decade (Zysman 1977: 70). Thus, although intensified in the mid-sixties as France's exposure to world markets increased, the state elite's rationalizing activities were not coincident with the internationalization effect. The second point to stress is that the campaign of economic modernization embraced objectives far wider than the creation of 'national champions': 'heroic firms, groomed, privileged and trained to carry the colors of France on the battlefield of the new international economic order' (P.A. Hall 1983: 183). In addition to encouraging larger firms to form giant, internationally competitive conglomerates, French planners also initiated fusions among small firms to create larger units. The state's modernizing impulse thus reached right into the heartland of France's highly efficient workshop economy. In Lyon, for instance, one of the most successful examples of flexible production, the state initiated a series of mergers which 'recast the region's productive structure' into a corporate, mass production mould (Sabel and Zeitlin 1985: 156–7). The aim was, in short, to remake France's artisanal economy in the Fordist image of American mass production (Piore and Sabel 1984: 141). The point can be made even more baldly: this was not just an attempt to create a more efficient, internationally competitive France. From its very inception it was above all an attempt to cast aside the nation's artisanal image.

The effects of these policies can be glimpsed in a variety of ways. The share of non-agricultural self-employment registered the most dramatic declines in all of Europe, plunging sharply, as we saw in chapter 2, from 17 to 6 per cent in the decade prior to 1972. Throughout the 1970s firms with more than 1,000 workers increased their share of employment – among firms employing more than ten people – by 20 per cent (Zysman 1977: 207). As Peter Hall has neatly encapsulated the transformation, in less than two decades 'France, once the nation of small, parochial firms, had the highest rate of mergers in Western Europe, and most large French firms were involved in an average of 20 joint ventures each' (1983: 182). It is ultimately impossible to quantify the state's contribution to industrial transformation. But it is equally difficult to deny its central role in that outcome.

We can now leave these observations aside and consider the central puzzle that must be posed for France. What is particularly striking in the Gallic context is the way post-war political economy broke radically with previous practice, shifting the focus of state concern from small business to the large industrial enterprise. The reason for this turnabout has been pondered before but it is usually considered in a narrower form: not 'why industrial concentration?', but 'why economic planning?' Consequently, the tendency has been to focus on what is unique and distinctive in French industrial policy, and on the internal factors that might account for it. 'Economic backwardness' (Birnbaum 1980: 108), the emergence of 'new men and ideas' and the 'organizational capacities' of the French state (Hall 1984) have been singled out by various commentators as the principal explanatory factors. Others, however, noting the strong geopolitical thrust of French policy, suggest a more plausible explanation in the role of external challenges mounted by military conquest (Hoffman 1962; Kuisel 1981). The suggestion then is that we look to international relations rather than internal factors. But before developing that argument let us dispense with the latter.

Economic arguments are the easiest to dispense with. They stress the need to overcome economic backwardness, to catch up and compete with rivals. Several objections can be made here. One problem is that France was not notably backward. In levels of per capita income, its pre-war position was well behind that of America and Britain, but well ahead of Germany and Italy (Clough 1964: 262). More strikingly perhaps, the French economy remained one of the *least* vulnerable to international pressures well into the sixties. Indeed in this respect it seemed much closer to America, exporting and importing a far smaller share of its gross national product (5 and 7.5 per cent respectively) than any other major European country (Piore and Sabel 1984: 139). Third, it seems difficult to attribute the 'deliberate destruction' of France's most famous region of small flexible producers to a struggle against the underdevelopment of capitalism. If this was indeed the case, then the 'industrial intelligence' so widely noted for the French state was on this occasion curiously absent. Finally, even if a sense of relative backwardness did prevail, it remains to be explained why this should become an issue in France and not, say, in Italy; and why in 1945, but not previously.

We can safely leave to one side the culturalist argument about 'new men and new ideas' since this has already been superseded by institutional explanations (see Hall 1984). The most sophisticated version of the latter stresses organizational features of the French state which ostensibly produced the will and the capacity to undertake major structural transformations (see, for example, Zysman 1983; Hall 1984). The availability of a solidary and well-trained elite socialized by the École nationale d'administration, together with the system of finance capital which gives officials control over allocation of investment funds, are two factors given special prominence in such accounts.

Now, it may be said that the value of the state capacities approach is clearly superior when considering national variations in the forms or effectiveness of intervention. But it is not a good predictor of the forms of capitalism likely to be promoted. After all, even states with the least capacity for detailed sectoral intervention can sponsor concentration – as we will see for Britain; while those with more formidable capacities may use them to strengthen small capital – as Japan has done since 1945 (Vepa 1971; Anthony 1983).[11] A more telling objection, however, is that it is very difficult to identify what policy instruments and resources a state may dispose of until they are mobilized and put to the test. Can it seriously be claimed that prior to 1945 the French state lacked the structural potential to recast national capital? If not, then the crucial issue is surely under what conditions such capacities are likely to be realized.

We can now leave these criticisms aside and offer an alternative explanation of the state's rationalizing objectives. The issues raised for both the economic and institutional accounts tend to point consistently beyond the nation-state to the international context and the role of military relations. Although nominally victorious, France emerged from the Second World War, once again, as the victim of a predatory industrial power – this time, however, as a conquered nation, its world status drastically diminished, its sovereignty in tatters.

The significance of that experience can be sharpened by way of comparison with the First World War.[12] Consider the striking parallels. In 1919 as in 1945, military relations had dramatized the links between industrial strength and national security, between economic overhaul and national regeneration. On both occasions, wartime experiments and above all the experience of German aggression had pushed into prominence a body of personnel poised to launch an aggressive industrial policy. Whereas prior to 1914, the Third Republic had done little to promote industrial expansion, by the end of the war, French officials were campaigning for an industrial base equivalent to Germany's and a managerial state to bring it about. As one Minister for Commerce put it, the aim of the new political economy would be to 'create in every corner of France the same great factories as those in Germany' (Kuisel 1981: 50). To that end, a special agency was created to foster mass production methods. But outside the emergent corporate sector boosted by the war effort, all such measures were widely resisted, and plans to reorder production quickly scuttled.

Such striking parallels between both periods testify to the impact of military relations on the government's relation to the economy. If the state succeeded in 1945, but not in 1919, this was partly because it was now able to exploit a much more thoroughgoing sense of crisis and national decline. Of equal importance, the state was now able to outflank capital which stood condemned for collaboration and associated with defeat. As Kuisel (1981: 188) has observed, 'The internal enemy, in economic terms, which was held heavily responsible for the defeat of 1940 and accused of being the mainstay of collaboration, was capitalism in general and the trusts in particular.' Politically, this implied a rupture with the pre-war liberal order. Economically, it meant the elimination of the nation's atomistic industrial structure.

It seems impossible, then, to understand the triumph of big business capitalism in France without reference to international relations. Weakness before German aggression in both world wars and, above all, wholesale defeat and occupation in 1940 helped to draw to conclusion the momentum stirred by 1914–18. Hence, well before the need to do battle in the new international order, the French authorities were responding to a different kind of struggle: the need to reassert France's political independence and restore its position in the world of nations. Consequently, when the planning elites looked to the industrial landscape, they did not see, as in Italy, a model suited to the national way of life. What they saw was only devastation and defeat: an artisanal economy and society destined to remain the '"prey" of industrial nations' (Kuisel 1981: 154).

## Germany

There are two important dimensions to the growth of industrial giantism in Germany which are directly related to an expansionist foreign policy. The first has roots in the state-building programmes of the nineteenth century. The second is closely related to sustaining a world role for Germany in the twentieth century. The former has been widely discussed in the literature and I shall not give much space to it here. As is well known, the German model of state-sponsored industrialism pioneered last century united Ruhr and Reich and tied heavy industry to the military and geopolitical programmes of the new empire. The German pattern of intervention, however, shared little in common with the intensively directive style of post-1945 France. It did not need to. By erecting tariff barriers, the state protected its infant industries. By contracting for the products of heavy industry (especially armaments), it underwrote the large-scale investments of the joint-stock banks in engineering, metals and chemicals. And by encouraging and legalizing combination, it provided a 'powerful institutional device' for concentration (Kemp 1969: 176; Trebilcock 1981: 68). The German economy thus very early acquired a highly concentrated sector of heavy industry, consisting of giant combines specializing in capital goods, nurtured by the investment strategies of the banks and nourished by the state-building programmes of the new Reich.

Beneath this top-heavy structure, however, lay a multitude of miniature concerns producing customized equipment and specialty items. It is the politically determined fate of that sector in Nazi Germany that has a direct bearing on the second dimension of German concentration. In view of the wide neglect and geopolitical significance of this second aspect, I use it as my central example of the 'replacement process'.

The important point to emphasize is that Germany's workshop economy did not simply wither away under the gradual onslaught of advancing concentration. Up to the early 1930s, the small business sector showed evidence of vitality rather than decay. Despite some contraction among the tiniest units (1–5 persons) during the First World War, on the whole the small firm sector held up rather well. It is highly probable that this was due to the way small-scale capacity was mobilized on that occasion (but not on the second). This took place not by direct incorporation (concentration), but by horizontal 'combination along co-operative lines', organized by a nation-wide network of artisan cooperatives (Grunberg 1942: 72). Thus, as late as 1926, firms with fewer than fifty employees still absorbed 53 per cent of all industrial labour. Moreover, the pattern for subsequent years is one of expansion, not contraction. From the mid-twenties to 1933, the proportion of self-employed in industry rose from 15 to 21 per cent (Hardach 1980: 218); and the number of independent craft concerns by 26 per cent (Grunberg 1941: 334). How much of this growth occurred before the 'flight into independence' of the Depression years is uncertain. What is clear is that when Germany entered the 1930s, a considerable portion of its national economic activity was still conducted in small units. Big business capitalism may have been dominant, but it was not yet preponderant.

The expansionist foreign policies and rearmament programmes of the Third Reich played a key role in reversing that situation. After 1934, as the country entered a state of continuous military preparation, the government introduced a series of measures to mobilize labour for the large industrial installations. Among the chief targets of the new regulations was the workshop economy. In order to reduce its overall labour force and to check the flow into independence, subcontracting arrangements were prohibited; tax and social security concessions for artisan industry were abolished; and stringent conditions of entry and licensing were enforced. As of 1935, registration of artisan concerns became compulsory. To obtain registration, however, all artisans, both prospective and established, now had to pass the mastership examination – and to do so by a specified deadline (1936). In addition, individual operators had to establish proof of general reliability and of public demand for the new business. With these onerous restrictions, the National Socialists were thus provided with a powerful means of limiting and eventually reducing the number of independent artisans (Grunberg 1942).

Some indication of that decline can be glimpsed in the sharp contractions that swiftly followed the period of small firm stability and growth. Whereas in the decade prior to 1936, the number of craft concerns grew by 26 per cent, between 1933 and 1939 they declined by 11 per cent (Grunberg 1941: 334). Over the same period, the share of industrial self-employment dropped dramatically from 21 to 9 per cent (Hardach 1980: 218). After careful analysis of the available data, Grunberg (1942: 67) concludes that the bulk of that decline must have occurred after 1936, hence directly attributable to the new legislation. Numerous long-established artisans, many of whom either failed to gain credentials by the deadline, or who failed the examination itself, were obliged to abandon business.

But efforts to narrow the space for small capital did not stop here. As Germany intensified its war production, the government renewed its campaign to mobilize artisan's as factory fodder. A 'Combing' Decree of 1939 ordered the compulsory closure of all workshops which did not meet the criterion of 'national signifi-cance'. As Winkler (1976: 13) has concluded: 'A privileged position in the Third Reich was only available to those who were indispensable for rearmament and war. The *Mittelstand* did not belong in this category.'

The German case thus offers a devastatingly clear illustration of calculated political decimation of the small firm sector and the geopolitical impulse behind it. If it is not easy to assess the immediate effects of the Reich's regulations, it is not difficult to appreciate their long-term consequences. Systematic 'combing' without compensation, plus the stringent conditions of small business entry (largely upheld by the new Republic), together expanded the space for big business capitalism much more effectively than in any previous period.

Turning now to the post-1945 economy, we may very well ask what there was left for the state to do. Governments could surely now sit back and allow the market to finish off what previous policies had begun. That they did not is of course an interesting comment on the dynamics of concentration itself. Why they did not is of even greater interest for our purposes. Let us review the conventional explanation first.

The dynamics of concentration in Germany after 1945 are usually analysed as part of a wider trend in the sixties when European governments set about creating firms of international stature that could fend off foreign subsidiaries and capture new commercial territory for the national economy. In practically all accounts, that story has been repeatedly told in narrowly economic terms: the American challenge and the integration of markets through the creation of the EEC are the favoured explanatory events which stride the pages of virtually all accounts of state-sponsored concentration (cf. Kuster 1974).

It is not that such accounts are wrong. The problem is that the 'international economy' argument is too simple. For in sponsoring the merger movement of the sixties, the federal government was merely making official and explicit what it had long been practising since the departure of the Allied powers in the late 1940s.

It may even be, as Stolper (1967: 26, 230–1) has suggested, that the German government was principally responsible for the marked trend towards concentration in the 1950s.[13] Between 1952 and 1961, for example, governments encouraged companies to merge their assets by granting generous tax benefits. To promote internal expansion through self-finance, the tax bill of large firms was significantly reduced and depreciation allowances rapidly increased. If companies then ploughed back their profits into large-scale investments, additional tax advantages were granted.

What accounts for these early policies? It would appear that realignments in the world economy played little part, since the general drive into foreign markets was not much in evidence prior to the mid-sixties. What then of the possibility that the new state centred on Bonn was simply building on familiar structures? Even this, however, overlooks the crucial historical point that those 'familiar structures' themselves became the subject of international controversy once the war had ended.

Indeed, for several reasons, these measures seem particularly puzzling in the German context. First, unlike France, Germany was not lacking in giant concerns. Second, German industry was not, as in France, blamed for defeat, but continued to be identified with national power. Third, and perhaps most important, as a direct consequence of the war the new republic was under considerable pressure to remove from its economy those aspects of industrial organization deemed violently expansionist, and to move towards a more decentralized productive structure.

In view of these considerations, and given the very strenuous efforts of the Allied powers to ensure the contrary, it is surely important to consider why German policy was even more aggressively concentrationist than ever. As in the case of France, the answer seems to lie in geopolitics. It is important to emphasize that Germany was now territorially divided, physically devastated and defunct as an independent military power. Thus, the last remaining sinew and symbol of national might was industrial giantism – but this too was under threat! During the Allied occupation, the US military government had taken action on three fronts to curb the nation's industrial power: several large industrial installations were dismantled; the Nazi restrictions on craft and retail trades were abolished; and a decree of 1947 provided for the imminent break up of cartels.

Under Erhard's 'social market' economy, some of these measures might well have proceeded, thus setting capitalist development in post-war Germany on a less uniform course. What happened of course was precisely the opposite. As soon as the Allies had departed, these measures went into reverse: the conditions for licensing new enterprise were again tightened up, this time in the name of 'preserving the middle class' (Stolper 1967: 259). Moreover, the German version of the cartel law, finally approved in 1957, contained so many exceptions and loopholes that its prohibitory essence was virtually non-existent.

But the Allied measures were not in themselves especially threatening. The challenge came in the form of a small but highly significant document: the preamble to the Decartelization Decree of 1947. This document aroused intense nationalist feeling and became the focus of a major political controversy, not simply because it overturned German legal tradition but because of the bald declaration of intentions which framed the document. Significantly, there was no trace here of the Anglo-American rhetoric of the free market, of the need to safeguard free enterprise, to improve competitiveness or to uphold anti-trust principles. On the contrary, the language of political economy was supplanted by the language of geopolitics: in stark terms, the Allied preamble proclaimed as the main purpose in breaking up giant combinations a desire to reduce Germany's industrial power (Stolper 1967: 258; Hardach 1980: 149).

As one historian has commented, 'These early decrees made it all the more difficult for Ludwig Erhard and his staff to take over the American heritage and to develop what in his judgment was appropriate in it for German requirements' (Stolper 1967: 258). Whether the power of capital would have prevailed with or without these difficulties, it is hard to know. The point is that for the political leadership the task of preserving and strengthening the organizational and structural features of German capitalism now became inextricably linked with the cause of national regeneration. Industrial giantism was no longer synonymous with the assertion of military power. None the less, it now figured as the key to Germany's resurgence as an independent nation.

## Britain

When compared with the political economies of France and Germany, the British experience seems so utterly different as to defy a state-centred analysis of capitalist development. Yet, in the struggles for national survival, those differences rapidly evaporated. Both in 1916 and again, more powerfully, in 1940, the British state demonstrated capacities for centralized economic management at least as impressive as those of its European neighbours. As in Germany and France, the need to maximize capacity and minimize the use of raw materials extended enormously the scope of government activity. But the British pattern of mobilization – for its insistence on the centralization of manufacturing facilities, on utility schemes for large-batch production and on the general exclusion of smaller plants (below fifty persons employed) from the military effort – tended to favour a much more rigorous concentration of the industrial economy (Allen 1951). In my discussion of the British case, then, the construction of war economies will figure as key episodes in the ascendance and consolidation of big business capitalism.

As we noted earlier, the economic impact of military competition was a devious one, producing both immediate and long-term changes. By the end of the war, the largest visible change in Britain could be seen in the permanently expanded role of government and the rise of large, mass production factories on a very broad front (Pollard 1960; Milward 1984). As to the magnitude of the structural changes involved, we lack the necessary data for a meaningful assessment. Nevertheless, in-depth studies of individual industries, such as the MacLeods' (1975) for optical glass and scientific instruments, afford a rare insight into the mechanisms and outcomes of government intervention in a wide range of industries crucial to the military effort. Analysing government activity in the science-based industries during the period 1914–18, the MacLeods show how the war bureaucracies mobilized public finance, technical assistance and entrepreneurial talent to create a mass production industry.

By setting up national factories and introducing standardized machinery, the government obliged existing producers 'to expand, collaborate and eventually form part of a great national network' (MacLeod 1975: 165). As a result, small producers deploying craft techniques were replaced by large manufacturers applying Fordist methods. In the optical glass industry, for example, one firm which on the eve of war supplied only 10 per cent of domestic needs, by 1918 was producing 'about twice the world's peacetime consumption'. Thus, virtually overnight, an industry consisting of little more than 'a fragmentary collection of craft-based family firms' had been transformed into a network of large, mass production companies (1975: 177).

Such examples could easily be multiplied beyond the science-based industries. Apart from illustrating the immediate effects of economic mobilization, they allow us to glimpse one of its long-term legacies. For the science-based industries – as with many of the state's other militarily motivated creations in the core sectors of engineering – emerged as 'victims of their own success'. Suffering from overcapacity and overcapitalization, firms in these rapidly extended industries were now reliant for survival on continuing government support (MacLeod 1975). Thus, rather than beating a hasty retreat, the state soon found itself involved in a further round of rationalization schemes to meet the new forces unleashed by the war economy.

To assist recovery (and later in coping with the Depression) government programmes tended to repeat the pattern of wartime economic management which had produced military victory (McNeill 1983: 346). Thus, rather than encouraging manufacturers to split up their assets, government now urged manufacturers to merge their interests in more permanent arrangements to take advantage of economies of scale (Pollard 1960: 170; Hannah 1983). Like the French state officials dazzled by the fruits of Fordism, British politicians too endorsed the view that the trend towards combination and concentration was 'both inevitable and desirable'.

Whether pushed by necessity or pulled by conviction, from the recovery years onwards governments increasingly took the initiative in promoting cartels and mergers across a wide range of industries. In aviation, electricity and railways, shipbuilding, textiles and steel, to mention but some of the targets, the state encouraged or compelled existing firms to associate and amalgamate, using contracts, subsidies, tariffs and tax concessions to achieve its objectives (Pollard 1960: 167-8; Aldcroft 1977: 142, 348–9; Bolton 1971: 282). While those aims shifted over the years, at first seeking to cheapen production costs, later trying to contain excess capacity and unemployment, on one point government policy did not vacillate: its avowed object of promoting concentration was consistently pursued (Aldcroft 1977: 348; Bolton 1971: 80).

That these measures added symbolic and material clout to the so-called 'rationalization movement' of the 1920s there can be no doubt. That they were solely responsible for the rise of Britain's corporate economy seems unlikely. What is clear is that after the war the state increasingly took the initiative to foster and facilitate concentration of its national capital; and that initiative itself was deeply inspired by the pattern of mobilization which helped achieve military victory.

But the inter-war picture of rapidly rising concentration needs to be qualified. On the whole, the merger movement of the 1920s bypassed the smaller establishments. Despite considerable cajoling from the sidelines and encouragement from above, Britain's still sizeable network of small, family-managed companies resisted amalgamation and rejected Fordist methods. That the resistance was at least as marked as in France can be gleaned from the stereotype of the British businessman to which it gave rise, now cast as the supreme amateur, profoundly conservative and irrationally wedded to feudal ways (Hannah 1983: 147). That small business still constituted a sizeable segment of the economy can be glimpsed in the employment data for manufacturing establishments. As late as 1935, small establishments still employed 44 per cent of the workforce.

But the days of stability were numbered. From the Second World War (right up to the late sixties) the trend is one of continuous contraction. What the years of merger and Depression had left untouched, the Second World War economy finally dislodged. Covering seventy branches of industry, the concentration schemes which were implemented in 1939 repeated in many respects the pattern of their predecessors. The firms which emerged most concentrated at the end of the war – in chemicals, scientific instruments, metals, aircraft and marine engineering – were of course those which military demand had done most to stimulate. Firms in this core engineering group of industries registered a remarkable expansion of personnel, ranging between 34 and 57 per cent of the insured labour force (Pollard 1960: 313; Hannah 1983: 156). The fortunes of the small firm population marginal to the war effort, largely colonizing the consumer goods industries, were precisely the reverse.

Generalizing from the case of the building industry to the small, consumer goods firms as a whole, Pollard (1960: 309) observes that capital was run down, employment and output dramatically reduced and, after a six-year interruption in the training and recruitment processes, skilled labour severely depleted. As 'official utility schemes introduced methods of mass production' craft practices were forgotten or abandoned. And as many of these concerns lost at least half their personnel, they were forced either to cease production or to merge with others (Allen 1951: 167, 178).

The Second World War economy thus helped finish off what the first had begun. Whereas between the wars the number of small establishments had declined only slightly, by the end of the war they had contracted by 30 per cent (Bolton 1971: 58). And despite a constantly expanding workforce, by 1951 the share of manufacturing employment in small firms had fallen to around 28 per cent, 10 points down on its pre-war (1935) level. These losses were neatly reflected in the gains of the largest firms (with at least 1,500 employees), where employment rose from an estimated 21 to 31 per cent over the same period.[14] From this analysis, it seems reasonable to conclude that the years of command mobilization and centralized economic management helped to concentrate British capital more successfully than in any time of peace. By the end of the war, Britain's big business economy was very firmly in place.

On the whole, the British government's relation to the industrial economy after 1945 is more likely to bore than to puzzle us with its passivity. As we move outside the hothouse environment of the war economy there is little in the way of state 'activism' to compare with either France or Germany. Indeed, when compared with those two countries where the crisis of defeat and occupation spurred economic rationalization and recovery, government efforts in victorious Britain seem remarkably restrained. There is, however, one very striking exception to that general pattern: the well-known modernization mania of the 1960s which infected Conservative and Labour governments alike. In pushing those events into focus my main concern here is not so much with the state's contribution to capitalist development. After all, the observation made for Germany applies equally to Britain: in view of the structures erected by 1945, subsequent interventions were at most extensions of, rather than contributions to, the existing framework. But why were those 'extending' activities undertaken? Why, at a certain point, did the cause of industrial giantism once again become the focus of political concern? These questions are of course similar to those posed for Germany. I pursue them in a similar manner, stressing the role of external political challenge to Britain's world role and the economic response this generated.

In contrast to the radicalism of economic overhaul in France, and the obsession with concentration in Germany, the central puzzle for British commentators has been the lack of state direction, the absence of economic nationalism and the subordination of economic growth to foreign policy. As much of the literature on Britain's economic decline emphasizes, the major difference is not that state elites are unconcerned with Britain's international position. Quite the reverse. It is precisely because that commitment has been so strong that the domestic economy has suffered. According to this view, successive governments after 1945 have been committed primarily to restoring and protecting Britain's position as a world power. In pursuing foreign objectives – maintaining an independent power base in the Commonwealth, sustaining the system of sterling, and keeping open links to the world economy – state elites have thereby overridden the interests and needs of the national economy (Gamble 1985; Blank 1986).

My interest here is not to question this interpretation, which I broadly support, but to use it as a means of posing a different question. In view of these more or less traditional interests and commitments, which amount to a kind of economic and political 'internationalism', what really needs explaining is the new 'rationalization restlessness' which gathered pace from the late 1950s onwards.

As is well known, in that period a new ideology of growth began to dominate political debate, eventually bringing Labour to power with a mandate to modernize the economy and society. Among the many agencies and ministries created in the sixties to manage these policies, the IRC (Industrial Reorganization Corporation) stood out as a shining symbol of the modernizing ethos. Established in 1966 to 'promote or assist the reorganization or development of any industry', the cornerstone of its industrial strategy was to reduce the number of competing operators in selected industries and thus create a few giant companies of international stature. At the end of a brief but active life, the IRC had financed around ninety large-scale ventures in more than twenty industries, including steel and shipbuilding, scientific instruments and ball-bearings, motor cars and machine tools, electrical engineering and computers (Broadway 1970; Williams et al. 1983).

Although the IRC's success in modernizing British industry was strictly limited, its activities added significantly to the list of giant national and multinational companies. Of course, in a big business economy already boasting the largest number of multinationals in Europe, the significance of those activities themselves is open to dispute. Economists are divided on the issue. Some argue that government policies significantly boosted post-war concentration (Aaronovitch and Sawyer 1975: 306); others claim that most mergers would have occurred with or without direct state support (Williams et al. 1983: 85). We do not need to enter that debate. The important point is that after 1945 – partly because it now stood at the core of a vast system of public provisioning – the British state was in a much stronger position to precipitate company mergers. And it did so, from the late fifties right up to the mid–seventies, with a gusto that, at least in terms of financial commitment, well surpassed its pre-war record (Hannah 1983: 171–3).

Now, when viewed in comparative perspective, there is nothing especially remarkable about these 'rationalizing' activities. Since many other European countries were similarly engaged, they might easily be explained as responses to the new economic challenges posed by increasing interpenetration of the industrialized economies. But our analyses of France and Germany have already indicated grounds for doubting that easy equation. From a different angle, the Italian experience too can serve as a useful check against that simple conclusion. As discussed in the previous chapter, the muted 'modern-izing' response of the Italians to realignments in the international economy ought at the very least to caution us against reading off state responses directly from competitive pressures. There is of course one final reason for doubting the primacy of the international economy. The new concentration imperative – variously formulated in terms of increased productivity, investment and efficiency – did not suddenly spring to life with the Labour administration in 1964. Although most energetically pursued by the latter, the new consensus on the need for economic overhaul from above was already forged in the late fifties and paved the way for a major policy shift in 1959 under the Conservatives.

These last points lead to a final set of considerations. When viewed in relation to the traditional patterns and priorities of government policy, is there not, after all, something truly remarkable in the intensity of the state's rationalization restlessness, in its explicit commitment to monumental enterprise and in the direct and systematic way it went about creating it? Could it not be that British society was undergoing a crisis of not dissimilar magnitude to the defeated nations of 1945, a crisis which the impending process of internationalization merely magnified?

Indeed it was, but the nature of that crisis was political not economic. Its immediate source was the Suez events of 1956 when the superior economic (and military) power of the United States forced Britain's retreat and precipitated its decline as a world power. Prior to that period, Britain could still maintain the trappings of a great power with a world role. The development of an independent nuclear deterrent, the maintenance of an extensive military presence overseas, together with a still sizeable empire and the international currency of sterling – all reflected and sustained those great power perceptions. Bur the Suez crisis and the collapse of empire which it triggered put that illusion to the test. Once the imperial links began to disintegrate and once the fears of becoming a client state began to mount, considerations of economic efficiency and competitiveness suddenly assumed the status of a national priority (cf. Gamble 1985: 206).

Thus began a period of intense scrutiny of the nation's economic problems at a time when Britain's growth rates and trading performance constituted dramatic improvements upon its pre-war position. As Gamble notes, 'taken on its own, [after 1945] the British balance of *trade* would have ensured balance of payments surpluses in every year up to 1973, with the possible exception of 1964' (1985: 110). As this suggests, the mounting political obsession with industrial competitiveness and the remorseless construction of comparative growth rates through the late fifties could not have been prompted by economic crisis. If the domestic economy had now become the main gauge of British morale, this was not due to a sudden reversal of economic fortunes. It was the direct outcome of Britain's severely diminished international role.

The parallels with Germany and France seem clear. In each case, the concentration imperative grew initially out of external political challenges. Although national power – its restoration and pro-tection – was the major driving force, that problem was formulated and pursued in terms of economic competitiveness. When the quest for national efficiency and regeneration dovetailed with structural changes in the world economy, the state's participation in capital concentration was even more powerfully reinforced.

## American exceptionalism

Before we turn to conclusions, let us consider objections, the main one here being the American case. This does not fit the overall argument. In the United States, the remarkable growth of big business preceded the state's participation in twentieth-century war, and did so without much direct encouragement from above. As is well known, the Americans not only spearheaded the develop-ment of the mass production corporation, they did so with a pace and alacrity unrivalled anywhere. Thus, already by the turn of the century a network of giant companies was organizing a significant part of the nation's manufacturing output. The question is of course what significance we should attach to the American experience. In the following section, I shall suggest two reasons for doubting the historical generalizability of the American model in the absence of the state. The first centres on the unique combination of 'society-centred' circumstances that the spread of mass production demanded. The second focuses on certain elements of the European developmental pattern which were shared by the United States. Taken together, this combination of the general and the unique in the American case adds weight to the overall argument of the chapter: historically, interstate struggle may not have been the only mechanism of big business consolidation. But it has been a major one.

Historians trace the rise of the corporate economy in America to the closing decades of the nineteenth century. It was soon after the Civil War that large companies first began to mushroom, rapidly gaining ground in two vigorous waves of concentration, variously described as the 'rise of the trusts' or the 'merger movement'. The first phase of concentration was typified by smaller consumer goods firms combining horizontally to form mass production corporations. The second saw mainly large firms in the producer goods sectors integrating vertically to form multidivisional conglomerates (Robertson 1973: 341-53). Overall, the years 1880–1904 witnessed the formation of 318 major industrial combinations, assimilating over 5,000 separate industrial establishments and holding around 40 per cent of total manufacturing capital (Bain 1968: 105). Later we will need to amend this picture of an established big business economy. But for now, let us turn to the arguments for American precociousness.

Why did American manufacturing move so early into a large-scale, mass production mould? According to the standard accounts, its development was conditioned by a very special environment. This environment combined both 'negative' and 'positive' features which 'predisposed the United States, more than other countries, to take the path of mass production' (Piore and Sabel 1984: 65). On the negative side, the New World possessed none of the historical legacies which in Europe set potential obstacles to the creation of a mass market and acceptance of standardized products. First, it lacked both the hereditary aristocracy and deeply class-conscious society whose finely variegated tastes might have sustained demand for differentiated goods. Second, it possessed neither institutional equivalents to the guild system nor a highly skilled workforce which might have resisted the overturning of craft traditions.

While these factors cleared the space for mass production, it was above all the railroads which helped chart its course. The railroads proved crucial in two respects. First, by bonding together a 'homogeneous but geographically dispersed demand' in one national economy, they allowed regionally based enterprise to exploit a vast and rapidly expanding domestic market. Second, and more crucially, railroad policy itself directly promoted concentration. To protect their large capital investments the railroads sought to stabilize and increase demand by promoting mergers among their principal customers. The corporations and trusts that emerged as a result of these schemes were then further favoured with special rebates. As Piore and Sabel (1984: 67) conclude, the railroads were thus 'the matrix of mass production industry' in the United States. If we accept the logic of these arguments, then the American model of society-led concentration begins to look more like the exception than the rule.

But is this the whole story? Was American capital exempt from the state-centred impulses noted for Europe? Is the precocious development and subsequent consolidation of big business in the United States explicable solely in terms of economy- and society-led forces? Much more research is required before these issues can be adequately addressed. Nevertheless, it is possible to suggest certain parallels with the European experience in the role of war and world struggle.

The main point to emphasize is the close connection between the establishment of a war economy and the extension of large-scale industry. In the American context, it seems no coincidence that mass producers began to multiply soon after the Civil War. For the striking feature of that long and bitter struggle was the scale and intensity of economic mobilization, comparable only with the kind of 'total' effort required in twentieth-century world war. Although it took at least a generation for this to be recognized, that protracted battle between north and south, as McNeill (1983: 242) has observed, was 'the first full-fledged example of an industrialized war, in which machine-made arms dictated new, defensive tactics, while railroads competed with waterways as arteries of supply for millions of armed men'.

The significance of America's first-comer status in pioneering total war is obvious. At the very least it suggests a key role for military demand and government direction in linking the organization of destruction with the organization of production. American precociousness thus begins to look less anomalous or extraordinary: exceptional social and economic circumstances may have helped to carry the mass production economy forward. But there seems little unique about its political–military impetus. In this respect, then, the American experience can add to the pattern unearthed for Europe.[15]

It is possible to extend this point, although in a highly cursory way, to the role of interstate struggle itself. For America, though, this would appear more contentious. After all, even if one could doubt the preponderance of large capital, the trend towards bigness was already strongly visible by 1914. On that basis, one might well reason that the effect of world war was at most to hasten the inevitable, to quicken an impulse whose outcome was assured. But even for the birthplace of Fordism, there are grounds for doubting that victory in the absence of international military struggle.

The main reason can be stated as follows. In the great phase of expansion of 1870–1900 small manufacturing, although gradually being outpaced by the growth of large enterprise, was still participating massively (Bruchey 1980). Even by 1914, three years before America became a belligerent, it was still possible to doubt the supremacy of big business. In manufacturing industry, for example, one in every three wage earners worked in small enterprise (with fewer than 100 personnel); and roughly one in every two in firms employing fewer than 250 workers. By contrast, the largest companies (with more than 1,000 workers) probably accounted for less than one-quarter of total manufacturing employment. On these indications, the level of American concentration well surpassed that of the pre-war European economies previously examined. But by the same token, big business had not yet conquered capitalist space. Indeed, when compared with the position in the late 1970s, by which time large enterprise absorbed an astonishing two-thirds of the entire manufacturing workforce, that battle had barely begun.[16]

In the thirty years between 1914 and 1944, however, the structure of American industry was substantially transformed and the triumph of giant mass production enterprise confirmed. This is nicely indicated by the census data for manufacturing establishments set out in table 8.1. Note in particular two patterns. First, in this period the respective shares of small and giant firms in overall manufacturing employment were more or less precisely reversed, the losses of the small sector being reflected in the gains of the large. The second, and much more significant, point is that this

Table 8.1   *Proportion of employees in US manufacturing establishments of various sizes, 1914–1947*

|      | Proportion in establishments fewer than 100[a] | | Proportion in establishments more than 1,000[a] | |
| ---- | --- | ------ | --- | ------ |
| 1914 | 35  | (33)   | 18  | (19)[b] |
| 1919 | 29  | (27)[b] | 26  | (27)[b] |
| 1923 | 29  |        | 24  | —      |
| 1929 | 29  |        | —   | —      |
| 1935 | 29  |        | —   | —      |
| 1939 | 30  | (26)   | 22  | (28)[b] |
| 1947 | 25  | (19)[c] | 33  | (35)[b] |

[a] Figures in parentheses refer to enterprises rather than establishments.
[b] Estimates.
[c] Represents share of employment in 1944.
*Sources*: Establishment figures from Granovetter (1984: 326); enterprise data from Vatter (1980: 154–5).

reversal of fortunes was accomplished almost entirely in two great bursts, each neatly bounded by the years of war production. This seems a most striking piece of evidence for the relationship between the competition of states and the concentration of capital. Of course it does not rule out the existence of long-term tendencies in that direction. But it does not support this either.

These rather dry observations could be fleshed out in a variety of ways. One might note, for instance, how the war effort strengthened the position of large capital not only structurally, but ideologically as well. On the structural side, McNeill (1983: 346) has emphasized the 'decisive impetus' that the First World War gave to the extensive industrialization of American agriculture. High prices, protected by government, and the insatiable demand of the Allied war economies together encouraged an enormous surge in output and investment in heavy capital goods. As a result, rural labour swelled the mass production industries and the family farm was transformed into agribusiness.

On the ideological side, these changes signalled a rather more novel development. This can be illustrated by way of contrast with the pre-1914 period. Up to that point, small farmers had provided the main stem of petit bourgeois ideology in the United States. The

Revolution, notes Berthoff (1980), 'turned peasant self-sufficiency into an explicitly republican ideal of personal independence'. Not surprisingly, small farmers have also been the traditional mainstay of American anti-bigness sentiment. In the late nineteenth century, for example, it was opposition from this quarter to the trusts and mergers encouraged by railroad policy which brought federal government into collision with big business in the Sherman Act of 1890.[17] By the 1920s, however, in stark contrast to the post-Civil War years which saw an 'extraordinary outpouring of anti-big business literature' (Chandler and Tedlow 1985: 553), it had become almost heretical to question its virtues and accomplishments (Beckman 1944: 99). As a result of its wide diffusion, its dazzling achievements and its spectacular contribution to American victory, the mass production corporation had become synonymous not just with commercial strength or national survival but with the American way of life itself (Carson 1973: 34; Berthoff 1980: 36). Big business – from the farm to the factory – had come into its own.

Now that picture may seem slightly puzzling in a context where small business has traditionally occupied a cherished place alongside 'motherhood and apple pie'. If small businesses were being crowded out why were they not protesting? The point of raising that question is to stress once again the formative importance of the war economy for American capitalism, this time by way of contrast with the Second World War. For it seems that during the first world struggle, small business was not noticeably threatened. It was losing out in relative terms, but its absolute position had not been eroded (see Mann: forthcoming, chapter 2). This, in particular, was the achievement of the Second World War economy, a far more protracted, highly planned and tightly managed affair than its predecessor.

The permanent crowding out of small manufacturing capital and the tendency for big business to become bigger and bigger are the well-noted legacies of that more recent experience. In view of what has already been said for the European countries, this seems a rather obvious and predictable outcome. At the same time, however, it must be remembered that, in stark contrast to Britain, for example, the United States placed great emphasis on the mobilization of small-scale capacity. The smaller war plants, as they were officially known, became an integral part of the system of military supply. In practice though their contribution was necessarily marginal since the top 500 corporations alone received 80 per cent of the prime contracts (Bernstein 1967: 162). Given the astounding increases in industrial output between 1940 and 1945, it takes little effort to appreciate the significance of that statistic for the growth of big business.[18] Indeed, as it suggests, the war agencies were granting dominant firms much larger shares of production than they had ever enjoyed in times of peace (Beckman 1944; Bernstein 1967; Vatter 1980). By contrast, small business was placed in the contradictory position of being mobilized for the national effort, yet denied sufficient orders for survival.

Ironically, it was this discrepancy between administrative principle and practice which served to politicize small business and to secure it a place in post-war policy – at the very moment when its economic base was being permanently eroded. This then was one further, if distinctively American, legacy of the war economy. Thanks to the world struggle, the historic importance of small business ideology to the United States had finally become an infrastructural reality, a point I shall return to in the final chapter.

This brief outline was intended to suggest and highlight ways in which the state's importance for capitalist development might be equally applicable to the United States. No doubt, as we have seen for Europe, the significance of the state is not restricted to those major 'reorganization episodes' of war. But I have presented sufficient indications here to cast doubt on the 'exceptionalism' of the United States. At the very least they force us to consider the possibility that, even in that bastion of the free market, the political–military impetus to industrial giantism has been paramount.


## Conclusion

We have travelled some distance in time and space in response to our initial question: Why has small capital been crowded out in most industrial economies? This chapter has set about that task by endeavouring to illustrate and to explain the state's formative role in the development of big business. Thus, it was not what governments failed to do for small capital, but rather what they did to favour large capital that mattered.

Stated more generally, the main argument has been that as states have responded to challenges emanating from the sphere of geopolitical and military relations, they have become major protagonists in the making of 'mature' capitalism. It must be said of course that any pattern of development is composed of many intricately connected elements and that perhaps no single one of these can ever claim exclusive weight. Nevertheless, this does not obviate the need to assign priorities. Hence, if the preceding analysis is accepted, it would seem that historically the concentration 'imperative' is linked more strongly to politics than to markets, and more clearly to the contest of states than to the competition of enterprises. It is above all the external challenges to state power – whether the threat of invasion, the crisis of defeat or the desire to act efficaciously in the international system – that have typically prompted rulers to rationalize their productive structures in more or less calculated ways.

Overall, then, my analysis suggests a primary and dynamic role for interstate relations in the determination of economic and political relations within nations. This has obvious implications for theories of the state's relation to capitalism. For it ties one of the most formative experiences in the making of twentieth-century capitalism to a sphere of activity quite independent of the power of capital. As the evolving literature on states makes clear (see Hall 1986: 1–21), it is precisely this international system which constitutes an autonomous arena of social action. To the extent that the rationalizing activity of states flows from that arena, it is therefore irreducible to capitalism. Consequently, it may well be that the logic of conventional theories needs to be reversed. For, as is well known, in these accounts the compulsive logic of economic relations creates a world dominated by big business which in turn dominates the state. In getting behind the present, however, we have seen how national political agencies have themselves contributed independently to the development of that world. In the process, it was not states undertaking functions for capital that seemed paramount, but the way in which capital has been called on to undertake tasks for the state.

If there is a single conclusion to the chapter as a whole, it is that capitalist development is by and large neutral about economic forms. Politics is not. The dispersed economy is therefore no mere exception to the Fordist rule, for no such rule exists. Just as there is nothing necessary about the general decline of small-scale production, so conversely, no capitalist law of motion, no industrial logic makes the spread and triumph of giantism irresistible. It does indeed depend significantly on what states do. Does this mean that small business can be re-created? Can the Italian model be replicated? If so, do its advantages outweigh possible disadvantages? These are the questions we must now take up in the final chapter.

# 9

# Re-creating micro capitalism

As in military matters, so in economic ones it once seemed that the states which did best were those which could mobilize capacity on a grand scale. In retrospect that equation was far too simple. The military victors of yesteryear are not the commercial conquerors of today. In a world where 'Japan, with its substantial small firm sector, flourishes' and 'Great Britain, with its highly concentrated economy, languishes', the relation between giantism and economic success is far from clear (Piore and Sabel 1984: 20). What is clear is that since the last world war and partly in consequence, the conditions of growth have been greatly altered and complicated by two developments: the establishment of a tightly integrated world economy and the emergence of a highly organized working class. This means that the days of the closed economy and of working class docility are over. States need to be effective in the international arena and this places a premium not on the size of industrial units, but on cohesive domestic relations which allow for flexible responses to rapidly changing markets.

While there can be no ready-made formula for achieving this combination, it appears that presently only two main possibilities exist. States can either travel the high road of corporatism, eliciting adjustive behaviour on the part of trade unions by building collaborative relations into their political systems, or they can pursue the low road of 'dualism', eschewing trade union participation by building such relations into the economic system itself. As we have seen, this was the 'solution' the Italian state – or rather its political managers – stumbled upon while pushing dispersion for political and social reasons.

Now it is generally agreed that big business corporatism and micro-capitalist dualism represent two extreme solutions – the one eliciting maximum participation of workers as citizens, the other revivifying a classical capitalist order of compulsive cooperation. It is also claimed that as the less competitive nation-states struggle to meet the costs of economic change and the crisis of social integration, there will be increasing pressure to opt for one of these outcomes (see Goldthorpe 1984). In view of that likelihood, it becomes important to ask whether the Italian recipe is of use to others and just what sort of solution it presents. Are the ingredients so special as to render futile all attempts to reproduce it? In particular, might the so-called 'small' business policies currently available in the United Kingdom and the United States, for example, eventually produce similar results? More generally, is extensive micro capitalism likely to square with the vision of social order such political economies uphold, as merely one more recipe for reproducing the rampant individualism that liberal democracies have not yet outgrown?

Taking up each of these issues, this chapter concludes the study on a practical note. It considers the lessons that Italy has to offer those countries which may seek to extend the 'dualist' track. Reviewing the arguments for and against the possibility of replication, I suggest that the main impediments to the resurgence of micro capitalism lie not so much in preconditions of social structure but in the conceptions of the small firm and the model of political economy that inform current policies. These two points are illustrated respectively with examples from America and Britain.

## The relative importance of state and social structure

Over the past decade, as markets for mass production have contracted, as the recession has deepened and unemployment soared, governments in many western democracies have begun to take a lively interest in ways of increasing the population of small firms (see Storey 1983). Whether small firms can offer solutions to such problems is, in the light of the Italian experience, not at issue. The important question is whether it is possible to re-create micro capitalism on an extensive scale in economies already dominated by big business. Can we be certain that what the state does will matter to the outcome? Or do these countries – in particular, America and Britain – lack certain features of social structure without which state activity is bound to fail?

Posing the problem thus forces us to consider the relative

importance of state and social structure. The question is how best to proceed? We will not learn much from countries like the United Kingdom whose small business measures are far too recent to permit any meaningful assessment. What then of the United States? From a superficial glance at the American experience it is tempting to conclude that it is not what the state does but what it has to work with that matters. For despite specific small business legislation and programmes stretching back over three decades, America's small manufacturing sector – already significantly reduced by 1945 – has not simply failed to expand. It has steadily declined. As we shall see, however, the matter is not so easily resolved since the conclusion rests on false premises. Indeed, the closer we examine those programmes, the more doubtful it becomes that the United States has a 'small' business policy at all!

The best way to proceed then is to revisit the home of micro capitalism and to identify what it is that is distinctive about the Italian recipe. At the outset we can acknowledge the obvious point that what the state can create is limited by the resources available in the first place. Certainly in terms of the sheer numbers and diffusion of petite producers in 1945, the Italians had a head start over the British and the Americans with their highly concentrated ownership patterns. A case might also be made that the social structure in which Italian producers are embedded confers additional advantages. Is it possible though to uphold the much stronger claim that there are indispensable preconditions in social structure which limit emulation of the Italian model (see, for example, Piore and Berger 1980: 9)? This view, I shall argue, tends to exaggerate the importance of nationally specific resources and, in some respects, to confuse preconditions with consequences.

### *Mezzadria* and artisan traditions

As we saw in chapter 2, small firms are abundant throughout the Italian peninsula, but they are especially characteristic of the industrial structure of Italy's central and north-eastern regions. This distinctiveness of the 'third' Italy has prompted a search for the common features of social structure which might facilitate entrepreneurship and the formation of new firms. In the ensuing research, two principal factors have been emphasized: the role of share-cropping agriculture and of artisan traditions in providing a reservoir of technical skill, entrepreneurial talent and family labour (Paci 1982).

Paci has suggested that diffuse industrialization finds its social basis above all in the *mezzadria* (share-cropping) system of agriculture which survived longer in the third Italy than elsewhere, in some parts until after the last war. This form of family-sized tenancy has supposedly acted as a forcing ground for small entrepreneurship in three main ways: by furnishing a mechanism for acquiring managerial experience; by transmitting technical skills; and by exploiting the pooled resources of the extended family unit (Paci 1982). A parallel role has been suggested for the presence of a long-established urban artisanry whose remarkable technical skills and innovative capacities received constant stimulation from the highly variegated tastes of a discerning landowning and professional clientele which spent its agricultural rents in the cities (Bamford 1984). Here too it would seem that the tradition of family enterprise, the propensity to work in and as a family unit, has acted as an historic conveyor belt for the craft principles and entrepreneurial spirit vital to the workshop economy.

Now if the familial organization of agriculture and craft skills were preconditions for small firm formation, then we would expect to find strong evidence of this in the data on intra- or inter-generational mobility. If there is such a relationship however, the causal links are not at all direct. Indeed, there is virtually no support for the hypothesized passage from sharecropper (or sons thereof) to independent entrepreneur (see Tousijn 1980; Bagnasco and Pini 1981). The role of artisan enterprise, while much more clearly reflected in the data, is not by any means overwhelming. What is particularly striking about the mobility data – whether at national, regional or sectoral level – is the significant proportion of small industrialists and independent artisans who were formerly skilled factory workers or of working class background. Again and again, the results show a consistently high 'working class' factor in the generation of small industry (see, for example, Ministero dell'Industria 1963: 465; Frijeni and Tousijn 1976). Moreover, that pattern extends well beyond the traditional artisan homeland of the 'third' Italy. In Lombardy, centre of heavy manufacturing in the 'first' Italy, where the bulk of artisan concerns have emerged since the last war, an astonishing 80 per cent of the owners operating in the 1970s were formerly wage earners, chiefly in the mass production or craft sectors of industry (Giunta Regionale della Lombardia 1974: 40, 234).

The significance of this data is clear: the routes to independence and the means of acquiring the necessary skills for it are not the monopoly of any one organizational form. Indeed, given the heterogeneity of the small firm sector itself – whether in degree of familialism, organization of production, or links with the market – it would be surprising if access to economic autonomy were so circumscribed. Moreover, the routes by which skill is acquired are no more clearly defined than are the paths to entrepreneurship. As Solinas (1982: 338) concludes from the career patterns of workers in Carpi's knitwear industry, 'Progress from semi-skilled to the craft level may be achieved by advance within a large firm, or between small firms, or by a sequence of changes between firms of different size.'

It may be that Italy is unusually blessed with traditions of familialism and craftsmanship and that these resources have been intensively mobilized for micro-capitalist production. But from the evidence indicated above, the most we can conclude is that their relationship is one of 'elective affinity', not that the resources in question are indispensable ingredients for that outcome.

If small firm formation is not restricted by special features of social structure, can the same be said of the way such an economy works once in place? Some writers have argued that the success of Italy's flexible economy is bound up with the social relations of community and that these tend to colour, rather than limit, its significance for other countries (Piore and Sabel 1983; 1984).[1] Since this touches on a crucial ingredient of the Italian recipe, let us consider it more closely.

### The social cohesion of flexible production

The popular image of small capital as deeply disorganized, in the sense of being predicated on 'competitive individualistic atomized markets', does not square well with the Italian regime of flexible production. For one thing, the 'territoriality' of the craft economy – dense regional conglomerations of firms specializing in one industrial sector – pulls the whole structure together in important ways. So too does the extensive collaboration that has come to characterize the relations both among and within small enterprise. Two close observers of this regime, Piore and Sabel (1983: 404), describe the defining characteristics of the small Italian firm thus: 'close collaboration between manufacturer and client; close collaboration between different groups within the firm, between the firm and its neighbours; and, as a corollary to these, general-purpose machines and a broadly skilled workforce'.

It appears then that the success of small-scale production depends on a degree of collectivism inconceivable in the orthodox understanding of small capital. This takes a variety of forms, from consultation on technical matters, to sharing the costs of new innovations, to guaranteeing each other orders to disperse the risks of investment in sophisticated technologies. As Piore and Sabel describe it, the mutual dependence of specialist producers is rather like the collegial relation between good university teachers who depend on the help of their neighbours with complementary specialties: 'each firm is jealous of its autonomy and proud of its capacities, but each is fully conscious that its success and even its survival are linked to the collective efforts of the group to which it belongs' (1983: 400–1).

Similar considerations govern the relations between skilled workers, technicians and owners within the small firm itself where the division of labour is extremely fluid, and where close collaboration between workers with different kinds of expertise is essential to the entire productive process (Brusco and Sabel 1981; Solinas 1982).

To these observations, we can add a third which again highlights the collective nature of the small producer regime: the numerous joint ventures, mentioned in chapter 4, which achieve for small firms economies of scale in administration, purchasing and marketing. As in Japan, these consortia, cooperatives and other associations of small producers organize marketing, bulk buy raw materials, prepare the pay slips, accounts and taxes, and negotiate cheap loans for their members. The building of industrial estates or 'parks' to house small workshops operating common facilities is one further development along these lines. And again, as in Japan (from whence the Italians not infrequently drew inspiration), many of these ventures have been initiated with the backing of national and local governments, including a notable input from the Communist administration.

The ability to cooperate with competitors is thus one important ingredient in the success story of Italian micro capitalism. How can it be explained? Generalizing, Piore and Sabel have argued that the collaborative regime of flexible production depends on prior socialization into some form of community, whether ethnic, political or religious (1984: 266, 278). But given the close parallels with the Japanese economy (Dore 1986), particularly the relationships between the corporations and their small flexible suppliers (see Friedman 1983), this seems doubtful. Indeed it may well be that 'solidarity and communitarianism' are consequences rather than causes of small firm organization (see Bonacich and Modell 1980).

It is possible to explain the collaborative character of craft production without recourse to prior conceptions of community. Basically, two elements are involved: first, a public infrastructure encouraging cooperative efforts (which is a function of politics); and second, the organization of specialist production (which is a function of market strategy). The first point has already been discussed. As to the second, suffice to recall that the core of craft production is continuous innovation. As Piore and Sabel themselves point out, it is the ability to constantly redesign products and to quickly reshape and rearrange the productive process that goes to the heart of its competitive strategy. Thus, whereas in mass production the definition of the product is fixed and the main obsession is to produce as much as possible at the lowest cost, in flexible production the strategy is completely reversed. Here, firms must permanently anticipate and accommodate change by continuous product differentiation. It is this strategic commitment to continuous innovation, to the ceaseless development of 'new product ideas into actual market offerings' that pushes the flexible producer to maximize cooperation both within the firm and with its specialist neighbours (Friedman 1983: 354–5).

We have, then, an explanation for social cooperation that does not depend solely on the fertility of Italian soil; the strategy of flexible production provides the driving force while infrastructure furnishes the material means. For the sake of completeness, we could add that settlement patterns (regional conglomerations) supply the opportunity. From this, incidentally, flows another feature of the small firm economy which, according to the 'dualist' interpretation, was not supposed to happen: its increasing cooperation with trade unions. Both the regional density and close proximity of productive units, organized into industrial estates, have steadily enhanced the presence of a trade union movement more committed to class than to sectional advantages. In some areas and sectors – the mechanical engineering industry in Emilia Romagna, for instance – the 'organized' sector extends right down to firms with thirty employees (Capecchi and Pugliese 1978; Brusco 1982). Even the tiniest artisan firms with fewer than fifteen employees, exempt by law from the more stringent labour legislation, have gradually extended wage agreements with unions. Whatever the reasons for these unanticipated developments – political in the case of trade unions, economic in the case of small employers (Federlombarda

1977: 64–81; Piore and Sabel 1983: 409–10) – the central point to emphasize is that the successful small firm economy thrives on a degree of collectivism that politicians and most academics outside Italy have thus far overlooked.

From this excursion into the economy of cooperation, we can extract two main points and begin to anticipate their wider significance. First, the small firm sector works best when competition is restrained by cooperation. As Piore and Sabel observe, in so far as the latter is vital to its success, 'flexible specialization works by violating one of the assumptions of classical political economy: that the economy is separate from society' (1984: 275). As we will see, however, this adds up to a world very different from the one envisaged and endorsed in the policies of the British government.

The second point to be made is that cooperative relations stem from organizational features of politics and market. They are not by any means restricted to a 'culture of community'. If this extends the significance of the Italian model, it also colours it in important ways: it is not that cooperation is impossibly difficult to achieve outside Italy, but that it is an outcome much at odds with the vision of industrial order that informs the political economy of 'deregulation'. To rephrase the point we must add to Piore and Sabel's previous observation. Micro capitalism works also by violating a much more central assumption of classical political economy: that the economy is separate from the power of politicians. One vital consequence of that power, discussed earlier, is the permanent provisioning of a collective infrastructure. This too has important implications for countries like Britain which have begun to champion small business initiatives in the wider cause of a deregulated economy. But there is an even stronger consequence of that political power, an anathema to marketeers, which has featured at the core of this book: the capacity to regulate the economy by shaping its activities in crucial ways. This goes to the very heart of the Italian recipe and returns us once again to the state.

## Politics as recognition and regulation

If the previous analysis is correct, then social structure will be less important in the long run than what national governments do to resuscitate or extend small-scale production. When contrasted with the Italian approach, however, it will be shown that current attempts in that direction, in both the United States and Britain, are bound to yield little since they eschew the political recognition and regulation that underlies much of the micro-capitalist order.

That point has been amply illustrated throughout the book. Here we need merely to foreground its significance by re-emphasizing that most remarkable feature of the Italian phenomenon: the fact that the vast majority of Italian firms are born small *and destined to remain small*. As we saw in chapter 2, Italian firms tend to share economic space rather than to vertically integrate, expand or amalgamate. One manifestation of that tendency is the proliferation of subcontracting arrangements within the small firm population – not just when orders are booming, but as a matter of routine practice. One answer to that puzzle was indicated in chapter 4. By remaining small, firms retain the special benefits that they would otherwise lose by expanding. As a special category in Italian law, small capital is thus the target of numerous privileges, exemptions and state-provided benefits – qualifications for which are crucially dependent on firm size (typically defined by number of workers employed).[2] The fact that the state recognizes small business as a special and separate category of economic activity and that it backs up that recognition with a precise targeting of benefits is thus what sets Italy apart from all other countries, with the single exception of Japan. It is highly significant that Japan, the only other major industrial country which matches Italy in this regard, legally specifying size limits for the purpose of extensive small business assistance, is also abundantly endowed with petite enterprise.[3]

## Lessons for America and Britain

This then can be considered as the major lesson of the Italian experience. The significance of such a regulatory system is that it not only ensures a constant replenishment of the small firm sector, but also encourages the small to remain small. If other countries have failed to find, adopt or stumble upon the Italian solution, this is in large part because they cannot agree on what constitutes a small business. But this is not simply a conceptual difficulty. It is also a cultural and political problem.

It is political in the sense that such a system involves a radical departure from market principles in regulation of the economy, hence an 'extreme' solution for advocates of deregulation. To this one might add that few governments in big business cultures would be prepared to counter the resistance mounted by the corporate sector against attempts to differentiate the entrepreneurial universe. In Italy and Japan special conditions have operated to help surmount or pre-empt such obstacles. As we saw in chapter 7, the constitution of a power base independent of big capital enabled the Italian political leadership to counter the effects of that opposition. In Japan, no such resistance has ever been mounted. The reason is simple. Despite the close relationship between the state and the corporations, the latter are structurally implicated in the fortunes of the small firm sector, via both widespread subcontracting links and extensive equity ties with a myriad of suppliers. Indeed so vital are these arrangements to Japanese industry that the state has developed over the last thirty years a strict set of codes to prevent abuse of superior bargaining positions. The result is a very tight regulation of relations between client enterprises and their subcontractor suppliers (see Vepa 1971; JETRO 1981).

There is also a cultural dimension to the problem in the sense that – in the United States and the United Kingdom at least – national economic history has furnished little in the way of models for valorizing small enterprise as a positive social and economic force in its own right.

To illustrate these points, we turn to two national settings where the development of Fordism has gone furthest, one in which small business offerings have long been vaunted (America), the other where these have only recently come into vogue (Britain).

### The United States: contradictory targets

Like Italy, America developed specific programmes for small business soon after the last war. In the United States, however, these initiatives arose in an attempt on the part of the federal government to redress the damage wrought by the war economy. Hence the curious inclusion within the Small Business Administration's (SBA) founding objectives that it would 'seek to insure the participation of small business enterprises in war, or mobilization of our economy for war' (cited in Carson 1973: 13). With the establishment of the SBA in 1953, the government thereby acknowledged the claim of small industry that its development had been compromised by the war agencies' preferential treatment for big business in allocating contracts. Thus, the birth of that agency was less a sign of client strength than a symptom of its decline, a situation which could only weaken the symbolic clout of a country determined to export its free enterprise ideology abroad.

The very title of the SBA, however, is in many respects a misnomer. Although its loan schemes are generous and its managerial and educational programmes sophisticated (Thompson and Leyden 1983), the fact is that most of the measures proposed to aid small enterprise 'have little or no direct relevance to the great majority of firms commonly included in the category of small business' (Phillips 1958: 88). This point is readily demonstrated in the SBA's definition of what counts as a small business in the manufacturing sector. Apart from being 'independently owned and operated, not dominant in its field', any firm with up to 1,500 employees is eligible for assistance! Clearly this renders the concept of small business altogether meaningless. One may well doubt the federal agency's small business credentials when in the 1980s American policy-makers are still debating the criteria for defining it; when almost half the states use no definition at all; when government agencies within the same state use conflicting definitions; and when most of these do so without any rationale. As the authors of these findings tellingly conclude: 'How can we be effective in assisting the small business sector if we do not know what it is?' (Nappi and Vora 1980: 26).

Why then is the task so difficult? Why has an agency, ostensibly geared to the needs of small capital, ended up with such a top-heavy definition? With the Italian approach very much in mind, Piore and Sabel go to the heart of the matter in suggesting that American policy makers lack the 'intellectual categories' in which to conceive of a form of business activity that achieves economic dynamism on a small scale (1983: 419). It is possible to push that point further by noting that economic and cultural history has furnished two contrasting models of independent business, each of which figures in the policies of the SBA. The first is based on the classical idea of peasant self-sufficiency and personal autonomy of the sort once valued by the Republican freeholder and early European immigrant (Berthoff 1980). Its closest contemporary equivalent would be the shopkeeper or provider of services, sectors where the American small business ethic still has a materiality and social resonance.

The second model of independence is the polar opposite. Drawing heavily upon the national myths concerning universal opportunity, the possibility of ever-upward economic mobility through one's own efforts, it converges with the notion of dynamic entrepreneurship. In this model, independence becomes incompatible with smallness, since it is only through ceaseless striving and rational restlessness – to grow and expand – that economic success can be verified (see Carson 1973: 33; Piore and Sabel 1983: 419). Its closest contemporary equivalent is probably the computer entrepreneur who, from modest beginnings, reaches the heights of the corporate sector.

In industry at least, the term 'small' is therefore little more than a catchword, a term which emerged historically simply to express a contrast with aggregations of capital and enterprise resulting in the cartel or trust (Phillips 1958: 90; Carson 1973: 74). Indeed, whether one examines the Congressional debates on anti-trust legislation, or the SBA programmes, or even the claims of captains of commerce and industry, 'small' is little more than a proxy for forms of enterprise that are carried forward by the skills, energy and daring of the independent entrepreneur: typically, it stands for both the large firm in embryo and the 'onetime small business grown commendably successful' (Berthoff 1980: 36).

Confronted with these two contradictory models, the SBA consequently 'found it difficult to comprehend, within a single definition of smallness, both the economic dynamism of the true entrepreneur and the classical stability of the artisan or shopkeeper' (Berthoff 1980: 40). One may venture, however, that the opposition between 'personal autonomy' and 'dynamic entrepreneurship' found an outcome in the clear bifurcation of SBA policy. Within retail and services, it is the genuinely small enterprise which receives federal support. In manufacturing industry, however, the emphasis is on encouraging 'relatively' small manufacturers to become even bigger, 'to the point where', as Berthoff comments, 'they might begin to be serious rivals of the established giants' (1980: 40–1).

The problem, then, is not that the United States lacks a positive conception of independent enterprise. The independent enterprise is popularly approved and admired – but less for what it *is* than for what, if successful, it is bound to *become*. Since this notion is also pervasive among small business groups, it is doubtful that a constituency for the kind of solution adopted by Italy exists. In a country which pioneered the mass production corporation, this is perhaps not surprising. Despite the break up of mass product markets, and despite signs of 'decentralizing' experiments within the corporate sector, it seems that Fordism still remains a powerful paradigm. It may well be, as Piore and Sabel's (1984) study suggests, that the historical success of Fordism in the United States will make that country's future 'hostage to its past'.

## The United Kingdom: *incongruous means and ends*

Whereas American policy valorizes an entity which it is inherently incapable of recognizing, let alone encouraging, in British programmes that contradiction tends to be reversed. As I shall presently suggest, the major problem for British government lies not so much in identifying an appropriate target for assistance (although this is far from settled). Rather, it consists in the incongruity of means (regeneration of small enterprise) and ends (extension of market principles).

Britain is unusual in having both the smallest small business sector in the developed capitalist world (Bolton Report 1971), and in being one of the latest starters in launching a small business programme. What counts as a small business? In a country where politicians have for the most part remained oblivious to small enterprise (Bolton Report 1971), the conceptual problem was quickly resolved by a statistical convenience. Although the size of manufacturing firms eligible for assistance ranges widely between 20 and 1,000 employees, most schemes tend to fasten on a category of enterprise, traditionally defined by the collector of statistics, with a maximum threshold of 200 employees.

As to preferential treatment for small enterprise, although widely identified with the Thatcher regime, this policy did not suddenly spring to life after 1979. The Conservatives merely took over the heritage of the previous Labour administration (Beesley and Wilson 1984: 123–4), pushed the trend further and donned the small business mantle with a partisan flourish. To the existing schemes covering training and advisory services, employment subsidies and export assistance, the policy of the present government has added three novel touches. First, it stresses the need to encourage the birth of small firms (not simply their survival and expansion). This has been accompanied by an extensive promotional campaign to resell the public on the virtues of self-employment (Beesley and Wilson 1984). Second, it identifies small business propagation with a wider non–interventionist policy. This finds extreme expression in the concept of 'enterprise zones', originally designated as 'zones of fairly shameless free enterprise . . . outside the scope of United Kingdom taxes, social services, industrial and other regulations' (cited in Stanworth and Curran 1984: 145). Although the full-blown version has been watered down in practice, it nicely captures the Lone Ranger conception of the small British firm in government thinking. The third and perhaps the boldest novelty (for Britain at least) is the introduction of direct financial assistance. Most important under this rubric is the Loan Guarantee Scheme under which the state guarantees a proportion of the loans to small enterprise from financial institutions. So popular was this measure, however, that the government responded not by increasing assistance, but by making it more costly to obtain, increasing premiums and reducing the proportion of the loan guaranteed from 80 to 70 per cent. In Britain, at least, a small business loan is a very expensive privilege (Woodcock 1986: 44).

The reasons for this reluctant commitment coupled with constant celebration of the virtues of small enterprise are not too difficult to discern. The Thatcher government is not primarily interested in regenerating a small business sector *per se*, nor indeed in propagating small industry throughout the economy. Rather, it seeks to re-create an economic culture purged of 'collectivist' elements, a culture which fits its philosophical vision of maximum market discipline and minimum state regulation. To the extent that small enterprise can help realize this wider project to 'depoliticize' the economy, it is thus worth promoting (but not too much).

However, if we have learned one lesson from the Italian case, it is surely that a small business solution is not an individualistic or market solution. On the contrary, securing it requires a good deal of intervention from above and, one might add, a considerable degree of 'collectivism' from below. In this light, the Conservatives' small firm policy is incongruent with the wider ends pursued. It is precisely for this reason that such a policy is misconceived and unlikely to succeed in its present form.

Since there are really two points here, it is important to be clear about them. The argument is that Britain's small business strategy is misconceived in two main areas: one regarding the state's relation to the economy; the other concerning the social relations of small-scale production itself. On the first, it needs to be stressed that contrary to current government understanding, the small firm 'solution' is not a recipe for the state's retreat from the market. If anything, the reverse is true, especially for Britain where the state has a much narrower base to work with. Indeed, in contexts like the British one – where work has long been carried out in bureaucratic organizations, where craft skills have largely been creamed off by Fordist techniques and where family members tend to strike out on individual career paths – there may be much less incentive or opportunity for people to aspire to economic independence. The significance of this point is not that small firm regeneration is impossible.[4] It is simply that the propagation of small enterprise is bound to be a long-term venture, requiring in turn a long-term commitment from the state on a number of fronts, not least that of education and finance.

. The second weakness – which has much more specific policy implications – stems from an antiquated stereotype of small-scale production reminiscent of nineteenth-century classical capitalism. Conceived as a means of widening the sphere of self-help and pushing back the frontiers of collective provisioning, the small firm in the Conservative project has little in common with the craft economy of the late twentieth century. As we have seen for Italy, and as others have reported for Japan, the core of modern micro capitalism is not competitive individualism but collective endeavour (Vepa 1971; Piore and Sabel 1984). It is not the Lone Rangers of the 'enterprise zone', but the collaborators of the 'industrial estate' who best capture its distinctive spirit. In policy terms, this implies *inter alia* infrastructural support for cooperative efforts of the kind mentioned earlier.

Re-creating micro capitalism is thus no policy for the Lone Ranger. On the contrary, it requires intensive cooperation from below and extensive regulation from above. In principle, that task clearly challenges the commitment to a *laissez-faire* Britain. In practice, however, to judge by the record thus far, we are more likely to see its confirmation.

## Conclusion

There is no conclusion. We do not know what kind of world we are likely to inhabit tomorrow. But if the preceding analysis is accepted, then the possibility of re-creating micro capitalism is by no means excluded. The irony is that the Fordist cultures most in need of the flexibility that craft production allows are those whose political economies are the least receptive.

No doubt there are other ways of achieving that flexibility, as the national varieties of corporatism indicate. But even these solutions should not be romanticized. Apart from being very tricky to transpose to other settings, each has its own disadvantages. Sweden, for instance, disperses the costs of economic adjustment externally, on to a non-unionized, low-wage periphery. To this extent, as Vogler (1985: 32) points out, 'The living standards of the whole Swedish working class are . . . subsidised by lower wages in the less developed countries.' Even the micro-corporatist arrangements that operate in Japan are not without costs. While the lifetime employment principle allows considerable corporate flexibility (Dore 1986), this privilege is probably only possible in a society that retires its workforce at fifty-five and – let us not forget – its women on marriage.

None of these observations, however, detract from the fundamental principle of their success: social cohesion is their life-blood. But it is no less true for micro-capitalist 'dualism'. The Italian solution fares better only in allowing a wider distribution of skills, property and investment decisions. While also demonstrating the capacity to pay decent, even high, wages and to create rather than shed employment, it is of course no match for the trade union protection that corporatism allows – at least not yet. But the signs are that this may be changing. As we have seen for Italy, small capital is not immune to 'primary' sector guarantees. Even in Japan, the lifetime employment principle has diffused right down to the small firm sector (Vepa 1971: 72; Dore 1986: 113).

From this view, then, the choice between the high road of big business corporatism and the low road of micro-capitalist 'dualism' begins to look much less sharply defined than commonly supposed. Either way, we must accept there is no road back to the stateless economy.

# Appendix I

Table A  Loans receiving interest subsidy, discount and state guarantee, 1953–1976

| | Subsidized loans[a] | | | | Discounted loans[b] | | | | State guaranteed loans | | | |
| | Ordinary | | Disaster | | Ordinary | | Disaster | | Ordinary | | Disaster | |
| Year | No. | Amount[c] | No. | Amount | No. | Amount | No. | Amount | No. | Amount | No. | Amount |
|---|---|---|---|---|---|---|---|---|---|---|---|---|
| 1953 | 270 | 415,768 | — | — | 172 | 257,122 | — | — | — | — | — | — |
| 1954 | 1,836 | 2,803,996 | — | — | 822 | 1,274,074 | — | — | — | — | — | — |
| 1955 | 2,658 | 4,288,273 | — | — | 1,870 | 2,960,607 | — | — | — | — | — | — |
| 1956 | 2,966 | 4,763,141 | — | — | 1,751 | 2,824,789 | — | — | — | — | — | — |
| 1957 | 4,393 | 7,330,417 | — | — | 3,294 | 5,413,834 | — | — | — | — | — | — |
| 1958 | 6,483 | 12,035,772 | — | — | 4,023 | 7,284,205 | — | — | — | — | — | — |
| 1959 | 7,900 | 16,450,716 | — | — | 3,696 | 7,423,805 | — | — | — | — | — | — |
| 1960 | 10,532 | 25,188,831 | — | — | 5,048 | 12,099,378 | — | — | — | — | — | — |
| 1961 | 15,069 | 38,994,292 | — | — | 2,458 | 5,671,487 | — | — | — | — | — | — |
| 1962 | 15,396 | 42,155,969 | — | — | 3,592 | 8,887,850 | — | — | — | — | — | — |
| 1963 | 14,682 | 45,137,308 | — | — | 4,454 | 12,628,537 | — | — | — | — | — | — |

| | | | | | | | | | | | | |
|---|---|---|---|---|---|---|---|---|---|---|---|---|
| 1964 | 12,398 | 38,786,747 | — | — | 3,368 | 9,862,290 | — | — | — | — | — | — |
| 1965 | 8,699 | 27,072,729 | — | — | 5,413 | 16,355,987 | — | — | — | — | — | — |
| 1966 | 5,572 | 17,904,675 | 131 | 707,539 | 2,315 | 7,169,449 | 31 | 187,794 | 55 | 143,552 | 64 | 304,410 |
| 1967 | 18,494 | 70,652,341 | 3,049 | 16,549,336 | 5,373 | 20,991,543 | 337 | 1,789,256 | 665 | 2,755,883 | 2,633 | 14,898,806 |
| 1968 | 24,263 | 120,008,606 | 164 | 1,090,692 | 5,039 | 24,198,335 | 16 | 115,800 | 1,634 | 8,647,847 | 131 | 904,900 |
| 1969 | 19,625 | 104,330,238 | 249 | 2,091,120 | 3,298 | 17,095,324 | — | — | 1,944 | 11,214,882 | 170 | 1,643,290 |
| 1970 | 16,525 | 92,630,640 | 48 | 761,900 | 2,837 | 16,068,656 | — | — | 1,387 | 8,732,045 | 33 | 723,600 |
| 1971 | 20,016 | 114,591,359 | 641 | 3,811,203 | 4,668 | 26,416,296 | 144 | 1,476,500 | 1,684 | 11,031,240 | 633 | 3,772,503 |
| 1972 | 25,969 | 182,548,582 | 19 | 140,300 | 3,911 | 26,467,283 | 3 | 38,000 | 2,323 | 17,908,785 | 19 | 140,300 |
| 1973 | 40,540 | 312,197,222 | 593 | 3,597,087 | 3,898 | 31,782,704 | 475 | 2,963,741 | 4,494 | 37,461,576 | 400 | 2,405,185 |
| 1974 | 17,796 | 148,745,423 | 169 | 1,506,712 | 3,937 | 30,596,088 | 147 | 1,314,212 | 2,386 | 21,496,513 | 89 | 909,914 |
| 1975 | 30,983 | 319,573,601 | 38 | 485,322 | 6,898 | 64,792,978 | 39 | 510,322 | 4,007 | 43,385,429 | 15 | 166,300 |
| 1976 | 47,052 | 605,984,705 | 65 | 1,677,154 | 8,688 | 105,742,655 | 13 | 271,267 | 6,399 | 83,670,607 | 57 | 1,564,800 |
| Total | 370,117 | 2,354,591,351 | 5,166 | 32,818,365 | 90,323 | 464,266,074 | 1,205 | 8,666,892 | 26,978 | 246,448,359 | 4,244 | 27,434,008 |

[a] Disaster and Guaranteed loans are included in the Subsidized loan operations.

[b] Clear of interest.

[c] Amount in thousands of lire.

Source: Artigiancassa, *Bilancio 1976* (1977: table 1).

Table B   Value of soft loans (thousands of lire)

| Value | No. | % | Amount | % | Average value |
|---|---|---|---|---|---|
| Up to L.10 million | 317,768 | 84.67 | 1,420,758,142 | 59.51 | 4,471 |
| L.10–15 million | 38,865 | 10.36 | 540,136,094 | 22.63 | 13,897 |
| L.15–20 million | 6,953 | 1.85 | 128,543,516 | 5.38 | 18,487 |
| More than L.20 million | 11,697 | 3.12 | 297,971,964 | 12.48 | 25,474 |
| Total | 375,283 | 100.00 | 2,387,409,716 | 100.00 | 6,361 |
| *Average value* | | | *6,361* | | |

*Source*: Aritigiancassa, *Bilancio 1976* (1977: table 10).

Table C   Artisan firms financed in relation to total sectoral growth

| | 1951 | 1971 | 1961 | 1971 | 1951 | 1976 |
|---|---|---|---|---|---|---|
| Firms censused | 650,700 | 877,400 | 742,200 | 877,400 | 650,700 | 1,057,500[a] |
| Sectoral growth | 226,700 | | 131,200 | | 406,800 | |
| Firms financed[b] | 171,400 | | 119,300 | | 300,500 | |
| As a percentage of sectoral growth | 75% | | 91% | | 74% | |

[a] 1976 figure is an estimate.
[b] From 1953 onwards, being the year the basic loan scheme was put into operation.
*Sources*: ISTAT, *Annuario di statistische industriali*, 1977 edn, vol. 21 (Rome, 1978); Artigiancassa, *Bilancio*, various years.

*Table D   Distribution of soft loans and investments realized, by project type, 1953–1976 (thousands of lire)*

| Project | No. | % | Amount | % | Amount | % |
|---|---|---|---|---|---|---|
| | | Loans | | | Investments | |
| Installation of workshops | 115,254 | 30.71 | 849,322,323 | 35.57 | 1,532,332,972 | 41.6 |
| Modernization and extension of workshops | 38,389 | 10.23 | 229,108,274 | 9.60 | 369,305,015 | 9.92 |
| Machinery and equipment | 202,257 | 53.89 | 1,223,263,962 | 51.24 | 1,706,934,242 | 45.86 |
| Stock | 19,383 | 5.17 | 85,715,157 | 3.59 | 113,747,379 | 3.06 |
| Total | 375,283 | 100.00 | 2,387,409,716 | 100.00 | 3,722,319,608 | 100.00 |

*Source*: Artigiancassa, *Bialancio 1976* (1977: tables 7 and 8).

*Table E   Employment by size of establishment and region, 971*

| Region | 1–19 | 20–99 | 100–500 | 500+ | Total |
|---|---|---|---|---|---|
| | % employed in manufacturing establishments with: | | | | |
| Piedmont ⎫ Val d'Aosta ⎭ | 19.2 | 17.0 | 21.6 | 42.2 | 100 |
| Lombardy | 23.8 | 25.3 | 27.1 | 23.8 | 100 |
| Liguria | 28.9 | 16.7 | 20.3 | 34.1 | 100 |
| Trentino-Adige | 37.9 | 21.6 | 24.3 | 16.2 | 100 |
| Friuli-V. Giulia | 26.3 | 23.1 | 19.7 | 30.9 | 100 |
| Venezia | 32.1 | 27.1 | 24.6 | 16.2 | 100 |
| Emilia Romagna | 38.2 | 27.4 | 23.6 | 10.8 | 100 |
| Tuscany | 43.2 | 26.1 | 16.0 | 14.7 | 100 |
| Marche | 44.7 | 30.2 | 18.3 | 6.8 | 100 |
| Umbria | 35.2 | 19.8 | 18.1 | 26.9 | 100 |
| Latium | 38.6 | 19.2 | 22.6 | 19.6 | 100 |
| Mezzogiorno | 48.0 | 17.2 | 16.1 | 19.8 | 100 |
| Italy | 31.7 | 22.7 | 22.2 | 23.4 | 100 |

*Source*: Tassinari (1975: vol. 2, 81).

Table F    Relation between firms registered and firms financed in each region, 1971, in rank order

| Regions | Firms registered[a] as at 31 Dec. 1970 | Firms financed as at 31 Dec. 1971 | % of regional firms financed |
|---|---|---|---|
| ★Marche | 41,353 | 14,637 | 35.4 |
| ★Emilia Romagna | 121,802 | 32,478 | 26.7 |
| ★Umbria | 18,767 | 4,366 | 23.3 |
| ★Veneto | 92,799 | 20,442 | 22.1 |
| Lombardy | 185,020 | 38,008 | 20.5 |
| ★Tuscany | 96,442 | 15,216 | 15.8 |
| ★Lazio | 74,232 | 9,609 | 12.9 |
| Piedmont | 103,380 | 13,433 | 12.9 |
| ★Friuli–V. Giulia | 26,881 | 2,894 | 10.8 |
| Abruzzi | 27,880 | 2,505 | 9.0 |
| Liguria | 39,028 | 3,387 | 8.7 |
| Molise | 8,506 | 662 | 7.8 |
| Calabria | 34,311 | 2,104 | 6.1 |
| ★Trentino–Adige | 17,882 | 1,060 | 5.9 |
| Campania | 72,247 | 3,060 | 4.2 |
| Puglia | 67,566 | 2,843 | 4.2 |
| Valle d'Aosta | 2,987 | 98 | 3.2 |
| Basilicata | 11,838 | 362 | 3.1 |
| Sicily | 131,551 | 3,943 | 3.0 |
| Sardinia | 31,009 | 281 | 0.9 |
| Italy | 1,205,481 | 171,389[b] | |

★ 'Third' Italy

[a] Artisan concerns registered with provincial Chambers of Commerce in December 1970.

[b] of which 29,842 firms received two or more loans.

*Source*: Artigiancassa, *Bilancio 1971* (1972: table P).

*Table G   Regional distribution of artisan proprietors and of firms financed, 1971*

| Region | Firms financed | Artisan proprietors |
|---|---|---|
| Piedmont | 7.8 | 9.0 |
| Valle d'Aosta | 0.1 | 0.2 |
| Lombardy | 22.2 | 16.7 |
| Liguria | 2.0 | 3.3 |
| Total North-west | 32.1 | 29.2 |
| Trentino–Adige | 0.6 | 1.5 |
| Venezia | 11.9 | 7.9 |
| Friuli–V. Giulia | 1.7 | 2.4 |
| Emilia Romagna | 19.0 | 10.2 |
| Tuscany | 8.9 | 8.3 |
| Marche | 8.5 | 3.3 |
| Umbria | 2.5 | 1.6 |
| Lazio | 5.6 | 6.0 |
| Total Centre-north-east | 58.7 | 41.2 |
| Abruzzi | 1.4 | 2.2 |
| Molise | 0.4 | 0.6 |
| Campania | 1.8 | 5.6 |
| Puglia | 1.7 | 5.4 |
| Basilicata | 0.2 | 1.0 |
| Calabria | 1.2 | 2.8 |
| Sicily | 2.3 | 9.6 |
| Sardinia | 0.2 | 2.4 |
| Total South | 9.2 | 29.6 |
| Total Italy | 100.0 | 100.0 |

(Italy = 100)
*Sources*: Artigiancassa, *Bilancio 1971* (1972: table P); Barberis (1980: 58).

Table H  Destination of Mediocredito finance to the SMI by size of loan, 1953–1969 (millions of lire)

|  | up to 5 million | 5–20 million | 20–50 million | 50+ million | Total |
|---|---|---|---|---|---|
| Amount | 22,140 | 126,811 | 162,106 | 144,501 | 455,828 |
| % | 4.9 | 27.8 | 35.6 | 31.7 | 100 |

Source: CENSIS (1972: table 40).

Table I   Results of Law 623 of 1959, 1960–1970 (millions of lire)

| Years | Mezzogiorno | | | Centre-north | | | Total | | |
|---|---|---|---|---|---|---|---|---|---|
| | No. of loans | Amount | Investment | No. of loans | Amount | Investment | No. of loans | Amount | Investment |
| 1960 | 510 | 54,665 | 107,871 | 1,560 | 104,475 | 210,739 | 2,070 | 159,140 | 318,610 |
| 1961 | 602 | 72,423 | 146,955 | 1,421 | 80,166 | 168,641 | 2,023 | 152,598 | 315,596 |
| 1962 | 785 | 79,990 | 183,739 | 1,216 | 75,830 | 158,779 | 2,001 | 155,820 | 342,518 |
| 1963 | 1,056 | 125,372 | 289,489 | 1,063 | 103,035 | 151,066 | 2,119 | 228,407 | 440,555 |
| 1964 | 1,109 | 130,977 | 323,456 | 1,048 | 57,544 | 139,354 | 2,157 | 188,521 | 462,810 |
| 1965 | 836 | 106,522 | 306,131 | 823 | 110,593 | 125,653 | 1,659 | 217,115 | 431,784 |
| 1966 | 862 | 131,481 | 403,963 | 1,743 | 126,027 | 275,321 | 2,605 | 257,508 | 679,284 |
| 1967 | 660 | 157,080 | 456,696 | 1,739 | 156,112 | 332,701 | 2,399 | 313,192 | 74,316 |
| 1968 | 853 | 180,428 | 460,594 | 2,410 | 199,785 | 402,501 | 3,263 | 380,213 | 863,095 |
| 1969 | 984 | 181,688 | 415,504 | 1,441 | 134,678 | 258,908 | 2,425 | 316,366 | 674,412 |
| March 1970 | 233 | 57,997 | 124,929 | 898 | 83,360 | 156,470 | 1,131 | 141,357 | 281,399 |
| Total | 8,490 | 1,278,623 | 3,219,327 | 15,362 | 1,231,605 | 2,380,133 | 23,852 | 2,510,228 | 5,599,460 |
| Estimated new jobs: | | 314,403 | | | 404,070 | | | 718,473 | |
| Average loan value: | | 150m | | | 80m | | | 105m | |
| % of investment financed (average): | | 39 | | | 52 | | | 44.8 | |

Source: CENSIS (1972: table 43).

*Table J Regional distribution of loans and finance granted by Mediocredito Centrale under Law 949 of 1952, 1952–1960[a] (thousands of lire)*

| Regions | Loans No. | % | Amount (thousand lire) | % |
|---|---|---|---|---|
| Piedmont | 978 | 43.6 | 13,045,938 | |
| Liguria | 190 | | 3,760,084 | |
| Lombardia | 3,395 | | 51,985,742 | |
| Total North-west | 4,564 | 43.6 | 68,791,764 | 44.7 |
| Trentino-Adige | 496 | | 8,710,077 | |
| Friuli-V. Giulia | 212 | | 2,695,246 | |
| Venezia | 868 | | 12,212,222 | |
| Emilia Romagna | 1,092 | | 14,974,404 | |
| Tuscany | 647 | | 10,298,558 | |
| Marche | 325 | | 3,155,036 | |
| Umbria | 120 | | 1,349,865 | |
| Latium | 1,077 | | 15,458,268 | |
| Total Centre-north-east | 4,837 | 46.2 | 68,853,676 | 44.8 |
| Abruzzi and Molise | 140 | | 1,174,984 | |
| Campania | 368 | | 6,282,049 | |
| Puglia | 101 | | 1,488,521 | |
| Basilicata | 19 | | 144,058 | |
| Calabria | 59 | | 749,097 | |
| Sicily | 338 | | 5,049,624 | |
| Sardinia | 35 | | 1,223,089 | |
| Total South | 1,060 | 10.2 | 16,156,422 | 10.5 |
| Total Italy | 10,460 | 100.0 | 153,801,862 | 100.0 |
| *Average loan value:* | | | *14,608* | |

[a] Includes 220 loans for 4,214,766 thousand lire relating to 1960 outlays under Law 623 of 1959.
*Source*: CNEL (1961: 24).

Table K  Firms financed under Mezzogiorno laws, by plant size, 1973
(millions of lire)

| Plant size | Firms financed | | Amount obtained | |
| | no. | % | million lire | % |
| --- | --- | --- | --- | --- |
| 11–100 | 687 | 73.5 | 100,180 | 3.3 |
| 101–500 | 161 | 17.2 | 145,841 | 4.3 |
| 500+ | 87 | 9.3 | 2,827,040 | 92.0 |
| Total | 935 | 100.0 | 3,073,061 | 100.0 |

*Source*: Mediocredito Centrale (1977: vol. 1, 85, table 42).

Table L  Loans to industry granted by the Cassa per il Mezzogiorno, 1961–1971, by size of investment

| Size of investment[a] | No. of loans | Small firms' share | Finance obtained[a] | Small firms' share | Investment | Projected employment |
|---|---|---|---|---|---|---|
| up to 40m | 2,711 | | 80,981 | | 50,259 | 16,394 |
| 40.1–80m | 1,842 | 8,510 | 59,873 | 554,666 | 110,576 | 26,706 |
| 80.0–300m | 3,255 | (83.2%) | 266,431 | (14.5%) | 507,228 | 89,703 |
| 300.1–500m | 702 | | 147,381 | | 270,865 | 35,684 |
| 500.1–1,000m | 619 | | 252,190 | | 441,368 | 44,979 |
| 1,000.1–3,000m | 610 | | 653,961 | | 1,115,235 | 88,109 |
| 3,000.1–6,000m | 303 | | 719,751 | | 1,310,610 | 48,627 |
| 6,000m+ | 175 | | 1,657,553 | | 3,651,291 | 75,136 |
| Total | 10,217 | | 3,838,121 | | 7,457,432 | 425,338 |

[a] millions of lire
Source: Comitato per il Mezzogiorno (1972).

# Appendix II

## (i)  *Artisan enterprise*

In order to ascertain what proportion of artisan concerns have benefited from one or more loans over the period, one is faced with the problem of which statistical source to use as an estimate of the size and evolution of the artisanat. There are, in fact, three principal sources: the official Industrial and Commercial Census; the Chamber of Commerce Provincial Registers (used by Artigiancassa); and the *Casse Mutue* (where artisans enrol for social security benefits).

For each one of these sources, a considerably different picture emerges. Take, for example, the years 1970–1. In the latter year the Industrial Census recorded 877,422 concerns (in all sectors); in the previous year, the Chambers of Commerce registered 1,205,481 artisan units; and in 1971 the *Casse Mutue* records showed a total of 1,266,000 artisans. In any given year, the difference between the census figures and those provided by the other two sources varies from 20 to 38 per cent.

Thus, depending on which source is used to document the size of the sector, quite different estimates of the proportion of beneficiaries will ensue. This disparity occurs also in connection with the geographical distribution of artisan enterprise. Where sources agree in registering an overall decline in the south's share of artisan concerns over the period, the distribution of north–south firms differs in each case (see overleaf).

The lower percentage of artisans censused in relation to those registered for tax and social security benefits in the south suggests the 'use' of the artisan classification against economic hardship. In Palermo alone it has been estimated that around 40 per cent of the registered artisans are false, 'presenting themselves as artisans only for purposes of assistance' (Chubb 1982: 126). Whilst this practice

| Source | North (%) | South (%) |
|--------|-----------|-----------|
| Chamber of Commerce (1970) | 68.1 | 31.9 |
| *Casse Mutue* (1971) | 70.4 | 29.6 |
| Census (1971) | 73.0 | 27.0 |

probably occurs to a much greater extent in the south, there is no way of knowing how much it inflates the number of national artisans.

There is, of course, another reason for the difference between the census data and that of other sources. As Barberis (1980: 52) points out, many artisans work at home, either for intermediaries or on a subcontracting basis (notably in the clothing industry). Being without business premises – the criterion of census taking – they therefore escape tabulation.

For these reasons, I have used the official census figures as the more meaningful basis upon which to assess the national proportion of artisans using subsidized credit. What seems to be the important point is that the majority of artisan concerns escaping the census taker's net represents an area of craft industry for which business finance – for the specified purposes of investment in workshops, machinery, etc. – would appear to be largely irrelevant.

### (ii)   *Small industry*

The overall figure of 25,000 small firm beneficiaries is a conservative estimate arrived at in the following manner: Under *Law 623/1959*, 80 per cent of the 24,000 loans allocated (Appendix I, table I) went to small firms, making a rough total of *19,200* loans. Under *Law 949/1952*, 10,220 loans were made by the end of 1960. Since there is no information on loans made, but only finance allocated, up to 1969, I have estimated this number on the basis of average loan values. Up to 1960, the average loan value was *c.*15 million lire; assuming that the average value had *tripled* over the next decade (i.e. 45 million), and given that 306 billion lire had been allocated between 1961 and 1969, then just under 7,000 new loans would have been allocated in this period – bringing the total loans for 1952–69 to 17,000. Although the proportion is probably higher, for reasons already mentioned, I have also assumed here that 80 per cent of these loans, that is, *13,600*, were destined to small firms. Together, then, the SMI laws account for a total of *32,800 loans* to small firms.

With regard to the number of actual *firms* receiving loans, however, the figure of 32,800 is deceptive, since the same firm may have recourse to more than one loan under a given provision over a period of time. To allow for the inflationary element of additional loans, I have based my calculations on Mediocredito's 1973 survey findings. These showed that 18 per cent of loans made under Law 949 and 29 per cent of those under Law 623 were additional loans. On this basis, 13,600 loans (law 949) were absorbed by some *11,200* firms; whilst 19,200 loans (law 623) were distributed to *c.13,600* firms. Overall, then, the SMI laws benefited about *25,000 small firms*.

### (iii)   *Small industry*

Several sources indicate that at least one-third of the loans granted under Law 623 were for *new* plant. Thus, of the 19,200 loans to small industry, approximately *6,400* would be for new installations (CENSIS 1972: table 45; Rampino 1967: 364; IASM 1969: Introduction). There are no figures available on Law 949 concerning new firms created. I have therefore assumed that a similar proportion of the 7,000 loans made between 1961 and 1969 – that is, at least *2,000* – would be for new plant. Regarding southern laws, the Casse records 8,510 loans to small firms, of which more than 40 per cent (*3,411*) were for new firms, created between 1961 and 1971.

Taking into consideration the three provisions, this brings the *total number of new firms financed in the space of a decade to just under 12,000*.

# Notes

### Chapter 1   Forms of capitalism and the state

1  As outlined below on p. 6. Fordism in the strictest sense refers to a system of production which eschews craft principles. Unless otherwise specified, however, I also use the term in a broader sense to indicate a range of phenomena associated with big business capitalism.

### Chapter 2   The problem: its contours and explanations

1  As a percentage of total exports of OECD countries between 1955 and 1973, whilst France's share remained static (at about 9 per cent), Britain's more than halved (from 18 per cent to 8.5 per cent), Germany's increased by 50 per cent (from 13 per cent to 19.6 per cent), but Italy doubled its proportion to 7.2 per cent (Conti 1978: 56).
2  Between 1950 and 1976, for example, the growth of employment in Italian industry at 2.3 per cent per annum was second only to Japan's with 3.3 per cent, as against 0.7 per cent for France, 0.8 per cent for Germany and -0.3 per cent for the United Kingdom (Grassini 1979: 10). Between 1970 and 1979 industrial employment in Italy rose by 9 per cent (second to Japan with 12 per cent); whereas France, West Germany and the United Kingdom registered significant declines (−4, −10 and −13 per cent respectively) (Schiattarella 1984: 70). More recent OECD (1986: 61) figures still show a higher than average job-creation record. Between 1973 and 1985, whereas employment 'remained virtually flat in the rest of Europe', in Italy it rose by 6.5 per cent.
3  The 1956 law establishes a maximum of ten persons employed and

ten apprentices (half this number if the work involves mass assembly), with exceptions for cooperatives and artistic trades 'as long as members are personally involved in the work, and as long as such work has a pre-eminent role over capital'. Registration with the provincial Chambers of Commerce is also obligatory.

4   Chapter 8 pursues this point in relation to the state's promotion of big business capitalism.

5   For further discussion of this point see chapter 5. One of the most publicized of the PCI's efforts in this direction was a study conference examining the problems and prospects of small and medium industry, proceedings of which are published in two volumes by the Istituto Gramsci–CESPE (1975). A succinct analysis of the PCI's alliance strategy can be found in Hellman (1975).

6   For a discussion of these issues see Salvati (1974). Capecchi and Pugliese (1978: 41) point out that at the beginning of the 1970s the PCI's support for the small business class was so unconditional that it frowned on trade union inquiries which sought to evidence the 'satellite' nature of small enterprise, and sought to distance itself from anything which seemed 'an intolerable criticism of the small entrepreneur'.

7   On the comparative performance of the third Italy see Bagnasco and Pini (1981: tables 3.1 and 3.2).

8   It is estimated that between 1961 and 1971 – despite significant increases nationally – artisan concerns in the Mezzogiorno declined by 11,000 units (Sicca 1981: 164). In the same period, the south lost *c.* 10,000 establishments in manufacturing industry, compared with increases elsewhere of 32,000 units, the majority of these in the third Italy.

9   It is worth pointing out that international data on the export structure of various OECD nations – their share of the market for products of different technological content ('mature', 'medium', and 'high') – between 1954 and 1973 fail to show any clear correlation between the relative importance of small firms in a given nation and the evolving pattern of exports. Japan is one case in point (cf. Conti 1978: 53, 56).

10  I am grateful to Michael Mann for reference to this general point.

11  Sabel dates the emergence of Italy's innovative craft sector to the mid-1970s, attributing it to a restructuring process of Italian industry, consequent to the Hot Autumn struggles and trade union gains of 1969. However, in view of the fact that Italy's predominantly small-scale mechanical engineering sector has led Italian exports and has accounted for the largest share of value added in the post-war period, it seems reasonable to assume that such firms had achieved a certain

level of technological sophistication well before the events which led to their 'discovery'.

12   Prato, if not the most outstanding, is certainly the most publicized example of the success of small entrepreneurship. The thriving centre of Italian textile production, Prato is an affluent provincial town of family mini 'factories', exporting some $1.5 billion of its products annually and with a per capita income 50 per cent higher than the national average. See the special report in *Time*, 17 August, 1981; also CENSIS (1980).

13   Cited in *Time* (ibid.: 14).

14   Evidence for the last decade shows that on a variety of dimensions – including job creation, profit margins, per capita investment, technological change, productivity and value added – small firms in all sectors have outperformed the big companies (Schiattarella 1984: 93ff).

15   Despite sweeping generalizations that the growth of small enterprise is the result of big business's 'decentralization' strategies, very little evidence has been forthcoming. In Lombardy, centre of large-scale industry, for example, surveys showed that more than 70 per cent of small industrial firms produce *directly* for the market. Furthermore, the proportion had increased by four points between 1969 and 1974, precisely in the period when larger firms were supposedly contracting out more work (cf. Gasparini's report in the Federlombarda study, 1977: vol. 1). A 1974 study of the artisanat in the same area produced similar results: 87 per cent of the region's artisanal production were finished products, of which only 13.6 per cent was destined to industry (Giunta Regionale della Lombardia assessorato all'artigianato 1974: 64).

16   A 1977 inquiry carried out by the Federation of Metalworkers in Bologna province showed that the smallest firms (20–49 employed) subcontracted out a much larger proportion of their total production (30 per cent) than those with over 1,000 employed (17 per cent) (cf. Capecchi and Pugliese 1978: 9). In the metallurgical sector, Brusco (1975, 1982) found that many *already* tiny factories (employing fewer than thirty workers) actually contracted out all or most of their production (for example, dishwashers and machinery for the textile and paper industries) to other small businesses, confining their operations to the construction of prototypes and final assembly (cf. also Capecchi and Pugliese 1978: 9). On this general point see also research into the knitwear industry in Prato (CENSIS 1980) and Carpi (Solinas 1982).

17   The best treatment of the problem and also the most representative of

the positons criticized in this book are the seminal essays of Berger (1974, 1980) and Pizzorno (1980).

18  First published in 1974. '*Ceti medi*' translates loosely as 'middle strata', referring to those who are neither capitalist nor working class.

## Chapter 3   The petite bourgeoisie on trial

1  This chapter is an expanded version of an earlier article (Weiss 1986).

2  As Linz (1976: 59) points out, it is more instructive to know the membership of the PNF *before* its consolidation as a regime. For once in power, other parties are outlawed and membership becomes largely indispensable for advancement, for privileges or simply for protection against harassment – hence the cynical designation of the PNF (Partito Nazionale Fascista) as 'Per Necessità Familiare' ('for family necessity').

3  I follow those writers who identify these three strata as constitutive of a distinctive middle class. For the most convincing sociological case to date, see Michael Mann's volume 2 of *The Sources of Social Power* (forthcoming: vol. 2, ch. 4).

4  At the closure of the debate on the government's programme, De Gasperi pointed out that 'it is not right to sit in Cabinet, participate in the responsibility of administration, have the advantages of the state apparatus, and at the same time oppose the government in the press and propaganda. This fractures democracy, annuls the democratic method and makes dictatorship inevitable' (published in *Il Popolo*, 26 June 1946, cited in Setta 1975: 178).

5  The MSI expanded, briefly, only in 1972 when it absorbed some of the electorate of the disbanded Monarchist Party, thus gaining its highest share of the post-war suffrage (8.7 per cent).

6  It is the traditional puzzle of Fascist research: why did the petite bourgeoisie support a party which acted against its interests? The answer suggested by Kater for Germany is that Nazi policies to eliminate non-economic businesses and to restrict entry ironically sponsored a consolidation process. By 'thinning out' the small business sector, the regime thus strengthened the positon of the surviving fittest (1983: 86ff). These policies, however, came into being after 1935, paralleling the so-called 'second wave' of German Fascism. In seeking to release manpower for strategic industries, National Socialism thus met one traditional claim of the *Mittelstand*: that entry to independent trade be strictly regulated by credentialism (see chapters 6 and 8).

7    As late as 1968 it was estimated that the independent middle class,
     together with family members, still accounted for around 30 per cent
     of the voting population (Sylos Labini 1978: 73).
8    Based on a study of the 1968–76 electoral data, the 'constant'
     electorate refers to those who voted for the same party in two
     successive elections. Sydney Tarrow (1979: 167) makes similar
     observations. Note that 'electoral stability' is intended in a statistical
     sense at a given ecological level, but does not exclude changes over
     time of individual units (commune or province) taken alone.
9    In 1953 the strongest force on the right was the Monarchist Party
     (PDIUM), which benefited from opposition to the land reform in the
     south. In 1963 it was the Liberals (PLI) in the north who gained most
     from opposition to the centre-left. Only the 1972 election appears to
     qualify this point, when the MSI gained its highest share of the post-
     war suffrage (8.7 per cent) by absorbing much of the electorate of the
     disbanded PDIUM.
10   On the varying importance of class and religion for electoral
     behaviour, see Barnes (1974). On the significance of organizational
     factors, see Germinio and Passigli (1968: 118–27). The organizational
     variable is often interpreted as a vote of *appartenenza* which translates
     roughly as 'group identification' or 'subcultural belonging'. On this
     point see Parisi and Pasquino (1979: 15–16).
11   According to a 1975 survey conducted nationally, the non-agricultural
     self-employed and salaried personnel accounted for around 22 per cent
     of both the Communist and Christian Democratic electorate. For
     references on the survey materials used, see Merkl (1980b: 657).
12   See, for example, the lively debates of 14 and 18 July 1961 on
     'Credito all'artigianato e piccola industria' in Camera dei Deputati,
     *Atti Parlamentari* (Discussioni).
13   For a similar argument in a comparative setting, see Mann, vol. 2
     (forthcoming: ch. 4).
14   On the ability of the PCI in Tuscany 'to maintain contact with the
     "new" entrepreneurs of popular origin and to make space for them
     within its breast', see Cavalli's Introduction and Giovaninni's research
     paper in Cavalli (1973).

### Chapter 4   Patterns of state support I: bountiful but bounded

1    Even in the mid-1960s when larger initiatives began to be funded,
     specifically to encourage industrialization of the south, firm size
     continued to be an important determinant of eligibility for state-

assisted schemes, giving more generous benefits to smaller enterprise.

2   Law 860 of 1956 establishes a maximum of ten persons employed (or twenty including apprentices), with exceptions for cooperatives, artistic trades (e.g. ceramics, fashion, etc.), limited companies and partnerships, 'as long as members are personally involved in the work, and as long as such work has a preeminent role over capital'. Artisan firms must also be registered with the provincial Chambers of Commerce.

3   Since 1956 the benefits have increased enormously. As early as 1952, tax concessions were granted and the minimum taxable income for artisans was raised. The general tax on income was reduced from 3 per cent to 1 per cent; in the field of social insurance, artisan employers, from 1954, could pay the lower contribution to family allowances for their workers (13 per cent as against 22.5 per cent for industrial firms). In addition, they are exempt from contributions to the workers' unemployment fund. Overall, such exemptions from contributions amounted to about 15 per cent. At the same time, responsibility for payment of insurance contributions for apprentice artisans was assumed by the state (Presidenza Consiglio Ministri 1958: 230ff). In 1968 artisans – both self-employed and employers – became eligible for the lowest category of income tax, placing them on the same scale as dependent wage earners.

4   This was of course precisely what the government intended with the 1956 Act. For discussions of this point and its effects on social mobility, see especially chapters 5 and 6.

5   Artigiancassa is a 'clearing house'. It finances banks and credit houses so that they in turn can furnish loans to artisans. With an initial endowment of 500 million lire and a further state guarantee fund of 5 billion lire, a total of 6,705 loans amounting to c.five billion lire were granted between 1948 and 1952 (Guidi 1954: 17ff; Presidenza Consiglio Ministri 1958: 230).

6   Unless otherwise specified, the term 'billion' denotes a 'thousand million', rather than a 'million million'. All calculations are based on data supplied by Artigiancassa, *Bilancio* (various years).

7   See Artigiancassa, *Bilancio* 1966 (1967: table D).

8   That is, a total of 2,388 billion lire in loans, leading to an overall investment of 3,722 billion lire. *Bilancio 1976* (1977: tables 8 and 9).

9   1971–6 data are not strictly comparable since they refer to *loans* made rather than *firms* financed. (Some firms obtain more than one loan, e.g., for purchase of stock, which are available only to those in receipt of finance for plant or equipment.) The above is a reasonably accurate estimate of firm beneficiaries, based on the fact that up to 1971, at

least 80 per cent of loans made annually are first loans, that is, going to *different* firms. Hence, of the total loans for the entire period, 80 per cent (300,500) would be first loans. Estimates for the 1971–6 period are based on a universe drawn from the 1976 Casse Mutue (social security) figures (1,410,000 being the number of artisans registered on social security rolls in 1976); however, since this source inflates the census figures by *c*.30 per cent, I have allowed for this in my estimate (see also note (i) in Appendix II).

10   Special benefits for small industrial concerns have generally evolved in conjunction with those for medium-sized enterprise, defined as those firms employing a maximum of 100 persons, and between 101 and 500 persons respectively. Since these provisions are generally legislated for together, they are referred to as the small and medium industry (SMI) laws. When examining the results of these incentives, I shall be chiefly concerned only with their application to small industry. Wherever the data cannot be disaggregated, I indicate this with the term 'SMI' rather than 'SI'.

11   Of course, small firms do not necessarily borrow their maximum entitlement. This disparity may be partly due to the fact that southern firms in receipt of soft loans can also obtain capital grants (of up to 20–30 per cent of fixed investment), and since together such awards cannot exceed 70 per cent of total investment expenditure, this reduces the proportion of subsidized credit that can be granted.

12   For one of the best analyses in Italian, see Saba (1969); for a comprehensive treatment in English, see Rodgers (1979); and for a comparison with French regional policies, Allen and MacLellan (1971).

13   In 1953, for example, the Interministerial Committee for Credit and Savings (CICR) established that the medium-sized firms were those employing a maximum of 500 persons, and having a fixed capital investment not exceeding 1.5 billion lire. In view of the need to finance the capital intensive projects of the state holding corporations (which is required by law to locate a major portion of its investments in the south), this limit has been sucessively raised. A further deliberation of CICR ruled that for investments located in the south, these requisites could refer to the single establishment, regardless of the size of the parent company.

14   For example, under Law 717 of 1965, special interest rates on individual loans are graded according to size of initiative: smallest investors pay 3 per cent, whilst larger pay 6 per cent; the value of the loan is similarly tapered. Capital grants similarly depend on project size: larger firms could obtain grants worth 15–20 per cent of fixed

investment; but the equivalent value for small firms was at least twice as great at 35–45 per cent. As SVIMEZ (1973: 15), the agency responsible for research and technical matters regarding southern development, has noted in this context, 'the general criterion informing the graduation of incentives in terms of size criteria is that of favouring in greater measure small and medium firms.'

15 In contrast to Artigiancassa's systematic coverage of loan operations, information on the SMI loan schemes is dispersed across several agencies, none of which provide a comprehensive account of the schemes they administer. The findings on small industry are the result of calculations I have made, using a variety of official documents, surveys and unpublished reports. These include: CNEL (1961); IASM (1969); Mediocredito Centrale (1971, 1977); CENSIS (1972). The rationale for various estimates is outlined in notes (ii) and (iii) in Appendix II.

16 Data culled from various official sources offer a more realistic view of loans granted over a given period; yet, this view suffers from a number of shortcomings. It indicates *loans* allocated rather than *firms* financed; it covers only certain periods, rather than the entire period of application of a given law; and it provides only a rough guide to loan distributions by firm size. By contrast, the survey material is more detailed and systematic, covering the major incentives on offer, the number and size of firms subsidized, as well as the regional distribution of loans. However, it lacks a dynamic view of loan operations, hence is of little validity as an absolute expression of firms financed over the post-war period. As a guide to the proportional distribution of loans by firm size and geographical area, however, the MC survey is excellent.

17 Of the 47,176 firms deemed eligible in December 1973, around 50 per cent appeared in the final survey. Whilst this may be sufficiently representative of the universe in the wider sense, small firms were ultimately under-represented because of their lower frequency of response. Ranked by size of firm (number of workers employed), the frequency of response was as follows: more than 500, 65 per cent; 101–500, 61 per cent; 51–100, 59 per cent; 11–50, 44.8 per cent.

18 A firm which obtained more than one loan from a given law is listed only once in the data, but is counted every time it uses a different law. However, the tendency for a given firm to have recourse to different laws for its financial requirements is very slight, compared with that of using the same provision for additional loans (see Mediocredito Centrale 1977: tables 74 and 75; also note (ii) in Appendix II).

19 In 1966 the Minister for Industry reported that 12,030 of the 14,550

loans allocated under Law 623/1959 (i.e. 82.6 per cent) were for the lowest category of loan values (up to 100 million lire). Since it is generally recognized that loans of this size are destined to the smallest concerns, we can therefore see that a good 80 per cent of the 623 loans were absorbed by small firms (see Camera dei Deputati, *Relazioni e Documenti*, no. 3607, 1 December 1966; also Rampino, 1967: 370).

20  See note (ii) in Appendix II for method of calculation.

21  According to Mediocredito's (1977: 336) estimate, 40,904 manufacturing firms in the 11–100 size category.

22  Note that even if such data were available, the amount obtained per employee as a measure of 'who did best' would not be very useful – primarily because in contrast to France, for example, incentives have not been based on job creation or numbers employed (see chapter 5). Data on jobs created are indeed often wildly inaccurate projections, since the recipient firm is not required to stick to them.

23  The figure is a minimal estimate because the periods referred to for each law do not cover the entire period of a given law's application. As set out in note (ii) in Appendix II, the 13,600 loans granted under Law 949/1952 refer to the period 1953–69; the 19,200 loans allocated under Law 623/1959 cover the years 1960 to March 1970; whilst the 8,500 southern loans cover only 1961–71, although the scheme began in 1957.

24  The universe here being the 58,700 manufacturing firms in the 10–100 size category, according to the 1971 Census. A small proportion of loans would have gone to non-manufacturing firms, hence this figure may be slightly inflated.

25  See note (iii) in Appendix II for the method of calculation.

26  The 1976 law (902), which reorganizes the credit system, appears to set out to rectify this disparity by specifying that in future, 65 per cent of loan finance be set aside for the south.

27  It should be emphasized that these figures are useful primarily for regional *comparisons*, but not as an accurate description of results in a given region. Whilst the survey gives a breakdown of the size of regional firms in a given area, it does not disaggregate loan operations on this basis, hence some medium-sized firms are also included in the above loan operations. The same point should be noted for the following section where 'SMI' stands as a reasonable proxy for small enterprise.

28  Among these must be included the very generous ten-year exemption from income tax for new small firms, as well as the ample technical, marketing and training assistance provided by state agencies and

government-sponsored schemes. Introduced in 1957, the tax concession for which only *new* small firms are eligible involves full tax
exemption for ten years for all profits arising from industrial projects
in designated problem areas of the centre-north (a similar measure
being available in the south). The classification of 'problem area' is
highly misleading, however, since around 75–80 per cent of all
communes in central and northern regions effectively have qualified
for the benefit, thus reflecting the popularity of the measure and the
successful lobbying of politicians to have their 'areas' so classified.
Although no information is available on the number of firms
emerging to take advantage of the concession, nor on the amount of
exchequer revenue forgone, studies undertaken at a provincial level
indicate that the tax measure has been a major inducement for small
enterprise. In the communes of Piedmont, for example, 82 per cent of
the small industrialists interviewed declared that the decisive factor in
setting up their firms had been the intention to take advantage of the
ten-year tax exemption (Guerra 1966: 142).

State agencies are additionally involved, both directly and indirectly,
in training schemes for craft trades. As well as sponsoring courses in
engineering, building, dressmaking and tailoring, the state provides
considerable financial support to charitable bodies, for example, the
Salesian Institutes which have functioned throughout the country
as training centres for high-grade printing and furniture-making
(Williams 1963).

### Chapter 5   Patterns of state support II: beyond employment

1   There seems here to be a contradiction in Berger's (1980) argument.
    On one hand, we are told that the traditional sector is 'functional' for
    the modern sector; on the other, that it has 'to pay high costs' for
    'protecting the traditional remnants'; on one hand, that the sector
    receives new life from the modern sector (via subcontracting
    practices); on the other, that it appears constantly on the verge of
    being weakened by the industrialization process.
2   See the government's report 'Norma per la disciplina giuridica delle
    imprese artigiane', discussed by the Commissione Industriale in the
    Chamber of Deputies on 20 April 1956.
3   Whilst stipulating that some part of the production process had to
    involve craft principles, the modernizing impulse of the 1956 law has
    encouraged significant innovations within the sector. To take one
    example, in the furniture industry, innovations in the 'moulding'

('*formatura*') phase reduced the labour time for a standard panel from 540 to 36 seconds; in the 'pressing' stage, innovations enabled a worker to increase average hourly production by 220 per cent between 1951 and 1971. On the impact of new technologies on small enterprise, see Bagnasco and Pini (1981: 103ff). On productivity increases between 1951 and 1961, see Profumieri's report in the Istituto Gramsci-CESPE studies (1975: vol. 2, 19).

4  See the government's report to the Commissione Industriale, on the Ministry of Industry's annual budget, debated in the Chamber of Deputies on 23 June 1954.

5  From Togni's report to the Chamber of Deputies on 22 February 1951. This accompanied the government's bill to give artisans representation in the Chambers of Commerce (see Camera dei Deputati, *Disegni di Legge – Relazioni*, no. 1841).

6  Thus, Italy's first economic plan, presented to the Economic Organization for the European Community, stated that 'Given the uncertainty of our knowledge of technical progress, it cannot be discounted that the process of remodernization that our economy requires is such as to render even smaller [than the estimated 10–15 per cent] the possibilities of further employment in industry, even with significant increases in production' (Saraceno 1969: 381).

7  See Longoni's report to the Chamber of Deputies on 23 June 1954, during debate of the Ministry of Industry's annual budget.

8  See Aldo Moro's address to the 1959 National Congress in Atti del 7°Congresso della DC (DC 1961: 265).

9  See Dosi's report to the Chamber of Deputies, Commissione Industriale, DDL no. 1524, on 20 April 1956.

10  Total employment in the south actually declined by half a million between 1951 and 1975, although its resident population has increased by *circa* one-and-a-half million. In 1976, 12 per cent of its workforce were registered as unemployed. This accounted for 60 per cent of the national figure, although the south has only about 34 per cent of the active population (Wade 1979: 199).

11  It would be quite legitimate to argue here that the traditional sectors got less because, for the same amount of employment, they require less capital – their investments being less capital intensive. However, this would still weaken the functionalist argument about privileging labour-absorptive enterprise. In fact, as the Salerno research revealed, the smallest category of firms financed (with 1–50 workers) had, on average, a higher per capita investment than that of firms with 51–200 employees, and firms with over 500 employees (Bonazzi et al. 1972: 232).

12 On the use of public enterprise in a manner congruent with the DC's small firm bias, see chapter 7.

13 The implication here is that it would have been far less rational to subsidize or sustain a network of firms whose products could not compete with those of their northern counterparts. The authors of the studies cited here do not, however, draw this conclusion, despite their numerous observations which point in this direction.

## Chapter 6  The social project

1 Since the term ideology has been used to indicate quite conflicting possibilities – from utopianism, altruism and the giving of meaning and morality on one hand, to the masking of interests and legitimation of power on the other – one is tempted to dispense with it altogether. But Mann's simple yet profound point, elaborated in the context of a grand argument, serves to forestall such despair precisely by reconciling that conflict. As he puts it, 'though ideologies always do contain legitimations of private interests and material domination, they are unlikely to attain a hold over people if they are merely this' (1986: 23). Happily, this also rescues my use of the term ideology from meaninglessness because most of the elements previously indicated apply to the DC's social project.

The important point to be made is that the political actors in question construed a world in which the class of small capital had especial moral and material significance, and that they acted in accordance with those presuppositions. My interest in the 'ideological' therefore transcends questions of normative ideals and political calculation. I use it in this context primarily as an indicator of goals independently formulated by significant state actors.

To retrieve the ideological basis of that project, I therefore proceed in two ways. The first involves identifying the fundamental goals of the party, by seeking out what remains constant in its policy statements and what is emphasized in its guiding principles. The first part of my analysis is therefore based on the 'founding' documents of the DC, those which were elaborated in the period 1943–6 spanning the collapse of Fascism and the formation of the new republic. These sources have a special significance in so far as they indicate the place of small capital in the DC's vision of industrial order and the party's commitment to securing it *before* becoming immersed in the world of political conflicts, power struggles and electoral contests.

An analysis of this kind, however, cannot rest exclusively on the most conspicuous ideological pronouncements. The more humble sources have the advantage of revealing that 'taken for granted' quality of ideology, the perceptions and presuppositions that are both frequently found and widely shared (Poggi 1963). Thus the second strategy is to supplement the 'founding' material wherever relevant with statements drawn from a variety of contexts: study conferences, party congresses, parliamentary debates, official reports and ministerial statements. In general, this material is drawn from contexts where policy matters are proposed, debated or defended. It will not be examined in isolation, but used in the course of this and the following chapter to support various points in my discussion.

2  Often implicit in these appeals was the notion that the proletarian who had renounced the 'wage-earning mentality', in the desire to escape from the working class, was already in some sense part of the *ceto medio*. This is evident, for example, in De Gasperi's statement in 1953 (1969: 551) that 'The *ceto medio* consists substantially of those who seek an autonomous means of employment to develop an activity of their own, like the artisan, farmer, shopkeeper, and entrepreneur.'

3  Thus the first programme of the Catholic movement carried the explicit title: 'The Programme of Catholics in Opposition to Socialism'. With reference to the wider social context – the spread of the socialist movement from the rural population to the cities and manufacturing centres – it asks 'What programme can Catholics counterpose to that of socialist doctrinaires?' (cf. Scoppola 1963: 77–83).

4  In fact, it was precisely these schemes (for worker participation in agricultural enterprise and profit-sharing arrangements) introduced by the *Popolari* in the Po valley which provoked a Fascist backlash by agrarian landlords. Refusing to abide by these agreements (drawn up by the *Popolari* and socialists), 80 per cent of the Cremona landlords combined in a Fascist syndicate and went into 'a state of permanent agitation', forcing new agreements to be drawn up (Tasca 1966: 196ff).

5  The main documents used in the following sections are as follows: *Idee Ricostruttive della Democrazia Cristiana* (1943); *Programa di Milano* (1943); *Il Programa della Democrazia Cristiana* (1944); *Per il solidarismo economico e la evoluzione sociale* (final motion approved by the DC Consiglio Nazionale in August [1945]); *Primo Congresso Nazionale della Democrazia Cristiana* (1946). All are contained in *Atti e Documenti*, vol. I, (1968). Page numbers cited in the text refer to the document's location in the 1968 volume. In addition, I have used two other

documents: *Riforme: Lavoratori e Imprese Industriali* (DC 1946); and *Codice di Camaldoli*, prepared between 1943 and 1944, the key extracts of which are published in Aga Rossi (1969: 320–30).

6  On the DC's ideas regarding worker participation in the firm's profits see *Rivista Internazionale di Scienze Sociale* for articles by F. Vito between between 1944 and 1946. According to the party document, *Riforme* (1946: 20), the DC had begun to set up 'schools of business orientation' in various cities so as to prepare workers for some future role in the firm's administration.

7  See Longoni's report to a parliamentary committee on 12 June 1954, deliberating the annual budget of the Ministry of Industry, Commerce and the Artisanat. I have drawn extensively on these discussions between 1950 and 1964, which are referenced in the bibliography under Camera dei Deputati, Stato di Previsione della Spesa del Ministero dell'Industria e del Commercio per l'Esercizio (various years).

8  For research on labour relations and workers' attitudes, which lend support to the 'solidaristic' view of small enterprise, see Bettin (1973); De Masi and Fevola (1974); Centro Studi Federlibro (1974: 102).

9  See Togni's opening address to the 1958 *ceti medi* conference attended by small business owners, DC Members of Parliament and government (1958: 30).

10  Somewhat ironically, it has fallen to Social Democratic governments of the 1970s to try to arrest this trend, for it was found that in Germany small firms 'account for a smaller share of industrial employment (12 per cent) and industrial production (10 per cent) than in any other OECD country' (Peacock 1980: para 4.25). Consequently, governments since 1975 have increased considerably the number of programmes and amount of expenditure for this sector.

11  Again, the context is a study conference to discuss the problems and policies regarding the *ceti medi* (see Lucifredi 1958: 82).

12  See the document elaborating the 'Tradition and Ideology of Christian Democracy' (1944), published in *Atti e Documenti* (1968: 41). The passage cited is taken from Toniolo, nineteenth-century exponent of Christian Democratic ideology.

13  As a sociological witness of those years, Pizzorno (1980: 64) recalls the 'enormous importance' of workers who had founded small industries in the 1950s, in providing a model and point of reference for others. His earlier study (1960) of industrial development near Milan suggests how deeply resonant within Italian society is the ideal of setting up independently, the phrase *mettersi in proprio* being one of the most frequently heard among the locals. Moreover, those who

managed to do so, more than being envied, were respected by almost everyone.

14  Unfortunately the survey did not include information on father's occupation, so we cannot ascertain how many of those 'previously unemployed' actually inherited their businesses. There is, however, considerable evidence in more recent studies to suggest that the 'inheritance' factor is not great, and that there is substantial mobility both across and within generations. One relevant finding reported in all the surveys is that the bulk of small firms operating in the 1970s were post-war creations. Even in the most mature industrial setting of Lombardy, around two-thirds of the small industrial firms surveyed in 1976 were established after 1945 (Tousijn 1980: 209); whilst for artisan concerns, the proportion was 88 per cent (Giunta Regionale della Lombardia 1974: 40). Of the 97,477 artisan concerns operating in Venezia in 1975, only 4.5 per cent were inherited (Barberis 1980: 42). In the Marche, almost 80 per cent of the 737 enterprises surveyed had emerged since 1950, of which only 12.4 per cent were run by 'inheritors' or persons other than the original founder. In this context, just under 60 per cent of all entrepreneurs had previously been wage-earners or without paid employment. For a comparison of survey material from several regions and a discussion of intragenerational mobility, see Tousijn (1980: 95–113).

15  Suzanne Berger (1980: 110–11) makes this point with regard to the 'functions' the traditional sector performs – especially for France – rather than to DC ideology.

16  Imberciadori's words based on interviews conducted among DC politicians in Tuscany in the early 1970s (1973: 148–9).

## Chapter 7    The internal challenge

1  For British research on effects of plant size on workers' political behaviour, see Ingham (1970) and Jessop (1974). While these earlier studies suggested deferential attitudes and conservative politics among small firm workers, later studies find no such evidence. For references see Curran and Burrows (1986).

   In Italy, the traditional entrenchment of the PCI and the DC in particular regions complicates the issue. The important point, however, is that worker–employer relations in small firms are more likely to be fraternal and collaborative than antagonistic (Bettin 1973;

De Masi and Fevola 1974: 775; Piore and Sabel 1983).

2   The very rebirth of Italian trade unionism as a paramilitary force in the resistance against Fascism ensured its politicization from the outset (Lama 1976: 8). But other factors sustained this orientation. Its leaders were themselves party men and their decisions were subordinated to party policy. Second, because the majority of workers were unorganized and employed in a multitude of tiny plants, pre-eminence had to be given to objectives that could be formulated at a national level. High unemployment, the priorities of national reconstruction and the Communists' collaboration in government also constrained unions to keep a tight rein on workers' specific economic grievances, and to direct them instead towards more diffuse political issues. For the early post-war years, the best account of the subject in English remains that of Salvati (1972a).

As the Christian wing broke away from CGIL and created its own independent organization, *Confederazione Italiano Sindacato del Lavoro* (CISL), trade union strategies in the 1950s became clearly divided – CGIL still pursuing a national political direction; CISL, a plant-focused action which emphasized the priority of claims formulated at enterprise level. For an account of 'The Two Logics of Class Action' (in Italian), see Pizzorno's 1980 volume, ch. 7.

3   By 1955, Communist strongholds in large northern factories had suffered a severe blow, especially so in the FIAT plants where the PCI had previously drawn some two-thirds of the workers' votes (in electing workers' representatives to shop floor committees). Here, its support declined sharply to 36 per cent, partly due to management's carrot and stick policy, but also to the PCI's neglect of workplace grievances which it openly admitted (see Sassoon 1981: 92–3). At the party's 1956 Congress, the trade union leader, Di Vittorio, therefore requested that the 'transmission belt' theory be abandoned.

4   Using Confindustria records, Zaninelli (1981: 434–5) reports a constant upward trend in strikes of a non-contractual nature: from 33 per cent of the total strikes in 1947 to 48 per cent in 1949. In 1951 the number of hours lost by strike activity which had no 'negotiable' ends (i.e. definite objectives) rose from 87 per cent in the previous year to 93 per cent of the total.

5   From about the mid-fifties onwards, trade union militancy declined (there were more strikes, but fewer workers involved) – thanks also to the repressive cold war climate and divisions within the labour movement. On strike activity see Neufeld (1961: 501, 547).

For the DC, these new trends were a sign that 'Italy's economic and social progress [was] helping the proletariat to finally appreciate the constructive methods of democracy' (Fanfani's report to the 1956 Party Congress, in DC 1976: 66).

6 From a letter of the President of Confindustria to the Prime Minister in September 1947 (see Abrate 1981: 478).

7 The so-called Costa–Pastore debate, in which open letters exchanged between the two leaders were published in Rome and Milan newspapers, is documented in Abrate (1981).

8 See De Gasperi's speech to the 1954 Party Congress in DC (1976: 55).

9 Where the average monthly wage for a skilled worker in private industry (1971) was 153 thousand lire, in the public sector equivalent it was 285 thousand lire. The disparity is similarly great for an unskilled worker: 128 as against 236 thousand lire in the respective sectors (Graziano 1978: 314).

10 A measure of their predominance is afforded by a series of 'special laws', from those designed to control collective action to the 1953 electoral law (eventually repealed), which proposed to create a 'protected democracy' by guaranteeing 65 per cent of the seats to the party or coalition which obtained an absolute majority. For a discussion of the 'exceptional' measures of the period, promulgated by the DC, see Scarpari (1977).

11 Cassano (1980: 57–9) makes this point when criticizing the conventional wisdom which tends to view the DC's activity in government as a vast operation of mass clientelism. As Cassano observes, the new power structure that the DC has created 'is rather different from and more complex than simple mass clientelism: it aims to organize consensus for the DC, but operates more profoundly in so far as it works to build a sytem of filters and barriers capable of splitting at the root every form of [class-based] action.'

12 A small, vocal minority – the so-called *Dossettiani* on the DC's left wing, who were forerunners of the neo-reformist deal struck with the Socialists in the early 1960s – battled within the party for an opening to the left and for greater emphasis to be given to the party's links with the labour movement. Because of the international and internal situation, however, the majority of delegates at the 1954 Congress rejected this request as an impossible one to enact in the short term; hence, the leadership's attempt to steer a centre course and defend the DC's interclass position by stressing its links with small employers and workers in the small sector (see below). On these points see Provasi (1976: ch. 3) and Manghetti (1975: 524).

13 From DC local party literature of 1952, cited in Graziano (1980: 154).

14 Support for this point can be found in Pizzorno's study of the response to industrial development of a community near Milan

(1960); and Bettin's research on the small entrepreneurial stratum in Tuscany (1973). An important aspect of this identification process is the fact that many small entrepreneurs are themselves of recent working class origin, which for the worker provides first-hand evidence of the very real possibility of one day following suit.

15  Data here refer to the mid-sixties (see Shonfield 1965: 185–6; Hildebrand 1967: 59). Since then, however, the state sector has extended to all the major industries, acquiring dominant shares in Olivetti (electronics) and Montedison, the major chemical group. By the early 1970s then, there were for all practical purposes only two major industrial and financial holdings in Italy: FIAT and the State Participation group (Salvati 1972b: 30).

16  The peculiar characteristics of the Italian financial market have given the state enormous powers over investment capital. In Italy, the stock market is only weakly developed, the major banks are publicly owned, and since the major banking crisis of the early 1930s, the banks have been confined by law to granting only short-term loans. For this reason, industrial investment loans have been provided only by specially created public institutions (Prodi 1974: 52).

17  The land reform, one of the DC's cardinal programmes since Sturzo, was initiated in 1950 against clamorous opposition from its Liberal coalition partners, from a group of southern DC deputies and their conservative agrarian supporters, and above all, from the Monarchists and neo-Fascists who subsequently gained the votes of many of the reform's adversaries (see Tarrow 1967: 293; Fonzi 1981: 800–5). Thus, although the reform eliminated the latifundia and swept away the old system of social relations in the countryside, it was never extended on the global scale originally planned. Adding fuel to the fire on the right was the sympathetic response from certain sectors of the ecclesiastical world. It judged Christian Democracy too weak towards communism and, instead, favoured a strong right-wing government which would include the minor parties of the far right (Fonzi 1981; Scoppola 1977).

18  See Abrate (1981: 515). The correspondence cited in this section is drawn from Abrate. Costa also complained simultaneously to the Vatican and to De Gasperi about a speech the latter had made to party colleagues concerning the need for workers' profit-sharing schemes. For Costa, this was pure demagogy, creating 'the false impression that through worker participation in profits one might solve the social problem'. De Gasperi responded that the Catholic movement had long upheld the principle of participation: 'But what then must we sustain, that the wage earner is the ideal system to oppose Communism?' For this exchange of letters in 1953 see Abrate (1981: 523).

19 Members of ACLI (Christian Association of Italian Workers).
20 From De Micheli's speech to the Annual Assembly of Confindustria in 1956, published in Provasi (1976: 160–2) along with other important documents of the period.
22 At the 1962 Congress (DC 1968: 1253–4), for example, Fanfani declared that the 'concentration of economic power' had to be controlled and that the democratic state 'must defend itself and political groups against the pressures of economic groups that in a roundabout way manage to disguise their true characteristics . . . the originating sources of these undue pressures . . . must be reduced to controllable proportions. Whoever does not effectively act on this terrain fertilises the field for Communist propaganda!'
22 See Senato della Repubblica (Atti Interni), 5° Commissione Permanente, DDL. no. 12, 25 November 1953.
23 Ibid.
24 There is some evidence to suggest that the distinction between the 'good' state enterprise and the 'bad' capitalist company exists also at a grass roots level. Following the installation of ENI's petrochemical plant in the southern town of Gela, Hytten and Marchioni found that 'the very fact of being an industry of the State conditions attitudes and industrial relations within the enterprise' (1970: 111). As the local population (and trade unions) saw it, the public corporation acted very differently from the 'speculator' capitalist: not only was it differentiated by a humane industrial relations policy; it was also struggling to end the dominion of private monopolies (e.g. the Montecatini petrochemical group) and to raise the standard of living of the community.
25 From Moro's address to the 1962 Party Congress (DC 1963: 350).
26 Ardigò's paper drew heavily on the Papal Encyclical's notion of *socializzazione*, defined as the new tendency of the modern world for organizations to increase in scale and number. Drawing out the implications of the Encyclical's point that it was necessary 'to extract the advantages and contain the negative effects of *socializzazione*', the sociologist argued for the social control of enterprise through economic planning. This way, the DC could overcome its mistrust of large 'rationalized' industry, which Ardigò saw as the 'historico-ideological obstacle' of the Catholic political movement (1962: 138–40). See also Saraceno's economic report, 'Lo Stato e l'economia', delivered at the same venue.
27 In English, a good discussion of the Italian planning experience can be found in Pasquino and Pecchini (1975: ch. 3).
28 This clause (cited in D'Antonio 1968: 38) is actually an amendment of

the original statement with regard to the artisanat. In the original draft, Socialists on the Planning Commission had emphasized the need to eliminate 'primitive forms of production' and 'unproductive' labour reserves which they saw existing not only in commerce, but also in the artisan sector (see Fuà and Sylos Labini 1963: 13–23; 28–33). However, this proposal was opposed in Parliament by a group of DC deputies who battled for the amended clause cited. For a résumé of the Christian Democrats' position, see the planning debates (and documents) in D'Antonio (1968).

29 Evidence for this view can be found in Colombo (1963: 636ff); in the annual budget debates for the Ministry of Industry, Commerce and Artisanat (Camera dei Deputati, *Discussioni della XII° Commissione Industriale*, 1958–63); and in the speech of Laforgia, DC MP and head of ACAI (Christian Association of Italian Artisans) to the 1967 Congress (DC 1969: 24).

30 The essentials of Tremelloni's discussion of the bill and its provisions in the Senate are reported in *Il Sole*, 11 March (1965: 1–2).

31 In the dichotomous conception of social structure, capitalists and workers constitute the fundamental classes, whilst the *ceti medi* comprise the spurious, unproductive categories – an obstacle both to political transformation and economic progress. See, for example, Pizzorno's (1980) interesting discussion of those in Italy – namely, Socialist planners and the extra-parliamentary left – who, for different reasons, have most upheld this 'dichotomous-productivistic' image. On the same point, Pasquino and Pecchini (1975: 75) observe that among the various reasons for the failure of economic planning in post-war Italy, the one 'insurmountable obstacle was . . . the fact that Christian Democrats and Socialists aimed at different types of society, whose foundations were to be built by planning, but they did not dare to express their models openly for fear of jeopardizing their cooperation. Thus the ideological call for a "socialist" society, or one based on collaboration between classes lost its appeal, and planning became a mere instrument for creating a welfare state.'

32 However, as late as 1966, Confindustria complained in its *Annuario* of the inadequacy of incentives to attract big private investors to the south, pointing out that if they were not improved, this would be positive proof 'of a political will aimed at favouring the expansion of public enterprise in the Mezzogiorno, drawing on the pretext of the inadequacy of private initiative' (CGII 1966: 287).

33 Under the revised southern legislation of 1965, for instance, 'large firms are also admitted to soft loans, but at interest rates hardly below those of the market. Consequently, the criterion of encouraging small

and medium units, which has been in operation over the 15 year period, 1950–1965, continues to prevail' (Saba 1969: 80).

The new 1971 law for southern development finally eliminated that formal preclusion of big enterprise. Once again, however, the legislation equivocates, by adding the disincentive of the need to obtain authorization from CIPE (Interministerial Committee for Economic Planning) for every investment project involving more than 7 billion lire (Amato 1976: 95).

## Chapter 8    Giantism and geopolitics

1   In the literature 'rationalization' stands for a hodgepodge of things. I use it in the most general sense to indicate attempts to increase the scale of enterprise and to concentrate national production whether via fusion of existing units, internal company expansion, freezing or eliminating the small firm sector.

2   The importance of state intervention for capitalist development has been well acknowledged for late industrializers ever since Gerschenkron's classical statement (1962). Nevertheless, the state's role in the latecomer theme tends to be strictly limited, the assumption being that if the state looms large in the industrialization process, this is because it is fired by a sense of economic backwardness and the need to 'catch up'. And if it favours bigness, this is because of the technological advantages available to late starters. The latecomer hypothesis, then, at least in its classical formulation, brims with economic–technological determinism. Not surprisingly, it has accommodated well to a structural Marxist interpretation of the state as a functional apparatus of capitalism, overcoming barriers to accumulation (see, for example, Birnbaum for France 1980: 108–9).

3   Several studies have begun to advance our understanding of the relationship between militarism and social development. On the relations between warfare and reformism see Mann (1987b); on class relations, Gallie (1983); and more generally, on economic and political development, Mann (1980, 1986), Giddens (1985) and Hall (1987).

4   As with most national statistics, French time series data measure establishments rather than enterprises. This is far from satisfactory for it tends to underestimate the actual levels of concentration, especially at the upper size levels where firms own more than one establishment. For lower size categories, however, the establishment is a reasonably good proxy for the enterprise.

5   Some caution is necessary here. German enterprise data deflate the

level of ownership concentration, treating subsidiary companies as separate legal units rather than grouping their activities together with the parent company. However, this would matter more for larger categories of enterprise, especially after 1945 with the more extensive development of the multi-establishment company.

6 The proxy for small enterprise used in virtually all the sources is the establishment employing fewer than 200 persons. British sources rarely disaggregate below this level.

7 For German data see Hardach (1980: 219); for France, Levy-Leboyer (1976: table 10). Japanese and American figures are supplied in Granovetter (1984: 326, 330). UK figures cover only the period after 1924 (Bolton 1971).

8 Establishment data of course hide significant shifts at ownership level, which took place between the wars as a result of mergers. Much of this movement was probably confined to the upper levels of enterprise size, hence without greatly affecting the weight of small firms in overall employment.

9 This section draws on Pearton (1982), McNeill (1983) and Milward (1984).

10 For the general perspective constructed here I have found particularly valuable the works of Vogler (1985), Strange (1986) and Poggi (1978).

11 While one reads much about MITI's big business strategies, this aspect of Japanese policy tends to be ignored in the literature. Japan may well be highly unusual in this regard, pursuing a dual strategy of assistance which has strengthened the corporate sector whilst simultaneously consolidating micro capitalism. This two-sided strategy, as the following chapter indicates, may stem from the highly interdependent nature of the two sectors in the Japanese economy.

12 The following section is based on Kuisel (1981).

13 Between 1952 and 1961 firms employing more than 1,000 persons increased their share of the industrial labour force from 34 to 40 per cent; and by 1960 Germany's 100 largest concerns employed one in three industrial workers and accounted for almost 40 per cent of total industrial turnover (Shonfield 1965: 241; Hardach 1980: 219).

14 My estimate based on figures supplied in the Bolton Report (1971). To obtain the enterprise figure establishment data need to be adjusted by *c*.5–7 per cent.

15 This is not to suggest that the scope of government intervention was extended as it was in Europe. But to look at the federal level is perhaps to look in the wrong place. As others have indicated, the states provided grants and legal advantages that privileged the formation of large companies (Bagwell and Mingay 1970: 174).

16 Data on small enterprise are from the Bruchey collection (1980: 154–5, 264). Figures for large enterprise are estimates, based on establishment data in Granovetter (1984: 326). These are obtained by adjusting downwards *c.*5 percentage points to allow for the difference between enterprise and establishment shares of employment.

17 This was at most a symbolic victory for small business since its prohibitory essence applied only to collusive agreements, not to mergers or other forms of combination.

18 For the United States at least, the Second World War was an astounding economic success. As Bond (1984: 178) observes, 'By the end of 1942 America was producing more war material than all the enemy powers combined . . . As much new plant was built in the first three war years as in the previous 15, and total production nearly doubled between 1939 and 1942.'

## Chapter 9   Re-creating micro capitalism

1 In certain of the following sections, I have leaned heavily on the work of Piore and Sabel who consider the implications of the Italian case for the United States from a slightly different perspective. My debt to their earlier paper (1983) and to their later path-breaking analysis of Fordist and craft systems of production (1984) will be apparent throughout, even where disagreements are registered.

2 One extreme consequence of such arrangements is the hiring of workers 'off-the-books', especially as outworkers (see Weiss 1987). The practice has been widely condemned for its exploitation of women. But for an analysis which challenges that generalization, see Solinas's (1982) study of the knitwear industry.

3 The fact that the Japanese government backs up that legal definition with an equally, if not more, generous set of financial and other programmes (Vepa 1971; JETRO 1981) reinforces my general argument. Nevertheless, the 'state' factor is not the only one at work in the Japanese context. First, in contrast to Italy, the degree of corporate dependence on small suppliers is unusually extensive. In 1976, for example, the proportion of small businesses in manufacturing which acted as subcontractors exceeded 60 per cent. Of these, the proportion of the tiniest industrial firms (1–19 employees) relying on subcontracting orders for at least 80 per cent of their production was 81 per cent (JETRO 1981: 24). The position of small suppliers is further reinforced by extensive ownership links to the corporate sector whose largest companies own at least 10 per cent of the capital in other firms

whose number ranges from 11 to 200 (Pempel 1978: 150). In distinction to the explanation offered for Italy, it may well be that this considerable interdependence lies at the root of the Japanese government's interest in its small business sector.

4   The trend since 1968 indicates a slight increase in the number of small manufacturing firms and in their overall share of employment (Stanworth and Curran 1984: 148). Chapman's (1981: 241) analysis of small firms in the textile industry suggests that some shift away from Fordist methods is occurring.

# Bibliography

For the sake of simplicity, sources are arranged under three main headings: Government sources, which include parliamentary papers and offical reports; Party literature; and Other sources.

## Government sources

### Parliamentary papers

Camera dei Deputati (*Atti Parlamentari*)
  Various years: Stato di Previsione della Spesa del Ministero dell'Industria. In *Discussioni della (X/XII) Commissione Industriale*, 1948–53, 1953–8, 1958–63. Rome.
  1950: Finanziamento alle piccole e medie industrie. In *Discussioni della X Commissione Industriale*. DDL no. 1032, 22 March and 18 April. Rome.
  1951: Partecipazione di rappresentanti degli artigiani e dei coltivatori diretti nelle giunte della Camera di Commercio, industria ed agricoltura. In *Disegno di Legge-Relazione*, 22 February. Rome.
  1956: Norma per la disciplina giuridica delle imprese artigiane. In *Discussioni della X Commissione Industriale*, 20 April and 21 June. Rome.
  1961: Credito all'artigianato ed alla piccola industria (M. Dosi's report). In *Discussioni*, 30 June. Rome.
  1966: Interventi Straordinari in favore delle aree depresse del Nord e del Centro-Nord d'Italia. In *Relazioni e Documenti*, no. 3183. Rome.
  1966: Proroga della legge 623. In *Relazioni e Documenti*, No. 3607, 1 December. Rome.
  1971: Indagine conoscitiva sulla piccola e media industria. In *XII Commissione Industriale*. Rome.

1972: Comitato per il Mezzogiorno, *Relazione sull' Attivazione del Piano di Coordinazione degli Interventi pubblici nel Mezzogiorno e sui Provvedimenti per le Aree Depresse del Centro-Nord*, doc. XVI, no. 5, vol. 3, Statistical App. Rome.

Senato della Repubblica (*Atti Interni*)
  1962: Le provisioni sugli investimenti industriali (Emilio Colombo's report). *Discussioni della Commissione Industriale*: Stato di Previsione della Spesa del Ministero dell'Industria per l'anno 1962–3, 30 October. Rome.
  1966: *Interventi Straordinari in favore delle aree depresse del Nord e del Centro d'Italia* (G. Pastore's report). DDL no. 1215, 16 May. Rome.


*Official reports*

Presidenza Consiglio Ministri 1958: *Politica di sviluppo, cinque anni di lavoro*. Rome.
CNEL 1961: *Osservazioni e proposte sui problemi delle minori imprese con particolare riguardo alle minori imprese industriali*. Rome.
  1966: *Parere in merito alle questioni relative alle possibilità, all'opportunità, ai criteri, ed ai parametri di una definizione o di una disciplina del'industria minore*. Rome.
Comitato Ministri Per Il Mezzogiorno 1961: *Relazione sulle attivita' di coordinamento*. Rome.
Lasorsa, G. 1963: *L'artigianato in Italia*. Rome: Ministero del'Industria.
Ministero dell'Industria (Direzione Generale dell'Artigianato e delle Piccole Industrie) 1961: *Provvedimenti per l'artigianato: raccolta di disposizioni legislativi ed amministrativi*. Rome.
  1962–3: *L'Artigianato in Italia*. Rome.
Presidency of the Council of Ministers 1964: Italian Artisan Trades. *Italy – Documents and Notes*, XII (6).
  1971: Artisan enterprise in Italy. *Italy – Documents and Notes*, XX (1).


**Party literature**

DC (Democrazia Cristiana) 1946: *Riforme: Lavoratori e Imprese Industriali*. Rome: SPES.
  Various years: *Atti del [number] Congresso della DC*. Rome: SPES.
  1956: *La Democrazia Cristiana per l'artigianato italiano*. Rome: SPES.
  1958: *Programma della DC per il Quinquennio 1958–63*. Rome: Cinque Lune.

1959: *Atti dei Congressi*. Rome: Cinque Lune.

1962: *Il Convegno di San Pellegrino*. Rome. Cinque Lune.

1963: *La Società Italiana*. Rome: Cinque Lune.

1964: *La Democrazia Cristiana di fronte al comunismo*. Rome: Cinque Lune.

1965: *La Democrazia Cristiana e Il Piano* (Atti del Consiglio Nazionale della DC, 28–30 April 1965). Rome: Cinque Lune.

1968: *Atti e Documenti* (1943–67). 2 vols. Rome: Cinque Lune.

1976: *I Congressi della Democrazia Cristiana* (1954–73). Rome: Cinque Lune.

1979: (L'Ufficio Programma economico della DC). *Primo Conferenza nazionale sull'-imprenditoria*, 4–5 March. Milan.

1982: I ceti medi protagonisti dello sviluppo. *Il Popolo*, 4 April.


### Other sources

Aaronovitch, S. and Sawyer, M. C. 1975: *Big Business: Theoretical and Empirical Aspects of Concentration and Mergers in the United Kingdom*. London: Macmillan.

Abrams, P. 1982: *Historical Sociology*. Shepton Mallet: Open Books.

Abrate, M. 1981: La politica economica e sindacale della Confindustria (1943–1955). In Zaninelli (1981).

Aga Rossi, E. 1969: *Dal partito popolare alla DC*. Bologna: Capelli.

Aldcroft, D. H. 1977: *The Inter-War Economy: Britain 1919–1939*. London: Batsford.

Allen, G. C. 1951: 'The concentration of production policy'. In D. N. Chester (ed.), *Lessons of the British War Economy*. Westport, Conn.: Greenwood Press.

Allen, K. and MacLellan, M. C. 1971: *Regional Problems and Policies in Italy and France*. London: Allen & Unwin.

Allen, K. and Stevenson, A. 1974: an *Introduction to the Italian Economy*. London: Martin Robertson.

Allum, P. 1973: *Politics and Society in Postwar Naples*. Cambridge: Cambridge University Press.

Alzona, G. L. 1975: 'Grande industria: sviluppo e strutture di controllo, 1963–1972'. In Graziani (1975).

Amato, G. 1972: *Il Governo dell'Industria*. Bologna: Il Mulino.

1976: *Economia, politica e istituzioni in Italia*. Bologna: Il Mulino.

Andrews, W. G. and Hoffman, S. (eds) 1981: *The Fifth Republic at Twenty*. Albany: State University of New York Press.

Anthony, D. 1983: 'Japan'. In Storey (1983).

Ardigò, A. 1962: 'Classi sociali e sintesi politica'. In DC (1962).

Ariotti, R. 1974: 'Scienze sociali e ceti medi: il problema del commercio'. *Il Mulino*, 23.

Artigiancassa [various years]: *Bilancio*. Rome.

Baget-Bozzo, G. 1976: 'Ceti medi e Mezzogiorno nella Lotta Politica Italiana' (1949). In Provasi (1976).

Baglieri, J. 1980: 'Italian Fascism and the crisis of the Liberal hegemony: 1901–1902'. In Larsen et al. (1980).

Bagnasco, A. 1977: *Tre Italie*. Bologna: Il Mulino.

Bagnasco, A. and Pini, R. 1981: 'Sviluppo economico e trasformazioni socio-politiche dei sistemi a economia diffusa'. *Quaderni fondazione Giangiacomo Feltrinelli*, 14.

Bagwell, P. S. and Mingay, G. E. 1970: *Britain and America, 1850–1939*. London: Routledge & Kegan Paul.

Bain, J. S. 1968: *Industrial Organization*. New York: Wiley.

Bamford, J. 1984: 'Small business in Italy – the submerged economy'. In Levicki (1984).

Banca d'Italia [various years]: *Relazione Annuale*. Rome.

Barbagli, M. 1979: *Fluidità elettorale a classi sociali in Italia: 1968–1976*. Bologna: Il Mulino.

Barberis, C. 1980: *L'Artigianato in Italia e nella Comunita' economica europea*. Milan: F. Angeli.

Barca, L. et al. (eds) 1975: *I Communisti e l'economia italiana, 1944–1974*. Bari: Laterza.

Barnes, S. H. 1974: 'Italy: religion and class in electoral behaviour'. In R. Rose (ed.), *Electoral Behaviour: A Comparative Handbook*. New York: Free Press.

Barucci, P. 1978: *Ricostruzione, pianificazione, Mezzogiorno*. Bologna: Il Mulino.

Beckman, T. N. 1944: 'Large versus small business after the war'. *American Economic Review*, 34 (March), pt 2, Supp.

Beesley, M. E. and Wilson, P. E. B. 1984: 'Public policy and small firms in Britain', in Levicki (1984).

Benedetti, M. 1979: 'Le tendenze della concentrazione industriale e le politiche al riguardo'. In Grassini and Scognamiglio (1979).

Berger, S. 1974: 'Uso politico e sopravvivenza dei ceti in declino'. In F. Cavazza and S. Graubard (eds), *Il Caso Italiano*. Milan: Garzanti.

—— 1977: 'D'une boutique à l'autre: changes in the organization of traditional middle classes from Fourth to Fifth Republics'. *Comparative Politics*, 10 (1).

—— 1980: 'The traditional sector in France and Italy'. In Berger and Piore (1980).

—— 1981: 'Regime and interest representation: the French traditional classes'.

In S. Berger (ed.) *Organising Interests in Western Europe*. Cambridge and New York: Cambridge University Press.

Berger, S. and Piore, M. 1980: *Dualism and Discontinuity in Industrial Societies*. Cambridge and New York: Cambridge University Press.

Berghahn, V. 1984: 'Ideas into politics: the case of Ludwig Erhard'. In R. J. Bullen et al. (eds), *Ideas into Politics*. London: Croom Helm.

Bergmann, J. and Muller-Jentsch, W. 1975: 'The Federal Republic of West Germany'. In S. Barkin (ed.), *Worker Militancy and Its Consequences, 1965–75*. New York: Praeger.

Bernstein, Barton J. 1967: 'Industrial reconversion: the protection of oligopoly and military control of the war economy'. *American Journal of Economics and Sociology*, 26: 159–72.

Berthoff, R. 1980: 'Independence and enterprise: small business in the American Dream. In Bruchey (1980).

Bettin, G. 1973: 'Gli imprenditori come classe dirigente'. In Cavalli (1973).

Birnbaum, P. 1980: 'The state in contemporary France'. In R. Scase (ed.), *The State in Western Europe*. New York: St Martin's Press.

Blackburn, R. and Mann, M. 1979: *The Working Class in the Labour Movement*. London: Macmillan.

Blackmer, D. L. M. and Tarrow, S. (eds) 1975: *Communism in Italy and France*. Princeton, NJ: Princeton University Press.

Blank, S. 1986: 'The impact of foreign economic policy'. In D. Coates and J. Hillard (eds), *The Economic Decline of Modern Britain*. London: Wheatsheaf Books.

Boissevain, J. 1984: 'Small entrepreneurs in contemporary Europe'. In R. Ward and R. Jenkins (eds), *Ethnic Communities in Business*. Cambridge: Cambridge University Press.

Bolton, J. 1971: *Report of the Committee of Inquiry on Small Firms*. London: Cmnd 4811, HMSO (The Bolton Report).

Bonacich, E. and Modell, J. 1980: *The Economic Basis of Ethnic Solidarity*. Berkeley: University of California Press.

Bonazzi, G., Bagnasco, A. and Casillo, S. 1972: *L'organizzazione della marginalità industria e potere politico in una provincia maridionale*. Turin: L'Impresa edizioni.

Bond, B. 1984: *War and Society in Europe, 1870–1970*. London: Fontana.

Braunthal, G. 1965: *The Federation of German Industry in Politics*. Ithaca, NY: Cornell University Press.

Broadway, F. H. 1970: *State Intervention in British Industry, 1948–68*. Madison: Fairleigh Dickinson University Press.

Bruchey, S. W. (ed.) 1980: *Small Business in American Life*, New York: Columbia University Press.

(ed.) 1981: *Petite entreprise et croissance industrielle*, vol. 1. Paris: CNRS.

Brusco, S. 1975: 'Economia di scala e livello technologico nelle piccole imprese'. In Graziani (1975).

1982: 'The Emilian model: productive decentralisation and social integration'. *Cambridge Journal of Economics*, 6 (2).

Brusco, S. and Sabel, C. 1981: 'Artisan production and economic growth'. In F. Wilkinson (ed.), *The Dynamics of Labour Market Segmentation*. London: Academic Press.

Cafiero, S. and Pizzorno, A. 1962: *Sviluppo industriale e imprenditori locali*. Milan: Giuffre.

Camp, R. L. 1969: *The Papal Ideology of Social Reform*. Leiden: E. J. Brill.

Capecchi, V. and Pugliese, E. 1978: 'Due città a confronto: Bologna e Napoli'. *Inchiesta*, 8.

Capuggi, L. 1981: 'The financing of industrial investment'. *Review of Economic Conditions in Italy*, 1 (1).

Carli, G. (ed.) 1978: *La struttura del sistema creditizio italiano*. Bologna: Il Mulino.

Carlini, D. 1972: *La politica del padronato italiano*. Bari: De Donato.

Carson, Deane (ed.) 1973: *The Vital Majority: Small Business in the American Economy*. Washington, DC: SBA.

Cassano, F. 1980 (2nd edn): *Il teorema democristiano*. Bari: De Donato.

Castronovo, V. (ed.) 1976: *L'Italia contemporanea*. Turin: Einaudi.

1980: *L'industria italiana dall'ottocento a oggi*. Milan: Mondadori.

Catalano, F. 1981: *Storia d'Italia, 1918–1860: Fascimo, guerra, repubblica*. Bergamo: Gruppo Ed. Walkover.

Catanzaro, R. 1979: *L'Imprenditore Assistito*. Bologna: Il Mulino.

Cavalli, L. (ed.) 1973: *Classe dirigente e sviluppo regionale*. Bologna: Il Mulino.

Cazzola, F. (ed.) 1979: *Anatomia del Potere DC*. Bari: De Donato.

CENSIS 1972: *La problematica economica delle piccole e medie imprese industriali*. Rome.

1980: *Il Caso Prato*. Milan: Etas Libri.

Centro Studi Federlibro 1974: *Piccola azienda, grande sfruttamento*. Verona: Bertani.

CGII [various years]: *Annuario*. Rome.

1956: *Atti del Convegno Nazionale per la piccola industria*. Rome.

1976: *Indagine conoscitiva sulla piccola industria*. Rome: unpublished report.

Chandler, A. D. and Tedlow, R. S. 1985: *The Coming of Managerial Capitalism*. Homewood, Ill.: Richard D. Irwin.

Chapman, S. D. 1981: 'Small firms in the British textile industries 1720–1978'. In Bruchey (1981).

Chubb, J. 1982: *Patronage, Power and Poverty in Southern Italy*. New York: Cambridge University Press.

Clapham, J. H. 1968: *The Economic Development of France and Germany 1815–1914*. Cambridge: Cambridge University Press.

Clough, S. B. 1964: *The Economic History of Modern Italy*. New York: Columbia University Press.

Coffey, P. 1973: *The Social Economy of France*. London: Macmillan.

Cohen, S. S. 1981: 'Twenty years of the Gaullist economy'. In Andrews and Hoffman (1981).

Colombo, E. 1963: *Lineamenti di una politica industriale, 1959–1962*. Bologna: Cappelli.

Comitato d'Intesa Unitaria del Ceto Medio 1958: *Una politica per il ceto medio*. Rome.

Confederazione Generale Italiana del Lavoro 1977: *I Congressi della CGIL*, vol. 3. Rome: ESI.

Confederazione Nazionale della Piccola e Media Industria 1965: *Una Politica Economica e Sindacale per L'Industria Minore*. Novara: Ed. Confapi.

Conti, G. 1978: 'Specializzazione e competitività internazionale dell'Italia'. In P. Alessandrini (ed.), *Occupazione e capacità produttive: confronti internazionali*, vol. 6. Bologna: Il Mulino.

Cova, A. 1981: 'Movimento economico, occupazione, retribuzioni in Italia dal 1943 al 1955'. In Zaninelli (1981).

Cross, M. 1983: 'The United Kingdom'. In Storey (1983).

Crouch, C. 1986: 'Sharing public space: states and organized interests in Western Europe'. In Hall (1986).

Curran, J. and Burrows, R. J. 1986: 'The sociology of petit capitalism: a trend report'. *Sociology*, 20 (2).

D'Antonio, M. 1968: *Commento al Programma Economico Nazionale*. Bologna: Cappelli.

De Felice, R. 1966: *Mussolini il fascista*, vol. 1. Turin: Einaudi.
  1977: *Interpretations of Fascism*. Cambridge, Mass.: Harvard University Press.
  1980: 'Italian Fascism and the middle classes'. In Larsen et al. (1980).

De Gasperi, A. 1955: *I cattolici dall'opposizione al governo*. Bari: Laterza.
  1969: *Discorsi Politici*. Rome: Cinque Lune.

De Masi, D. and Fevola, G. 1974: *I lavoratori nell'industria italiana*, vol. 1. Milan: F. Angeli.

Denton, G. 1968: 'Germany'. In G. Denton et al. (eds), *Economic Planning and Policies in Britain, France and Germany*. London: Allen & Unwin.

De Rosa, G. 1966: *Storia del movimento cattolico in Italia: Dalla restaurazione all'eta' giolittiana*. Bari: Laterza.

1973: *I partiti politici in Italia*. Bergamo: Minerva italica.

Di Palma, G. 1977: *Surviving without Governing: The Italian Parties in Parliament*. Berkeley: University of California Press.

Di Vittorio, G. 1955: *I Sindicati in Italia*. Bari: Laterza.

Dogan, M. 1967: 'Political cleavage and social stratification in France and Italy'. In S. M. Lipset and S. Rokkan (eds), *Party Systems and Voter Alignments*. New York: Free Press.

Donati, P. 1976: 'Ceti medi e struttura a dominanza: il caso dell'Emilia Romagna'. *Analisi e Documenti*, 12.

Donato, R. 1967: 'La nuova legge per il finanziamento della media e piccola industria'. *Rassegna Economica*, 2.

Donolo, C. 1972: 'Sviluppo ineguale e disgregazione sociale'. *Quaderni Piacentini*, 11.

Dore, R. 1986: *Flexible Rigidities*. London: Athlone Press.

Du Preez, P. 1980: *The Politics of Identity*. Oxford: Basil Blackwell.

Ehrmann, H. W. 1957: *Organised Business in France*. Princeton, NJ: Princeton University Press.

Einaudi, L. 1947: 'L'avvenire dei ceti medi'. *Il Nuova Corriere della Sera*, 16 March.

Ente Palazzo della Civiltà del Lavoro 1969: XII Convegno Nazionale, *Le Imprese Minori Fattore Insostituibile nel sistema economico*. (XII Convegno Nazionale). Rome.

Evans, P. B., Rueschemeyer, D. and Skocpol, T. (eds) 1985: *Bringing the State Back In*. Cambridge and New York: Cambridge University Press.

Fanfani, A. 1959: *Da Napoli a Firenze, 1954–1959: proposte per una politica di sviluppo democratico*. Milan: Garzanti.

Farneti, P. 1970: *Imprenditore e società*. Turin: L'Impresa Edizioni.

Federlombarda (ed.) 1977: *La piccola e media industria in Lombardia*, vol. 1. Milan: Ed. Industriali.

Ferraresi, F. 1980: *Burocrazia e politica in Italia*. Bologna: Il Mulino.

Ferrero, F. and Scamuzzi, S. 1979: *L'industria in Italia: la piccola impresa*. Rome: Riuniti.

Field, G. L. and Higley, J. 1978: 'Imperfectly unified elites: the cases of Italy and France'. In R. F. Tomasson (ed.), *Comparative Studies in Sociology*, vol. 1. Greenwich, Conn.: JAI Press.

FLM di Bologna 1975: *Ristrutturazione ed organizzazione del lavoro*, vol. 1. Rome: Ed. Seusi.

Florence, P. S. 1972 (3rd edn): *The Logic of British and American Industry*. London: Routledge & Kegan Paul.

Fonzi, F. 1981: 'Mondo cattolico, Democrazia Cristiana e sindacato (1943–1955)'. In Zaninelli (1981).

Foresi, P. 1958: 'Il Ceto Medio e l'unione Europea'. In Comitato d'Intesa Unitaria del Ceto Medio (1958).

Friedman, D. 1983: 'Beyond the age of Ford: the strategic bases of the Japanese success in automobiles'. In J. Zysman and L. Tyson (eds), *American Industry in International Competition*. Ithaca, NY: Cornell University Press.

Frigeni, R. and Tousijn, W. 1976: *L'industria delle calzature in Italia*. Bologna: Il Mulino.

Fuà, G. 1976: *Occupazione e capacità produttive: la realtà italiana*. Bologna: Il Mulino.

Fuà, G. and Sylos Labini, P. 1963: *Idee per la programmazione economica*. Bari: Laterza.

Fuscagni, C. 1973: 'Il recupero del ceto medio'. *La Discussione*, 23 (7 June).

Galli, G. 1966: *Il bipartismo imperfetto*. Bologna: Il Mulino.

 1968: *Il comportamento elettorale in Italia*. Bologna: Il Mulino.

Galli, G. and Facchi, P. 1962: *La sinistra democristiana: storia e ideologia*. Milan: Feltrinelli.

Galli, G. and Prandi, A. 1970: *Patterns of Political Participation in Italy*. New Haven: Yale University Press.

Gallie, D. 1983: *Social Inequality and Class Radicalism in France and Britain*. Cambridge: Cambridge University press.

Gamble, A. 1974: *The Conservative Nation*. London: Routledge & Kegan Paul.

 1985 (2nd edn): *Britain in Decline*. London: Macmillan.

Gasparini, I. 1977: 'Relazione generale'. In Federlombarda (1977), vol. 1.

Germinio, A. and Passigli, S. 1968: *The Government and Politics of Contemporary Italy*. New York: Harper & Row.

Germozzi, M. 1956: 'La funzione dell'artigianato nell'economia moderna'. *Rivista di Politica Economica*, 7–8.

 1972: 'Per una nuova politica per l'artigianato'. *La Discussione*, 20 April.

 1974: 'Gli artigiani vogliono regolare i conti'. *La Discussione*, 1 April.

 1978: 'Craft industry in the Italian economy'. *Review of the Economic Conditions in Italy*, 32 (4).

Gerschenkron, A. 1954: 'Some further notes on "Social attitudes, entrepre-neurship, and economic development"'. *Explorations in Entrepreneurial History*, December.

 1962: *Economic Backwardness in Historical Perspective*. Cambridge, Mass.: Belknap Press of Harvard University.

Giddens, A. 1985: *The Nation-State and Violence*. Oxford: Polity Press.

Giunta Regionale della Lombardia 1974: *Indagine conoscitiva sull'artigianato lombardo*. Milan: Zanolla.

Glisenti, M. and Elia, L. (eds) 1961–2: *Antologia di Cronache Sociali,*

*1947–1951.* San Giovanni Valdarno: L. Landi, 2 vols.

Goldthorpe, John H. 1984: 'The end of convergence: corporatist and dualist tendencies in modern western societies'. In J. H. Goldthorpe (ed.), *Order and Conflict in Western European Capitalism.* Oxford: Oxford University Press.

Gramsci, A. 1964: 'Alcuni temi della questione meridionale' (1926). In N. Gallo and G. Ferrata (eds), *2000 pagine di Gramsci.* Milan: Il Saggiatore, vol. 1.

Granovetter, M. 1984: 'Small is bountiful: labour markets and establishment size'. *American Sociological Review,* 49 (3).

Grassini, G. 1979: 'Introduzione'. In Grassini and Scognamiglio (1979).

Grassini, G. and Scognamiglio, C. (eds) 1979: *Stato e industria in Europa: L'Italia.* Bologna: Il Mulino.

Graziani, A. 1972: *L'economia italiana, 1945–1970.* Bologna: Il Mulino.

(ed.) 1975: *Crisi e ristrutturazione nell' economia italiana.* Turin: Einaudi.

1978: 'Piccola impresa e industrializzazione nel Mezzogiorno'. In C. Capecchi et al. (eds), *La piccola impresa nell'economia italiana.* Bari: De Donato.

Graziano, L. 1978: 'Centre–periphery relations and the Italian crisis: the problem of clientelism'. In S. Tarrow et al. (eds), *Territorial Politics in Industrial Nations.* New York: Praeger.

1980: *Clientelismo e sistema politico.* Milan: F. Angeli.

Gros-Pietro, G. M. and Boni, M. 1967: *La concentrazione industriale in Italia.* Turin: Einaudi.

Grunberg, E. 1941 and 1942: 'The mobilization of capacity and resources of small-scale enterprises in Germany'. *Journal of Business of the University of Chicago,* 14 (October): 319–44, and 15 (January): 56–89.

Gualerni, G. 1976: *Industria e fascismo.* Milan: Vita e Pensiero.

Guerra, E. 1966: *Lo sviluppo industriale delle aree depresse del Piemonte.* Milan: Franco Angeli.

Guidi, R. 1954: 'Lo sviluppo del credito alle imprese artigiane'. Convegno per lo sviluppo del credito alle imprese artigiane, July 17–18. Rome.

Hall, J. A. 1983: 'The conscious relegitimation of liberal capitalism'. In Adrian Ellis and Krishan Kumar (eds), *Dilemmas of Liberal Democracies.* London: Tavistock.

1985: *Powers and Liberties.* Oxford: Basil Blackwell.

(ed) 1986: *States in History.* Oxford: Basil Blackwell.

1987: 'War and the rise of the West'. In Colin Creighton and Martin Shaw (eds), *The Sociology of War and Peace.* London: Macmillan.

Hall, P. A. 1983: 'Economic planning and the state: the evolution of economic challenge and political response in France'. In Gosta

Esping-Andersen and Roger Friedland (eds), *Political Power and Social Theory*, vol. 3. Greenwich, Conn.: JAI Press.

—— 1984: 'Patterns of economic policy among the European states: an organizational approach'. In B. Bornstein, D. Held and J. Krieger (eds), *The State in Capitalist Europe*. London: Allen & Unwin.

Hannah, L. 1983 (2nd edn): *The Rise of the Corporate Economy*. London: Methuen.

Hardach, K. 1980: *The Political Economy of Germany in the Twentieth Century*. Berkeley: University of California Press.

Harris, N. 1972: *Competition and the Corporate Society*. London: Methuen.

Hayward, J. and Watson, M. (eds) 1975: *Planning, Politics and Public Policy*. Cambridge: Cambridge University Press.

Hellman, S. 1975: 'The PCI's alliance strategy and the case of the middle classes'. In Blackmer and Tarrow (1975).

Hildebrand, G. H. 1965: *Growth and Structure in the Economy of Modern Italy*. Cambridge, Mass.: Harvard University Press.

Hine, D. 1976: 'The labour movement and communism in France and Italy'. In M. Kolinsky and W. E. Paterson (eds), *Social and Political Movements in Western Europe*. London: Croom Helm.

Hoffman, S. 1962: 'The effects of World War II on French society and politics'. *French Historical Studies* (April).

—— 1963: 'Paradoxes of the French Political Community'. In S. Hoffman et al. (eds), *France: Change and Tradition*. London: Victor Gollancz.

Hudson Report 1986: 'The wasting of assets'. In David Coates and John Hillard (eds), *The Economic Decline of Modern Britain*. Brighton: Wheatsheaf.

Hull, C. 1980: 'Regional incentives in France'. In D. Yuill, K. Allen and C. Hull (eds), *Regional Policy in the European Community*. London: Croom Helm.

Husbands, C. T. 1981: 'Contemporary right-wing movements in Western European democracies: a review article'. *European Journal of Political Research*, 9.

Hytten, E. and Marchioni, M. 1970: *Industrializzazione senza sviluppo*. Milan: F. Angeli.

IASM 1969: *Indagine sugli effetti della legge 30 lulio 1959, n.623 nel Mezzogiorno*. Rome: unpublished report.

ICAS 1951: 'Le classi medie'. Special conference issue (August) of *Orientamenti Sociali*.

Imberciadori, F. 1973: 'Il gruppo dirigente democristiano'. In Cavalli (1973).

Ingham, G. 1970: *Size of Industrial Organisation and Worker Behaviour*. Cambridge: Cambridge Univerity Press.

Irving, R. E. M. 1979: *The Christian Democratic Parties of Western Europe.* London: Allen & Unwin.

ISTAT 1978: *Annuario di statistiche industriali,* vol. 21. Rome.

Istituto Gramsci-CESPE 1962: *Tendenze del capitalismo italiano,* vol. 2. Rome: Riuniti.

    1975: *La piccola e la media industria nella crisi dell'economia italiana.* Rome: Riuniti, 2 vols.

Jessop, B. 1974: *Traditionalism, Conservatism and British Political Culture.* London: Allen & Unwin.

JETRO 1981: *Promotion of Small and Medium Enterprises in Japan.* Tokyo.

Kater, M. H. 1983: *The Nazi Party: A Social Profile of Members and Leaders 1919–1945.* Cambridge, Mass.: Harvard University Press.

Katzenstein, P. J. 1985: *Small States in World Markets.* Ithaca, NY: Cornell University Press.

Kemp, T. 1969: *Industrialization in Nineteenth Century Europe.* London: Longman.

Kogan, N. 1981: *A Political History of Postwar Italy.* New York: Praeger.

Kuisel, R. F. 1981: *Capitalism and the State in Modern France.* Cambridge: Cambridge University Press.

Kuster, G. H. 1974: 'Germany'. In Vernon (1974).

Lama, L. 1976: *Intervista sul sindacato.* Bari: Laterza.

La Palombara, J. 1963: 'La Confindustria e la politica in Italia'. *Tempi Moderni* (October).

    1964: *Interest Groups in Italian Politics.* Princeton, NJ: Princeton University press.

Laqueur, W. (ed.) 1976: *Fascism: A Reader's Guide.* Berkeley: University of California Press.

Larsen, S. U. et al. (eds) 1980: *Who Were the Fascists?* Bergen: Universitetsforlaget.

Lauber, V. 1981: 'The Gaullist model of economic modernization'. In Andrews and Hoffman (1981).

Levicki, C. (ed.) 1984: *Small Business Theory and Policy.* London: Croom Helm.

Levy-Leboyer, M. 1976: 'Innovation and business strategies in nineteenth- and twentieth-century France'. In E. C. Carter II, R. Foster and J. N. Moody (eds), *Enterprise and Entrepreneurs in Nineteenth- and Twentieth-Century France.* Baltimore/London: Johns Hopkins University Press.

Linz, Juan 1976: 'Some notes towards a comparative study of Fascism in sociological historical perspective'. In Laqueur (1976).

Lucifredi, R. 1958: 'Problemi giuridico-amministrativo'. In Comitato d'Intesa Unitaria del Ceto Medio (1958).

McArthur, J. H. and Scott, B. R. 1969: *Industrial Planning in France*. Boston, Mass.: Graduate School of Business Administration, Harvard University

MacLeod, R. and K. 1975: 'War and economic development: government and the optical industry in Britain, 1914–18'. In J. M. Winter (ed.) *War and Economic Development*. Cambridge: Cambridge University Press.

McNeill, W. H. 1983: *The Pursuit of Power*. Oxford: Basil Blackwell.

Manghetti, G. 1975: 'Ideologia e politica della DC verso le piccole e medie industrie'. In Istituto Gramsci-CESPE (1975), vol. 2.

Mann, M. 1980: 'State and society, 1130–1815: an analysis of English state finances'. *Political Power and Social Theory*, vol. 1. Greenwich, Conn.: JAI Press.

   1984: 'The autonomous power of the state: its sources, mechanisms and results'. *European Journal of Sociology*, 25 (2).

   1986: *The Sources of Social Power*, vol. 1: *A History of Power from the Beginning to 1760 AD*. Cambridge: Cambridge University Press.

   1987a: 'War and social theory: into battle with classes, nations and states'. In C. Creighton and M. Shaw (eds), *The Sociology of War and Peace*. London: Macmillan.

   1987b: 'Ruling class strategies and citizenship'. *Sociology*, 21 (3).

   (forthcoming): *The Sources of Social Power*, vol. 2: *A History of Power in Industrial Societies*. Cambridge: Cambridge University Press.

Maraffi, M. 1980: 'State/economy relationships: the case of Italian public enterprise'. *British Journal of Sociology*, 31 (4).

Martinotti, G. 1978: 'Le tendenze dell'elettorato italiano'. In A. Martinelli and G. Pasquino (eds), *La politica nell'Italia che cambia*. Milan: Feltrinelli.

MEC 1962: *Situazione dell'artigianato nei Paesi della Comunita' Europea* (March–April). Milan.

Mediocredito Centrale 1971: *Indagine sulle imprese industriali*, 2 vols. Rome.
   1977: *Indagine sulle imprese maniffaturiere*, 3 vols. Rome.

Merkl, P. H. 1980a: 'Comparing Fascist movements' and 'Introduction to part III'. In Larsen et al. (1980).

   1980b: 'The sociology of European parties'. In P. H. Merkl (ed.), *Western European Party Systems*. New York: Free Press.

Merusi, F. (ed.) 1974: *La legislazione economic italiana dalla fine della guerra al primo programma economico*. Milan: F. Angeli.

Milward, A. S. 1980: 'Towards a political economy of Fascism'. In Larsen et al. (1980).

   1984 (2nd edn): *The Economic Effects of the Two World Wars on Britain*. London: Macmillan.

Montalenti, P. 1978: Stato democratico e partecipazioni statali. In G. Cottino (ed.), *Ricerche sulle partecipazioni statali*, vol. 1. Turin: Einaudi.

Nappi, A. T. and Vora, J. 1980: 'Small business eligibility: a definitional issue'. *Journal of Small Business Management*, 18 (4).

Neufeld, M. F. 1961: *Italy: School for Awakening Nations: The Italian Labor Movement in its Political, Social and Economic Setting from 1800 to 1960*. Ithaca, NY: Cornell University Press.

OECD (Industrial Committee) 1971: *Problems and Policies Relating to Small and Medium-Sized Business*. Paris.

    1984: *Economic Survey: Italy*. Paris.

    1986: *Economic Survey: Italy*. Paris.

Paci, Massimo (ed.) 1978: *Capitalismo e classi sociali in Italia*. Bologna: Il Mulino.

    1979: 'Class structure in Italian society'. *European Journal of Sociology*, 20 (1).

    1982: *La struttura sociale italiana*. Bologna: Il Mulino.

Parisi, A. and Pasquino, G. 1979: 'Changes in Italian electoral behaviour: the relationships between parties and voters'. *West European Politics*, 2 (3).

Pasquino, G. and Pecchini, U. 1975: 'Italy'. In Hayward and Watson (1975).

Pastore, G. 1955: *I Sindacati in Italia*. Bari: Laterza.

Payne, P. L. 1967: 'The emergence of the large-scale company in Great Britain, 1870–1914'. *Economic History Review*, 2nd series, 20 (3).

Payne, S. G. 1976: 'Fascism in Western Europe'. In Laqueur (1976).

    1980: *Fascism: Comparison and Definition*. Madison: University of Wisconsin Press.

Peacock, A. 1980: *Structural Economic Policies in West Germany and the United Kingdom*. London: Anglo-German Foundation for the Study of Industrial Society.

Pearton, M. 1982: *The Knowledgeable State*. London: Burnett Books.

Peggio, E. 1973: 'Dieci anni di politica economica democristiana'. *Critica Marxista*, 3–4.

    1975: 'La piccola e media industria nella crisi dell'economia italiana'. In Istituto Gramsci-CESPE (1962).

Pempel, T. J. 1978: 'Japanese foreign economic policy'. In Peter J. Katzenstein (ed.), *Between Power and Plenty*. Madison: University of Wisconsin Press.

Peschiera, F. 1979: *Sindacati, industria e stato negli anni del centrismo*. Florence: Le Monnier, 2 vols.

Petriccione, S. 1976: *Politica Industriale e Mezzogiorno*. Bari: Laterza.

Phillips, J. D. 1958: *Little Business in the American Economy.* Urbana: University of Illinois Press.

Piore,.M. J. and Sabel, C. F. 1983: 'Italian small business development: lessons for U.S. industrial policy'. In J. Zysman and L. Tyson (eds), *American Industry in International competition.* Ithaca, NY: Cornell University Press.

1984: *The Second Industrial Divide.* New York: Basic Books.

Pizzorno, A. 1960: *Comunità e razionalizzazione.* Turin: Einaudi.

1980: 'I ceti medi nei meccanismi del consenso'. In *I soggetti del pluralismo.* Bologna: Il Mulino.

Podbielski, G. 1974: *Italy: Development and Crisis in the Postwar Economy.* Oxford: Clarendon Press.

Poggi, G. 1963: 'Studio dell'ideologia nella sociologia dei partiti politici'. *Rassegna Italiana di Sociologia*, 205–20.

1968: *Le preferenze politiche degli italiani.* Bologna: Il Mulino.

1978: *The Development of the Modern State.* London: Hutchinson.

1983: *Calvinism and the Capitalist Spirit.* London: Macmillan.

Pollard, S. 1960: *The Development of the British Economy, 1914–1950.* London: Edward Arnold.

Prais, S. J. 1976: *The Evolution of Giant Firms.* Cambridge: Cambridge University Press.

Pridham, G. 1976: 'Christian Democracy in Italy and West Germany: a comparative analysis'. In M. Kolinsky and W. E. Paterson (eds), *Social and Political Movement sin Western Europe.* London: Croom Helm.

1977: *Christian Democracy in Western Germany.* London: Croom Helm.

1981: *The Nature of the Italian Party System.* London: Croom Helm.

Prodi, R. 1974: 'Italy'. In Vernon (1974).

1980: 'Il quadro economico'. In Rossini (1980), vol. 2.

Provasi, G. 1976: *Borghesia industriale e Democrazia Cristiana.* Bari: De Donato.

Pugliese, F. 1974: 'Il governo dell'industria tramite incentivi, 1946–1965'. In Merusi (1974).

Radi, L. 1973: 'La Democrazia Cristiana: i suoi iscritti e i suoi elettori'. *La Discussione*, 13 (29 March).

Rampino, D. 1967: 'La nuova legge per il finanziamento della media e piccola industria. *Rassegna Economica*, 24.

Ravalli, S. 1967: 'La distribuzione al dettaglio'. *Mondo Economico*, 23 December.

Ray, G. F. 1966: 'The size of plant: a comparison'. *National Institute Economic Review*, 38.

Roberts, D. D. 1980: 'Petty bourgeois Fascism in Italy: form and content'. In Larsen et al. (1980).

Robertson, R. M. 1973 (3rd edn): *History of the American Economy*. New York: Harcourt Brace Jovanovich.

Rodgers, A. 1979: *Economic Development in Retrospect*. New York: John Wiley.

Romagnoli, U. 1970: 'La politica sindacale dell'industria di Stato'. *Il Mulino*, 19 (209).

Romeo, R. 1972: *Breve storia della grande industria in Italia 1951–1961*. Bologna: Cappelli.

Rossini, G. (ed.) 1980: *Democrazia Cristiana e costituente*. Rome: Cinque Lune, 3 vols.

Rubinacci, L. 1958: 'Problemi sociali e economici del ceto medio'. In Comitato d'Intesa Unitaria del Ceto Medio (1958).

Saba, A. 1969: *La politica di incentivazione degli investimenti industriali in Italia e Europa*. Rome: Ateneo.

Saba, V. 1981: 'Verso un nuovo sindacato (luglio 1948–1955)'. In Zaninelli (1981).

Sabel, C. 1982: *Work and Politics*. Cambridge and New York: Cambridge University Press.

Sabel, C. and Zeitlin, J. 1985: 'Historical alternatives to mass production: politics, markets and technology in nineteenth-century industrialization'. *Past and Present*, 108 (August).

Salimbeni, R. 1974: 'Le agevolazioni fiscali alle attivita' industriali'. In Merusi (1974).

Salvati, M. 1972a: 'The rebirth of Italian trade unionism'. In S. J. Woolf (ed.) *The Rebirth of Italy, 1943–50*. New York: Humanities Press.

1972b: 'The impasse of Italian capitalism'. *New Left Review*, 82.

1974: 'Subordinazione o autonomia delle piccole imprese: politica o economia?' *Economia e Politica Industriale*, 2 (7–8).

Salvatorelli, L. 1923: *Nazionalfascismo*. Turin: Einaudi.

Samuels, J. M. and Morrish, P. A. 1984: 'An analysis of concentration'. In Levicki (1984).

Sani, G. 1978: 'La composizione degli elettorati communista e demo-cristiano'. In A. Martinelli and G. Pasquino (eds), *La politica nell'Italia che cambia*. Milan: Feltrinelli.

Saraceno, P. 1962: 'Lo stato e l'economia'. In DC (1962).

1969: *Ricostruzione e pianificazione (1943–1948)*. Bari: Laterza.

Sarti, R. 1971: *Fascism and the Industrial Leadership in Italy, 1919–1940*. Berkeley: University of California Press.

Sasso, G. 1978: 'Partecipazioni statali e politica del lavoro'. In G. Cottino (ed.), *Ricerche sulle partecipazioni statali*, vol. 1. Turin: Einaudi.

Sassoon, D. 1981: *The Strategy of the Italian Communist Party*. London: Frances Pinter.

Sauer, W. 1984: 'Small firms and the German economic miracle'. In Levicki (1984).

Scarpari, G. 1977: *La Democrazia Cristiana e le leggi eccezionali 1950–1953*. Milan: Feltrinelli.

Scase, R. and Goffee, R. 1980: *The Real World of the Small Business Owner*. London: Croom Helm.

— 1982: *The Entrepreneurial Middle Class*. London: Croom Helm.

Schiattarella, R. 1984: *Mercato del lavoro e struttura produttiva*. Milan: F. Angeli.

Scoppola, P. 1963: *Dal neoguelfismo alla Democrazia Cristiana: antologia de documenti*. Rome: Ed. Studium.

— 1977: *La proposta politica di De Gasperi*. Bologna: Il Mulino.

Seravalli, G. 1977: 'Credito agevolato, medie e piccole imprese'. *Economia del Lavoro*, 2.

Serrani, D. 1978: *Il potere per enti*. Bologna: Il Mulino.

Setta, S. 1975: *L'uomo qualunque*. Rome: Laterza.

Sheahan, J. 1963: *Promotion and Control of Industry in Post-War France*. Cambridge: Cambridge University Press.

Shonfield, A. 1965: *Modern Capitalism*. New York: Oxford University Press.

— 1974: 'L'impresa pubblica: modello internazionale o specialità locale?' In F. L. Cavazza and S. R. Graubard (eds), *Il caso italiano*. Milan: Garzanti.

Sicca, L. 1981: 'Rapporto tra incentivazioni e sviluppo del sistema industriale del Mezzogiorno'. *L'Industria*, 2.

Skocpol, T. 1985: 'Bringing the state back in: strategies of analysis in current research'. In Evans et al. (1985).

Smith, E. O. 1983: *The West German Economy*. London: Croom Helm.

Smith, T. 1974: 'The United Kingdom'. In Vernon (1974).

Solinas, G. 1982: 'Labour market segmentation and workers' careers: the case of the Italian knitwear industry'. *Cambridge Journal of Economics*, 6 (4).

Spano. P. 1979: 'Gli enti del settore creditizio'. In Cazzola (1979).

Stanworth, J. and Curran, J. 1984: 'Small business research in Britain'. In Levicki (1984).

Stolper, G. 1967: *The German Economy 1870 to the Present*. New York: Harcourt Brave & World.

Storey, D. J. 1982: *Entrepreneurship and the New Firm*. London: Croom Helm.

— (ed.) 1983: *The Small Firm*. London: Croom Helm.

Strange, S. 1986: 'Supranationals and the state'. In Hall (1986).

Sturzo, L. 1923: *Riforma statale e indirizzi politici: discorsi.* Florence: Vallecchi.

1926: *Italy and Fascism.* London: Faber & Gwyer.

1957: 'Indagine sociologica sulle classi medie'. *Sociologia,* 2 (1).

1968: *Politica di questi anni (1950–56).* Bologna: Zanichelli.

Suleiman, E. 1975: 'Industrial policy formulation in France'. In Warnecke and Suleiman (1975).

SVIMEZ 1973: *Gli investimenti industriali agevolati nel Mezzogiorno, 1951–1968.* Milan: Giuffrè.

Sylos Labini, P. 1972: 'Sviluppo economico e classi sociali in Italia'. *Quaderni di Sociologia,* 4.

1975 (rev. edn): *Saggio sulle classi sociali.* Bari: Laterza.

1978: 'Sviluppo economico e classi sociali'. In Paci (1978).

Tarrow, S. 1967: *Peasant Communism in Southern Italy.* New Haven, Conn.: Yale University Press.

1975: 'Communism in Italy and France: adaptation and change'. In Blackmer and Tarrow (1975).

1977: 'From Cold War to historic compromise: approaches to French and Italian radicalism'. In S. Bialer (ed.), *Radicalism in the Contemporary Age,* vol. 1. New York: Westview Press.

1979: 'Italy: crisis, crises or transition?'. *West European Politics,* 2 (3).

Tasca, A. 1966: *The Rise of Italian Fascism, 1918–1922.* New York: Howard Fertig.

Tassinari, F. 1975: 'Dinamica dell'occupazione e dimensione degli impianti produttivi nell'industria manifatturiera'. In Istituto Gramsci-CESPE (1975), vol. 2.

Templeman, D. C. 1981: *The Italian Economy.* New York: Praeger.

Thompson, J. H. and Leyden, D. R. 1983: 'The United States of America'. In Storey (1983).

Togliatti, P. 1970: *Lezioni sul fascismo.* Rome: Riuniti.

Togni, G. 1958: 'Discorso inaugurale'. In Comitato d'Intesa Unitaria del Ceto Medio (1958).

Tousijn, W. 1978: 'La piccola impresa in Italia: divisione internazionale del lavoro e rapporti tra le classi sociali'. *L'Impresa,* 20 (4–5).

1980: 'Imprenditorialità e struttura di classe'. *Quaderni di Sociologia,* 29 (1).

Trebilcock, C. 1981: *The Industrialisation of the Continental Powers, 1780–1914.* London: Longman.

Valli, V. 1976: *L'economia e la politica economica italiana (1945–1975).* Milan: Etas.

Vatter, H. G. 1980: 'The position of small business in the structure of

American manufacturing, 1870–1970'. In Bruchey (1980).

Vepa, R. K. 1971: *Small Industry in the Seventies*. Delhi/London: Vikas Publications.

Vernon, R. (ed.) 1974: *Big Business and the State*. London: Macmillan.

Vito, F. 1961: '"Mater et Magistra" e i nuovi termini delle questioni sociali'. *Vita e Pensiero*, August.

Vogler, C. M. 1985: *The Nation State*. London: Gower.

Wade, R. 1979: 'Fast growth and slow development in south Italy'. In D. Seers et al. (eds), *Underdeveloped Europe*. Brighton: Harvester Press.

Warnecke, S. J. and Suleiman, E. N. (eds) 1975: *Industrial Policies in Western Europe*. New York: Praeger.

Webster, R. A. 1960: *Christian Democracy in Italy*. New York: Stanford University Press.

Weiss, L. 1986: 'Demythologising the petite bourgeoisie: the Italian case'. *West European Politics*, 9 (3).

1987: 'Explaining the underground economy: state and social structure'. *British Journal of Sociology*, 38 (2).

Williams, G. 1963: *Apprenticeship in Europe*. London: Chapman & Hall.

Williams, K., Williams, J. and Thomas, D. 1983: *Why Are the British Bad at Manufacturing?* London: Routledge & Kegan Paul.

Winkler, H. A. 1976: 'From social protectionism to national socialism: the German small business movement in comparative perspective'. *Journal of Modern History*, 48.

Woodcock, C. 1986: 'The financial and capital environment of the small firm'. In James Curran, John Stanworth and David Watkins (eds), *The Survival of the Small Firm*, vol. 1. London: Gower.

Zaninelli, S. (ed.) 1981: *Il sindicator nuovo: politica e organizzazione del movimento sindacale in Italia negli anni 1943–55*. Milan: F. Angeli.

Zysman, J. 1977: *Political Strategies for Industrial Order: State Market and Industry in France*. Berkeley: University of California Press.

1983: *Governments, Markets and Growth*. Oxford: Martin Robertson.

# Index